Clear Path or Jungle in Commercial Arbitrators' Conflict of Interest?

ASA Special Series

VOLUME 48

Introduction

The Swiss Arbitration Association (ASA, Association suisse de l'arbitrage) is Switzerland's leading arbitration organization. With more than a thousand members, it brings together the world's most eminent arbitration practitioners from six continents and 50 + jurisdictions.

Since its foundation in 1974, ASA helps shape the development of international arbitration for the benefit of users worldwide. Its signature Annual Conferences in Zurich and Geneva explore topical issues with high-calibre experts from all over the world. The papers and materials are subsequently published in the ASA Special Series.

Editors

Each volume of the ASA Special Series is edited by different editors from among the ASA members and who have been the (co-)organizers of the pertinent ASA Annual Conference or are specialists in a particular topical issue to which a volume is dedicated.

Objective

The ASA Special Series are published to foster innovation in and to promote international arbitration globally.

They contain the full edited versions of the papers of the ASA Annual Conferences as well as ad hoc arbitration brochures published by ASA.

Frequency

One to two volumes per year, with one volume typically published following the ASA Annual Conference.

The titles published in this series are listed at the end of this volume.

Clear Path or Jungle in Commercial Arbitrators' Conflict of Interest?

Edited by

Felix Dasser

Wolters Kluwer

Published by:
Kluwer Law International B.V.
PO Box 316
2400 AH Alphen aan den Rijn
The Netherlands
E-mail: international-sales@wolterskluwer.com
Website: lrus.wolterskluwer.com

Sold and distributed by:
Wolters Kluwer Legal & Regulatory U.S.
7201 McKinney Circle
Frederick, MD 21704
United States of America
E-mail: customer.service@wolterskluwer.com

Printed on acid-free paper.

ISBN 978-94-035-3541-8

e-Book: ISBN 978-94-035-3542-5
web-PDF: ISBN 978-94-035-3543-2

Printed and bound by CPI Group (UK) Ltd, Croydon, CR0 4YY

Programme of the Conference

ASA Annual Conference
Clear Path or Jungle in Commercial Arbitrators' Conflict of Interest?
Disclosures | Objections | Challenges
Friday, 7 February 2020
Zurich, Switzerland

PRESIDENT'S WELCOME WELCOME ADDRESS AND INTRODUCTION TO THE CONFERENCE TOPIC	**Felix Dasser,** ASA & Homburger, Zurich **Wolfgang Peter**, Peter & Kim, Geneva
PANEL 1 – THE VIEW FROM THE USERS	MODERATION: **Wolfgang Peter**, Peter & Kim, Geneva
How much independence and impartiality do users seek? What expectations do users have from the different members of the tribunal? How important is a right of each party to appoint an arbitrator? When and why should an arbitrator be objected against/challenged?	SPEAKERS: **Jan Michael Ahrens**, Siemens Mobility GmbH, Munich **Ulrich Hagel/James Menz**, Bombardier Transportation, Berlin **Gottlieb Keller**, Roche Holding AG, Basle **Pierrick Le Goff**, De Gaulle Fleurance & Associés, Paris (previously Alstom, Paris) **Nishtha Kharb Shukla**, Association of Corporate Counsel, Singapore
PANEL 2 – PRACTICAL EXPERIENCE: THE VIEW FROM MAJOR INSTITUTIONS	MODERATION: **Pierre Tercier**, Independent Arbitrator, Fribourg

What is the threshold for disclosure? What is the procedure for objections/challenges? Is it effective? Is there any difference between party-appointed arbitrators and chairpersons? Is there an impact of the internal 'knowledge' of the institutions on appointments?	SPEAKERS: **Claudia Annacker,** SIAC Court of Arbitration & Cleary Gottlieb, Paris **Alexander Fessas**, ICC, Paris **Jamie Harrison**, LCIA, London **Gabrielle Nater-Bass**, SCAI & Homburger, Zurich
PANEL 3 – PRACTICAL EXPERIENCE: THE VIEW FROM STATE COURTS	MODERATION: **Felix Dasser**, ASA & Homburger, Zurich
What is the threshold for independence and impartiality? Is there a specific threshold for disclosure? What is the relevance of the IBA Conflicts of Interest Guidelines and other private instruments? Is there a duty of parties to investigate? How successful are challenges in court and on what grounds?	SPEAKERS: **Diana Akikol**, ABR Avocats, Geneva **Laurent Gouiffès**, Hogan Lovells, Paris **Paula Hodges QC**, Herbert Smith Freehills, London **Laurence Shore**, BonelliErede, Milan
PANEL 4 – THE DEBATE: IS THERE ENOUGH UNIFORMITY? NOT ENOUGH? MORE THAN ENOUGH?	MODERATION: **Charles Kaplan**, Orrick, Paris
IBA Guidelines versus ICC Notes and everything else? Are there conflicts between guidelines? Do we need harmonized standards for disclosure? How to deal with tactical challenges? Are there lessons to be drawn from other types of arbitration (investor-state, sports and others)? To what extent does the perception of independence and impartiality vary in different legal cultures?	SPEAKERS: **Alexander Fessas**, ICC, Paris **Paula Hodges QC**, Herbert Smith Freehills, London **Álvaro López de Argumedo Piñeiro**, Uría Menéndez, Madrid **Nathalie Voser**, Schellenberg Wittmer, Zurich
CLOSING REMARKS	**Felix Dasser**, ASA & Homburger, Zurich

Editor

Felix Dasser is a partner at Homburger in Zurich since 2000. He is a senior member and former head of the dispute resolution team. His practice focuses on litigation and arbitration of international commercial and investment disputes, as well as white-collar crime and investigations. Professor Dasser acts as counsel and arbitrator (sole arbitrator, co-arbitrator and chairman) in international arbitration cases under various arbitration rules. He is President of ASA, the Swiss Arbitration Association. He also advises Swiss companies on international litigation strategies and on the impact of foreign regulatory proceedings and represents Swiss and foreign companies before Swiss courts and authorities. His range of expertise covers, in particular, banking and insurance, M&A, commodity trades, distribution agreements, IT, engineering, investment, and international legal assistance. Professor Dasser lectures and regularly publishes in the fields of international commercial dispute resolution and international business law. He is teaching international dispute resolution at the Universities of Zurich and Bern, is visiting professor at the China University of Political Science and Law and, in 2018, taught at the Hague Academy of International Law on soft law in international commercial arbitration. He also frequently appears as an expert witness on Swiss law in foreign court and international arbitration proceedings. Professor Dasser studied at the University of Zurich, where he obtained his PhD, and at the Harvard Law School (LLM '90). In 1999, he received the *venia legendi* (Habilitation) from the University of Zurich for private law, international private and procedural law and private comparative law, and became an adjunct professor (*Titularprofessor*) in 2005.

Contributors

Dr Diana Akikol is a partner at Walder Wyss based in the Geneva office. She represents clients in international arbitration proceedings and frequently sits as arbitrator. Both as counsel and arbitrator, she has been involved in ad hoc (including UNCITRAL) and administered arbitrations (under the Swiss, ICC, LCIA and DIS Rules). She has particular experience in disputes involving sales, mergers & acquisitions, shareholder agreements, joint ventures, construction and engineering, agency agreements, licence and distribution agreements. Dr Akikol is member of the ICC Commission on Arbitration and ADR (Paris), the Swiss ICC Commission of Arbitration and ADR, and the ICC Swiss National Committee. She furthermore serves on the Arbitration Court of the Swiss Arbitration Centre, the International Advisory Board of the Vienna International Arbitral Centre (VIAC) and the Board of the Swiss Arbitration Association (ASA). Diana Akikol holds a law degree from the University of Fribourg and a doctorate degree from the University of Lucerne, both summa cum laude. She was admitted to the bar in 2002, ranked first of her class.

Claudia Annacker is a partner at Dechert LLP based in the Paris office. Her practice focuses on international arbitration and public international law matters, including investor-State disputes, disputes involving international organizations, State succession issues and State immunity, as well as disputes before the European Court of Human Rights. Dr Annacker received a PhD in 1992 and the *venia legendi et docendi* (Habilitation) for public international law in 1997, both from the University of Vienna, where she is an adjunct professor. She has also been a visiting professor at the Paris Ouest Nanterre La Défense University and at the National University of Singapore. Dr Annacker is a member of the Paris Bar, the ICSID Arbitrator Panel, the Court of Arbitration of the Singapore International Arbitration Centre, the Board of the Vienna International Arbitral Centre, the International Law Association, the American Society of International Law, the European Society of International Law and the German Society of International Law. She speaks and regularly publishes on investment and commercial arbitration and also sits as an arbitrator.

Álvaro López de Argumedo Piñeiro is a partner in the Madrid office of Uría Menéndez, and he focuses his practice on international arbitration, international commercial litigation and mediation. He has recently been appointed as a new Court Member of the LCIA Board. He was an officer of the IBA Arbitration Committee from 2017 to 2019, chair of the Arbitration Guidelines and Rules Subcommittee and co-chair of the IBA Task Force for the revision of the IBA Rules on the Taking of Evidence in International Arbitration. He is also a member of the Steering Committee of the UIA (*Union Internationale des Avocats*) Arbitration Commission. He was appointed "stakeholder expert" for the preparation of the Common Frame of Reference by the European Commission as part of the European Civil Code project. He is also an arbitrator at numerous institutions and a member of the Board of Directors and the Mediation Committee of the Spanish Arbitration Club (*Club Español de Arbitraje*). He regularly represents clients in arbitration proceedings before the main international and Spanish arbitration institutions (such as the ICC, LCIA, SCAI, CIMA, and the Madrid Arbitration Court), in addition to ad hoc arbitrations. He has extensive experience in contract law, real property rights, construction and energy matters, distribution and agency contracts, representing national and international clients. He frequently participates as a speaker at conferences and seminars pertaining to his areas of expertise (international arbitration and international commercial litigation) and has published several articles in these areas.

Federico Alberto Cabona is an associate with BonelliErede (international arbitration department) and a member of the Milan Bar.

Alexander Fessas is the Secretary General of the ICC International Court of Arbitration. As Secretary General, he is responsible for the operational management and coordination of the ICC Court's Secretariat and other dispute resolution services in Paris, Hong Kong, New York, Sao Paolo and Singapore. He joined the Secretariat in late 2011 and held consecutive positions in three case management teams, of which two as counsel. Prior to his appointment as Secretary General, he was the Secretariat's Managing Counsel over a three-year term. Mr Fessas studied Law at the University of Athens, Greece, having specialized in international commercial transactions and conflict of laws. Prior to joining the ICC Court, he practised as counsel out of Athens, where he established a sole practice in 2008. He was previously an associate at an Athens-based law firm. During the same period, he was also the editor-in-chief of the Revue hellénique de droit international. He is a member of the Athens Bar.

Laurent Gouiffès leads Hogan Lovells' International Arbitration group in Paris as a partner with over twenty years of experience representing major industrial groups and States in high-profile, complex international arbitrations and mediations. He has extensive experience of arbitration under the rules of the ICC, LCIA, ICSID and UNCITRAL and has also acted in a number of disputes brought under the Energy Charter Treaty. With a focus on energy-related, technological and investment disputes, he regularly acts on behalf of clients in the oil and gas, mining, electricity, nuclear, aerospace and telecommunications and transport industries, as well as on behalf of the States. He also acts as arbitrator in cases before the ICC, the LCIA and the Chamber of

Arbitration of Milan (sole arbitrator, co-arbitrator and chairman). Mr Gouiffès regularly speaks and publishes on topical issues in arbitration, energy and public and private international law and gives lectures on energy arbitration at the London School of Economics and Political Sciences and Sciences Po in Paris. He is admitted to the Paris Bar as well as the Bar of England and Wales.

Ulrich Hagel is Chief Compliance & Security Officer and Global Head of Litigations at Bombardier Transportation. After having worked as an Attorney at Law in Stuttgart, he joined Bombardier Transportation in 1998. He is working conceptually on conflict management processes and tools but also operationally leading complex disputes in negotiations, ADR processes, arbitration and court litigation. Since 2010, he is also a partner at KonsensKanzlei in Berlin. Dr Hagel has published on Conflict Management, Contract Management and Compliance. He is co-editor of the German Arbitration Journal (SchiedsVZ), founding member and member of the Board of the Round Table Mediation and Conflict Management of the German Industry (RTMKM). He is also a member of several advisory boards (German Arbitration Institute DIS, Eucon and the Online-Magazines AnwaltSpiegel and Dispute Resolution). Since 2014, he is the Academic Director of the MBA-Program 'International Commercial & Contract Management' at the Dresden International University. Dr Hagel studied Law and Business Administration at the University of Bayreuth, where he also obtained his PhD.

Jamie Harrison FCIArb is Deputy Director General of the London Court of International Arbitration (LCIA), a role that he took up in June 2019. He joined the LCIA after nearly eight years in Singapore, where he set up and managed the Singapore office of Addleshaw Goddard LLP, leading the firm's Asian arbitration practice. Mr Harrison qualified as a solicitor with Freshfields in 1992 and worked in the arbitration team in London and Hong Kong until 1999 when he joined the London office of US firm Morgan Lewis LLP, where he was made a partner in 2002. He joined the London office of Winston & Strawn LLP in 2005, where he founded and led the dispute resolution practice, working closely with established arbitration practices in Paris and Geneva. As a practising international arbitration lawyer, Mr Harrison acted as Counsel on general commercial disputes, principally arising in developing markets in Asia and West Africa under the rules of LCIA, ICC, SIAC, HKIAC, CIETAC, JAMS, UNCITRAL and ICSID. He is qualified to practice as a solicitor in England & Wales and Hong Kong and has been a registered foreign lawyer with full registration before the International Commercial Court in Singapore.

Paula Hodges QC heads Herbert Smith Freehills' Global Arbitration Practice and has over thirty years of experience advising on international disputes, particularly in the energy, telecommunications and technology sectors. She specializes in international arbitration and has represented clients in many jurisdictions (including London, Paris, Geneva, Zurich, Stockholm, the US, Canada, Dubai, Africa, Asia, Russia and the CIS) in ad hoc arbitration and proceedings under the auspices of the major arbitral institutions. She also sits as an arbitrator. Ms Hodges has been closely involved in several high-profile cases before the High Court in London and has also appeared before the Court of Appeal and House of Lords (now the Supreme Court). She became a QC in 2014 and President of the LCIA Court in May 2019. Ms Hodges frequently publishes and lectures in the field. She studied law at the University of Cambridge.

Charles Kaplan is a partner in the Paris office of Orrick. A highly specialized arbitration lawyer, he has conducted arbitrations on gas pricing disputes, investment disputes, disputes relating to tax stabilization and renewable energy incentives, international joint ventures, as well as aircraft development programs, in France and elsewhere. Highly regarded in the international arbitration market, Charles is consistently recognized as a key practitioner particularly in Europe, Africa and the Middle East. In particular, Charles advises French and international energy majors, and industrials. He has extensive experience of arbitration under ICC, ICSID, French Arbitration Association, LCIA and Milan Chamber rules. He regularly sits as arbitrator. He originally qualified as an English barrister and then as a French avocat. In addition to investment disputes, he has handled civil as well as common law disputes in a number of jurisdictions in Europe, Africa, the Middle East and Asia. Before he joined Orrick, he was co-head of Herbert Smith Freehills LLP's Global Arbitration practice and led the Paris Arbitration group.

James Menz is a founding partner of rothorn legal. With over fifteen years of experience, his practice focuses on complex disputes in the construction, engineering, energy, transportation, pharmaceutical, and biotechnology sectors. He has acted as counsel, arbitrator, and arbitral secretary in dozens of proceedings under a variety of applicable institutional rules and substantive laws. Most recently, Mr Menz worked in-house as a senior litigation expert for Bombardier Transportation, managing a range of domestic and international project and construction litigations and arbitrations and advising the business on dispute avoidance and resolution strategies. From 2016-2018, Mr Menz was Deputy Secretary General and Head of Case Management at the German Arbitration Institute (DIS), where he supervised hundreds of arbitration and ADR proceedings and served on the drafting committee for the revised 2018 DIS Arbitration Rules. Previously, for over ten years, Mr Menz practiced international arbitration, litigation, and competition law with major law firms in New York and Zurich. A graduate of the George Washington University Law School and admitted to the New York Bar, Mr Menz regularly sits as an arbitrator and publishes and speaks on issues in international commercial arbitration.

Gabrielle Nater-Bass is a partner at Homburger in Zurich. Her practice focuses on arbitration and litigation. She is an experienced party counsel and arbitrator in international commercial arbitration proceedings, ad hoc and institutional. Ms Nater-Bass also advises clients in investment treaty arbitrations and represents clients in complex cross-border litigations. She is a board member of the Swiss Arbitration Association (ASA) and a member of the LCIA Court. She served as President of the Arbitration Court of the Swiss Chambers' Arbitration Institution (SCAI) from 2016 to 2020. Ms Nater-Bass is listed on the panel of arbitrators of the ICC National Committee (Switzerland), the Hong Kong International Arbitration Centre (HKIAC) and the Singapore International Arbitration Centre (SIAC). Furthermore, she co-chairs the ICCA-ASIL Task Force on Damages in International Arbitration and is a member of the

SIAC Users Council, the advisory board of ArbitralWomen (former vice president) and the steering committee of the Equal Representation in Arbitration Pledge. Ms Nater-Bass received the Client Choice Award 2020 in the category Arbitration & ADR (Switzerland). She is a frequent speaker at international arbitration conferences and regularly publishes in the field. She studied at the University of Zurich and the Virginia School of Law and is admitted to the Swiss bar.

Wolfgang Peter is a founding partner of Peter & Kim with offices in Geneva, Seoul, Bern, Sydney and Singapore, specializing in international commercial and investment arbitration. Dr Peter represents major companies from Europe and overseas as counsel in large and complex international arbitrations. Dr Peter is particularly active in cases involving complex issues of valuations, including post-M&A disputes, joint ventures and projects stemming from the heavy industry. He has decades of expertise in cases involving gas & oil contracts, including upstream and downstream projects, as well as price reviews under long-term gas supply agreements. Dr Peter regularly advises third-party funding companies in evaluating the merits of the Claimant(s)' cases, especially with regard to the damages. An active speaker and contributor to the arbitration community at large, he is a member of the LCIA Board of Directors and of the ASA Board. Prior to his new venture, Dr Peter founded Peter & Partners, a boutique law firm specialized in arbitration, headed the arbitration group of Python & Peter and acted as a CEO of two luxury watch-making companies for twelve years. He studied at the Universities of Lausanne and Frankfurt as well as the Graduate Institute of International Studies in Geneva. Further, he was a visiting scholar at Harvard Law School. Dr Peter is admitted to the Swiss Bar.

Laurence Shore joined BonelliErede-Milan in September 2017, after practicing in London, New York City, and Washington, DC. He is the head of the firm's international arbitration department. Laurence sits as an arbitrator in addition to his counsel practice. He has been a tribunal member or lead advocate in cases under the LCIA, ICSID, AAA, ICDR, ICC, CRCICA, UNCITRAL, SIAC, HKIAC, Swiss Chambers, LMAA, and Society of Maritime Arbitrators' Rules, involving a wide array of industry sectors. He serves on the Institute for Transnational Arbitration's Executive Committee and previously served on the LCIA's North American Users' Council. From September 2012 to May 2014, Laurence chaired the New York City Bar's International Law Committee. He is a co-author of International Investment Arbitration: Substantive Principles (Oxford University Press). Laurence studied Law at Emory University and earned a PhD in American History from Johns Hopkins University; his undergraduate degree is from the University of North Carolina at Chapel Hill, where he graduated with the highest honors. He is a solicitor of the Senior Courts of England & Wales and a member of the New York, District of Columbia and Virginia Bars.

Summary of Contents

Table of Contents

Preface

COVID-19 delayed the publication of this volume, but the conference theme is as topical today as a year ago, if not more so. Arbitrators' conflicts of interest seem to exercise arbitration specialists as barely any other issue. The last months alone witnessed seminal decisions by several supreme courts that grappled with the issue. In England, the Supreme Court finally handed down its long-awaited decision in the *Halliburton* case, clarifying certain aspects of English law, but requiring sixty-one pages to do so.[1] For the first time ever, the Swiss Federal Supreme Court set aside an award due to objectively justified doubts as to the impartiality of an arbitrator.[2] The reports about these two jurisdictions had to be updated accordingly.[3] Conversely, in the US, the Supreme Court declined to review a controversial decision by the Ninth Circuit in the *Monster Energy* case, thus wasting an opportunity to finally settle the law on disclosure obligations and conflicts of interest in the US.[4] On a lighter note, the Austrian Supreme Court held that alleged eye-rolling by an arbitrator during oral pleadings cannot justify a challenge of the arbitrator even if proven.[5] This will come as a relief to all arbitrators who struggle with remaining poker-faced throughout sometimes rather tedious hearings. There remain more serious issues to be addressed, though. Just recently, the European Court of Human Rights felt compelled to weigh in, holding that Italy had violated Article 6 § 1 of the Convention for having refused a remedy against a particularly egregious case of apparent lack of independence.[6]

The conference approached the tangled topic from various sides. After an introduction by co-organizer *Wolfgang Peter* setting the scene, the most important stakeholders in arbitration, the users, had their say. *Jan Michael Ahrens*, *Nishtha Kharb Shukla*, *Gottlieb Keller*, *Pierrick Le Goff* and *James Menz* (standing in for *Ulrich Hagel*, who was prevented on short notice but contributed in writing), representing major

1. *Halliburton Company v. Chubb Bermuda Insurance Ltd*, 27 November 2020, [2020] UKSC 48.
2. Decision of the Federal Supreme Court 4A_318/2020 of 22 December 2020.
3. *See* below the chapters by Paula Hodges QC and Diana Akikol.
4. *See* below the chapter by Laurence Shore and Federico Alberto Cabona.
5. Austrian Oberster Gerichtshof, 23 July 2020, Case No. 18 ONc 3/20s, consid. 12.
6. ECHR, Case No. 5312/11, 20 May 2021, *Beg S.p.a. v. Italy*.

arbitration users in Europe and Southeast Asia, respectively, discussed under the moderation of *Wolfgang Peter* what impartiality and independence mean for users. A second panel under the moderation of *Pierre Tercier* reported from major institutions, namely *Claudia Annacker* (SIAC), *Alexander Fessas* (ICC), *Jamie Harrison* (LCIA), and *Gabrielle Nater-Bass* (SCAI). Then, it was the turn of the states: introduced by myself, *Diana Akikol* reported from Switzerland, *Laurent Gouiffès* from France, *Paula Hodges QC* from England & Wales and *Laurence Shore* from the US. The final panel, moderated by *Charles Kaplan*, tried to bring together the various views and aspects to answer the thorny question of whether there is enough uniformity. From their various vantage points, *Alexander Fessas*, *Paula Hodges QC*, *Nathalie Voser* and *Álvaro López de Argumedo Piñeiro* engaged in what was widely expected to be a mission impossible.

Is there enough uniformity? Even if not, is there are least a clear path? Or are we confronted with a jungle and a patchwork of diverging, competing and often nebulous standards? The conference did not provide all the answers to these ultimate questions, but as the chapters and summaries published in this book testify, it could raise awareness of the issues and provide answers at least to many of the countless aspects. As the saying goes: we might still be confused but on a much higher level. Or put differently: if there be a jungle, at least we have an idea where the snakes may be lurking.

This conference was perfectly organized by our Executive Director *Alex McLin* and his Assistant, *Songea Dehne*. Alex McLin has since moved on to a new challenge. He deserves all our gratitude for all he has done over more than eight years as Executive Director of ASA.

Special thanks to *Robyn Nott* for the again impeccable transcription services and to my Personal Assistant, *Jessica Wiederhold,* for her careful editing of the manuscripts.

Felix Dasser
Zurich, May 2021

CHAPTER 1

Introduction

Wolfgang Peter

Why do we have this subject? Has not enough been written on disclosure, objections and challenges? So many conferences have already dealt with these issues. So why do we propose this somewhat provocative subject? Today we intend to adopt a different approach, shedding light on a confusing situation which arbitration professionals must increasingly face. So let me lay out the approach of our Conference.

In a *first step,* the panelists of Panels 1-3 will describe how they have treated the issues of disclosure, objections and challenges under a comparative analysis from:

(1) the point of view of the users who are the drivers of arbitration;
(2) the viewpoint of the arbitration institutions; and finally
(3) the practice of state courts.

In a *second step*, Panel 4 will engage based on the results of the work of Panels 1-3 in a discussion on the question of whether there is enough uniformity, in other words, if there is a clear path or a jungle in determining commercial arbitrators' conflicts of interest. These issues relate, in particular, to the constitution of the arbitral tribunal, which is the most crucial step in the arbitral process.

The right of a party to appoint its arbitrator is a key aspect of arbitration. A party relies on its appointee with the expectation that its arguments on facts and law will be duly examined, will be considered on the basis of the arbitrator's experience, that the appointed arbitrator will be convincing in the discussions with the other members of the tribunal, that the arbitrator knows the file and is well prepared. Against the background of this legitimate expectation, we increasingly realize that tools are used against those nominated arbitrators that an opposing party does not want in the arbitration for opportunistic rather than legitimate reasons. Thus, the appointment becomes all too often the legal battlefield. This deplorable state of affairs is favored by a growing jungle of rules and guidelines on disclosure, objections and challenges. This undermines the fundamental right of the parties to appoint their arbitrator. The alleged fear of bias is, in reality, all too often a pretext to manipulate the appointment process in one's own favor. Moreover, rules and guidelines become stricter and, unfortunately, divergent and allow unscrupulous parties to fabricate reasons for objections and challenges, thus, undermining the process. We can just look at IBA Guidelines—the most respected global standard—which deals with the permissible frequency of arbitrator appointments. They impose disclosure time limits, for instance, the lapse of three years in certain instances and application lists, so-called red, orange and green lists. Other sources of rules lack such comfort and clarity. With the guidelines of the ICC, for instance, there is no threshold for frequency of appointments; there are no time limits, and application lists do not exist. Such sweeping rules can be abused by those parties who want to prevent the appointment of arbitrators who are not to their liking. Is this too provocative, too negative? Let me give you some flavor of objections and challenges which have seriously sought to disrupt the process and which exploited the lack of guidance and clarity in disclosure matters.

(1) In an ICC arbitration, the Respondent nominates its arbitrator, an M&A specialist, who meets with objections from the Claimant's side. As it turns out, the Claimant had appointed an industry specialist as arbitrator and realized too late that the disputed issues were not industry-specific but of an accounting and valuation nature. Fearful of an imbalance between the two arbitrators, the Claimant used various pretexts relying on the ICC Guidelines to prevent the appointment of an M&A professional because it needed to get rid of somebody dangerously competent.

(2) A four-month battle because the two nominated arbitrators were both members of the Board of an arbitration institution. This would not have been an issue under the IBA Guidelines, but the ICC Guidelines opened up the arbitration to the possibility of multiple objections.

(3) A chairman was appointed by an arbitration institution and was challenged by one party because he was, allegedly, of too advanced an age for the position. As it turned out, the reasons for the objection were not the age or medical condition (there was no medical condition) but the fact that the objecting party wanted a lawyer trained in common law. Again, the application of IBA Guidelines would have led to a far more expeditious decision.

(4) The alleged professional relationships between the arbitrator and the appointing law firm. The strange argument has been made by a party that an arbitrator sitting in two successive unrelated cases should disclose the fact that counsel to his appointing party appeared as counsel in the previous case, although it did not appoint him in that arbitration. Irrespective of who the appointing party is, the mere fact of sitting in a case supposedly creates a disclosable professional relationship between an arbitrator and a law firm. The fact that this surprising argument is not supported by any guidelines did not prevent the objecting party from accusing the arbitrator of failing to disclose a "professional relationship."

(5) An article written jointly by an arbitrator and counsel seventeen years prior to the nomination was used as an objection against the arbitrator because it had not been disclosed.
(6) And finally, as the cherry on the cake, in cases where the objections process has become extended and acrimonious, some counsel do not hesitate to state that, after having gone through this process, they would no longer expect the arbitrator to remain unbiased and their objection to his appointment should be upheld.

In reality, many of these objections and challenges are emergency breaks pulled by a party that fears being put at a disadvantage. The fear of arbitrator bias often misses the target. Legitimate independence is not the issue when absurd disclosure issues are fabricated. Parties should rather fear the truly independent arbitrator, who with an unobjectionable professional background may, for personal reasons, nevertheless be partial or become partial in the course of the arbitration, and who knows how to efficiently conceal his mindset. And parties should not fabricate biased arbitrators by using leeway under all too generous guidelines in order to raise abusive objections and challenges.

Moreover, the objection and challenge process works to the disadvantage of the arbitrator, who must absolutely refrain from showing the slightest sign of irritation when provocative language is deliberately used to produce a negative reaction. Even where counsel in a recent case called a nominated arbitrator "incompetent and dishonest" without advancing any proof, the arbitrator was confined to strict, measured and polite language if he/she did not want to provide a basis for objection/challenge.

Arbitral institutions like to point out that the vast majority of objections and challenges are rejected. They indeed are. But loose, open-ended guidelines assist abusive parties in creating objection/challenge processes that are disruptive, time-consuming, create tensions and help in fabricating allegations of arbitrator bias.

Thus, I suggest that the lack of harmonization among guidelines, the permissiveness of loose guidelines favor a jungle, which should be addressed by harmonizing guidelines and by establishing clear and reasonable criteria, as the IBA Guidelines have largely done. That is my view, based on my personal experience over the years, but let us now hear the view of the panelists.

PANEL 1 The View from the Users

CHAPTER 2

The View from the Users: Summary

Felix Dasser

1. INTRODUCTION

Who are the users? The users are those without whom there would be no arbitration, no arbitration specialists and no arbitration conference like this one. But who are they really? In-house counsel of global enterprises? The managers of these enterprises? Owners of small and medium enterprises that may not even have in-house counsel? Western, Eastern or Southern companies? Listed companies or privately-held companies? Parties with a single arbitration case or with dozens of pending cases?

There is no average or archetypal user. Any panel of users cannot cover the whole universe. This panel is representative of serial users. Each panellist can draw upon vast experience with arbitration cases. In alphabetical order, they are **Jan-Michael Ahrens**, Principal Counsel Litigation, Siemens Mobility GmbH, Germany; **Gottlieb Keller**, General Counsel, Roche Holding AG, Switzerland; **Nishtha Kharb Shukla**, Director, Association of Corporate Counsel, Singapore chapter; **Pierrick Le Goff**, Partner, De Gaulle Fleurance & Associés, Paris since 2019 after twenty-five years in-house, including as Group General Counsel of Alstom, France, 2015-2019; and **James Menz**, Senior Expert Litigations, Bombardier Transportation, Germany, stepping in for Ulrich Hagel, Global Head of Litigations and General Counsel Office, Bombardier Transportation, who was prevented at the last minute. Their views represent a significant share of the arbitration users and cases that participants at this conference are likely to be involved with and thus of eminent importance.

2. HOW MUCH INDEPENDENCE AND IMPARTIALITY DO USERS SEEK?

The requirement of independence and impartiality of the arbitrators is a fundamental tenet of arbitration laws as well as the rules of institutions. Among arbitration specialists, it is nowadays undisputed.[1] This was not always the case. In some jurisdictions, namely in the U.S., it was quite common to have non-neutral party-appointed arbitrators with the chair being the only neutral member of the tribunal and, therefore, aptly called "the neutral."[2] The general counsel of a major U.S. company once complained about this indirect system of arbitration, where in effect, the counsel present their case to their arbitrators, who then advocate on behalf of their respective party before the neutral.[3] Today, too much bias does not seem to be favored. However, is there also such a thing as too much independence and impartiality? Do users seek perfection?

Ahrens opens the discussion with a strong avowal of independence and impartiality as "cornerstones of international arbitration" and, thus, of fundamental importance. According to him, users expect from arbitration a process that is conducted fairly before decision makers who are open-minded and independent of the parties and impartial and who will then consider the parties' position in a way that would hopefully lead to a fair result. Independence and impartiality being so important, they need to be protected by the entire system, including legislators, courts, and arbitrators. Siemens Mobility and the Siemens group take these requirements very seriously when appointing arbitrators. There are not, in the least, very practical reasons for such care: if an in-house counsel appoints an arbitrator who is then successfully challenged, he or she may face serious questions by the management. The worst case would be a successful challenge of an award by the opponent. In one case, Siemens won the award, but the award was challenged due to an alleged lack of independence and impartiality of the arbitrator appointed by Siemens. The challenge was rightly dismissed by the Supreme Court of a major European jurisdiction. It could have been difficult for the in-house counsel to explain if the positive award had been set aside after five years of proceedings due to his or her unwise or uninformed choice of an arbitrator.

Menz confirms that in his experience, sophisticated users in particular value independence also of the arbitrator appointed by themselves, while less sophisticated users are sometimes more tempted to appoint a partial advocate. Since the appearance of impartiality is key, users would expect prospective arbitrators to err on the side of caution and to broadly disclose facts. Arbitrators tend to be somewhat too careful in this respect for fear of challenges. The flip side of erring on the side of the disclosure are parties that do not abuse the right to challenge and institutions that do not grant

1. *See* the contributions on the institutions and state courts in this volume.
2. *See, e.g.*, Gary Born, INTERNATIONAL COMMERCIAL ARBITRATION, Vol. II, 1801 et seqq. (Wolters Kluwer, 2014).
3. Panel contribution at the 2018 Cravath Summit on Global Dispute Resolution, New York, April 26, 2018.

frivolous challenges. Issues that users are interested in but are often not disclosed are informal relationships between arbitrators and also between arbitrators and counsel: Who likes to sit with whom on a tribunal? Who regularly appoints whom? What are their procedural leanings? Do they have a more dogmatic view or are attuned to business realities? What are their psychological predispositions? These issues may have a substantial impact on the conduct and outcome of a proceeding but are not usually disclosed and difficult to find out. Experienced users can gather some information either internally or through their networks; less experienced users do not have that benefit. New tools, such as the ones in investment treaty arbitration,[4] are helpful, but no comparably insightful tools are available for commercial arbitration yet.

Keller provides a good reason for choosing an unbiased arbitrator: at Roche, they first determine whether a case is good or bad. If they determine that they have a really good chance of winning, they go for arbitration and choose an experienced arbitrator known for quality and independence. Keller cares less about the independence of the arbitrator chosen by the opponent as he counts on the president of the tribunal to appreciate the merits of the case. If the case is difficult to arbitrate, for whatever reason, Roche prefers to negotiate, thus avoiding arbitration altogether.

Having just made the transit from in-house counsel to the independent practitioner, **Le Goff** realized that even experienced in-house counsel tend to underestimate the complexities of the issues around conflicts. The approach of in-house counsel is largely process-oriented, e.g., making sure that any arbitrator he or she selects has no link to any of the group's affiliates and divisions, including through his or her law firm. In global companies, this already presents a challenge but is important to prevent objections or challenges later on. What is often overlooked is that this must be an ongoing process for the whole duration of the arbitration proceedings.

It was for the last speaker, **Kharb Shukla**, to introduce a new perspective. In the Asian culture, the focus of users is less on impartiality and independence than on familiarity: an arbitrator is first of all expected to be familiar with the culture of the parties and with the type of dispute. In-house counsel need to balance this expectation with the usual standards of independence and impartiality. This is a difficult balancing act with the in-house counsel additionally being under substantial pressure from management in any dispute situation.

In sum, experienced in-house counsel agree that independence and impartiality, including the appearance of it, is crucial. The main reason is a very practical one: lack of independence and impartiality may lead to a challenge, thus disrupting the proceedings, adding to time and costs, and in the worst case, annihilating an award that had already been won at substantial cost. In-house counsel do not want to end up in a situation where they have to explain such an outcome to management. For prospective arbitrators, this means that they have to be very careful in checking potential conflicts and being very frank about disclosing any potential conflict at the very outset even if they feel fully unbiased and even if that means to risk losing an appointment on a perceived triviality. The same diligence is required from outside counsel.

4. For example, ArbiLex (https://www.arbilex.co/); Jus Mundi (www.jusmundi.com); Investor-State Law Guide (www.investorstatelawguide.com).

On the other hand, it also transpires that there is no such thing as the typical user with typical concerns. Counsel and arbitrators have to take into account the different expectations of different types of users with different cultural backgrounds and different levels of experience.

3. WHAT EXPECTATIONS DO USERS HAVE FROM THE DIFFERENT MEMBERS OF THE TRIBUNAL?

Independence and impartiality taken together are only one element in a whole bouquet of characteristics that users might expect from arbitrators. Taking one step back, therefore, and looking at the whole picture, what are users expecting and to what extent do expectations differ with regard to the "own" arbitrator, the arbitrator appointed by the opponent and the chairperson?

Le Goff points first to expertise in the field. Arbitrators are expected to possess a general understanding of the business field concerned. Second, expertise alone does not do the trick if an arbitrator does not look at the file; he or she, therefore, also needs to be willing to be close to the file. Third, users look at the overall dynamic of the tribunal. For example, if the claimant appoints a professor who can bring the academic edge into the deliberations, the respondent may opt for a practitioner to bring the practical angle.

Keller echoes the requirement of experience and, in addition, emphasizes general quality and timely availability. He notes that the best qualified and most experienced arbitrators are typically also very busy, which creates a certain tension.

From an Asian perspective, **Kharb Shukla** notes the need for time efficiency. Users expect predictability of the time it takes for the proceedings. To successfully compete against litigation in state courts, arbitration needs to be more efficient in time.

According to **Ahrens**, the LCIA Notes for Arbitrators sum it up nicely: "Parties to arbitrations are entitled to expect of the process a just, well-reasoned and enforceable award. To that end, they are entitled to expect arbitrators: to disclose possible conflicts of interest at the outset; to avoid putting themselves in a position where conflicts will arise during the course of the proceedings; to conduct the arbitration fairly, in a timely manner and with careful regard to due process; to maintain the confidentiality of the arbitration; and to reach their decision in an impartial manner."[5] Users expect the presiding arbitrator to be the guardian of these principles and to ensure that the award is taken in an impartial and timely manner. Conversely, they expect from the arbitrator they themselves have appointed to be well prepared and to ensure the effective consideration of their position both on the facts and on the law. In that context, the dynamics of a tribunal also play a role. One of the most dangerous situations is perhaps a tandem of arbitrators: when the arbitrator appointed by the opponent is closely related to the chairperson, for example, by having studied together at law school and then sat together on several arbitrations. At the same time, these situations are quite difficult to find out in time.

5. LCIA Notes for Arbitrators, 2017, Title 2 Independence and Impartiality, note 6.

Menz adds that the chairperson, in particular, needs to have management skills to keep the time schedule, to set the right expectations from the outset, and to manage the co-arbitrators. In addition, he or she needs to have increasingly important IT skills. Conversely, all arbitrators should be business savvy, industrious, and also curious. Many cases turn on the facts rather than on the law and thus require the arbitrators to spend considerable time studying the facts even though not all of that time may be compensated under an ad valorem system. Users expect an arbitrator to spend the necessary time anyway or otherwise decline to be appointed in the first place.

In sum, it appears indeed that independence and impartiality are only one element in a whole bouquet. And even though the laws on independence and impartiality typically do not distinguish between co-arbitrators and presiding arbitrators, users' expectations do differ a bit: while they expect the presiding arbitrator to be neutral and impartial, they understand that the co-arbitrators would lean towards their respective party and that these tendencies are ideally balanced out within the tribunal. Experienced users do not expect their arbitrator to be biased in his or her judgment but to ensure that the position of his or her party is heard and duly taken into consideration.

4. HOW IMPORTANT IS A RIGHT OF EACH PARTY TO APPOINT AN ARBITRATOR?

In international arbitration circles, a debate has been raised about the sense or nonsense of party-appointed arbitrators. Party appointments carry an obvious risk of impacting the arbitrator's independence and impartiality. There are more than enough examples of such arbitrators who were blatantly biased, or potentially more dangerous for the integrity of the process, totally biased but try to hide it the best they can. In 2010, Jan Paulsson called for the abolition of party appointments (except, of course, joint appointments by the parties).[6] In response, Alexis Mourre noted that there are issues with party appointments, but these can be addressed by "education and dissemination of the international arbitration culture" and do not require a ban.[7]

What do the users think about party-appointed arbitrators? After all, arbitration is a creature of contract, as we all know; it depends upon the will of the users and, thus, whatever the users want should be implemented within the very broad framework of the state arbitration laws.

The right of each party to appoint an arbitrator requires, of course, that there be a three-member panel (or more than three, although few practitioners would recommend larger panels given the likely impact on cost and time). Three-member tribunals are not a given, though. On the contrary, many arbitration proceedings are conducted

6. Jan Paulsson, *Moral Hazard in International Dispute Resolution, Inaugural Lecture U. of Miami School of Law 29 April 2010*, https://www.arbitration-icca.org/media/0/12773749999020/paulsson_moral_hazard.pdf.

7. Alexis Mourre, *Are unilateral appointments defensible? On Jan Paulsson's Moral Hazard in International Arbitration*, Kluwer Arbitration Blog, October 5, 2010, http://arbitrationblog.kluwerarbitration.com/2010/10/05/are-unilateral-appointments-defensible-on-jan-paulssons-moral-hazard-in-international-arbitration.

by a sole arbitrator, be it because of a regional tradition of sole judges or because of a need to reduce the cost of proceedings in smaller cases.[8]

Some institutions also have a list system that may go as far as limiting the choice of the parties to accredited arbitrators.[9] The idea behind such lists systems in general and a closed list in particular is to raise the quality of the proceedings and to reduce potential conflicts of arbitrators. Recently, diversity concerns also reinforced calls for institutions appointing all arbitrators. Statistics show that parties tend to appoint experienced arbitrators, think the archetypal gray-haired men from Europe or North America, while some institutions take great strides to increase diversity.[10]

Menz speaks for the whole panel when he describes the right of each party to appoint an arbitrator as "absolutely critical" and a "key advantage" of arbitration. He considers any discussion to shift the right of appointment to the institutions as "misguided" from a users' perspective.

Le Goff adds that from a philosophical standpoint, it seems somewhat contradictory to acknowledge the contractual fundament of arbitration but to try to curtail the parties' right to appoint the arbitrators. He refers to Prof. Daniel Cohen, who argued that party appointments do create issues but that this should not be a ground to deprive the parties of that right and that issues need to be addressed otherwise.[11]

Keller puts the position more starkly by noting that, in his experience, a sole arbitrator is even less predictable than a jury in the U.S. For him, the right to appoint a member of the tribunal is nonnegotiable.

Ahrens confirms that also for Siemens, that right is crucial and that, in case of an ICC arbitration, they insist on specifying that the two co-arbitrators have the right to appoint the chairperson, possibly in consultation with the parties.[12] He is doubtful about list systems; as such, a system does not guarantee a neutral and effective panel while severely restricting the parties' choice. To have an arbitrator of one's choice and trust on the panel is regarded as a protection against surprises and potential bias.

8. *See, e.g.*, the expedited proceedings under Article 42 of the Swiss rules: if the amount in dispute does not exceed CHF 1 million, the institution appoints a sole arbitrator unless otherwise provided for by the parties. In 2018, e.g., 42% of the ICC arbitral tribunals were constituted by a sole arbitrator (International Chamber of Commerce, *ICC Dispute Resolution 2018 Statistics*, www.iccwbo.org/dr-stat2018, 10).
9. *See, e.g.*, Article R33(2) of the Code of Sports-Related Arbitration of the Court of Arbitration for Sport; *see also* the non-mandatory list systems of the ICDR (Article 12(6) of the ICDR International Arbitration Rules) or CIETAC (Article 26 of the CIETAC Arbitration Rules 2015). These non-mandatory list systems require special attention at the time of executing the arbitration clause as a later agreement between the parties on the set up of an arbitration once a dispute has erupted is notoriously difficult.
10. *See, e.g.*, Lacey Yong, *Swiss Chambers releases gender diversity stats*, GAR & Investment Law Newsletters, August 17, 2016; Markus Altenkirch & Jan Frohloff, *Gender Diversity in International Arbitration—Statistics*, in: Global Arbitration News, July 3, 2017 (https://globalarbitrationnews.com/gender-diversity-in-international-arbitration-some-statistics/); LCIA 2019 Annual Casework Report, 16 (https://www.lcia.org/lcia/reports.aspx).
11. David Cohen, *Indépendance des arbitres et conflits d'intérêts*, Revue de l'arbitrage 2011, 611 et seqq.
12. Pursuant to Article 12(5) of the ICC Arbitration Rules, the presiding arbitrator is appointed by the Court unless the parties have provided otherwise.

Kharb Shukla adds a slightly different perspective from Asia, though. For her, the freedom of the parties is overrated. In Singapore, for example, most appointments are made by an institution. Freedom to choose also means to be confronted with the choice by the opponent and the questions how that choice might impact the proceedings and whether to challenge that arbitrator. She recalls cases where the parties fiercely fought for their rights to appoint and, in the end, agreed to delegate the appointments to the institution.

In sum, the verdict seems clear: The right of each party to appoint one member of a three-member panel is crucial, at least in most parts of the arbitration world. To take that right from the parties would jeopardize a core advantage of arbitration over litigation. Experienced users would have none of it. It is different in smaller cases, where sole arbitrators, typically appointed by the institution, seem to be well accepted by users if only for efficiency reasons.

5. WHEN AND WHY SHOULD AN ARBITRATOR BE OBJECTED AGAINST/CHALLENGED?

Challenges are rare. SCAI, e.g., received nine challenges over the course of eight years.[13] SIAC received six challenges over three years.[14] The ICC saw substantially more challenges, forty-five in 2018 alone,[15] but also administers more proceedings. Challenges are not only rare but also rarely successful. SCAI and SIAC each maintained one challenge out of the eight and six, respectively, and the ICC maintained seven out of the forty-five. Consequently, the vast majority of challenges are unsuccessful, meaning that the arbitrator who was personally attacked by one of the parties remains on the tribunal (unless he or she has decided to step down in the course of the challenge). Challenges of arbitrators may not have become more frequent over the years, but awareness of challenges as a bane of arbitration certainly has become more acute.

What is the experienced users' approach to this?

Kharb Shukla reports two conclusions from a survey that she undertook from Singapore. First, challenges of an arbitrator typically occur at the end of the proceedings, when a party is losing or has lost the case. In this situation, pressure on the in-house counsel by management increases and arbitrators may be tactically challenged for being biased or not acting independently. Second, a challenge is often based on information gathered from the Internet. **Keller** confirms, adding that time is of the essence: any challenge has to be raised immediately once a situation of bias is realized.

Ahrens emphasizes that management expects in-house counsel to run disputes in a professional manner. In-house counsel need to investigate potential conflicts early on before the tribunal is constituted and the arbitration proceedings get started. It is also easier to lodge an objection early and informally before an appointment has been confirmed, i.e., when an arbitrator may still reconsider and withdraw. Later, Siemens

13. *See* Nater-Bass, Chapter 6, in this volume.
14. *See* Annacker, Chapter 4, in this volume.
15. *ICC Dispute Resolution 2018 Statistics*, *supra* n. 8, 10.

would only challenge when they are reasonably certain to win. Otherwise, there would be a risk of having an arbitrator on the tribunal who might be holding a grudge against the challenging party.

Menz echoes the reluctance expressed by Ahrens. Any objection or challenge reflects a breakdown of the system. After all, the parties agreed on each party's right to appoint an arbitrator and should respect that right in the absence of grievous factors. That does not mean that users take conflicts lightly. On the contrary, Bombardier is critical of "Chinese walls" within large law firms and, incidentally, of the case-by-case analysis espoused by the Swiss Federal Tribunal in the recent CMS case.[16] Drawing on his experience at the German Arbitration Institute DIS, he notes, however, that in practice, most cases are either black or white and the system as a whole, therefore, works rather well. Looking at the recent developments in the courts of several jurisdictions, he observes a certain trend to become a bit stricter with regard to disclosure of potential conflicts, a trend he welcomes.

Le Goff points out the difficulty of any test that involves a high level of subjectivity, namely when you would have to determine what constitutes a reasonable doubt in the eyes of the parties. He personally applies a "remoteness" test: how close or remote is a relation? It is difficult to avoid any relation. Some arbitrators have been challenged for the most remote relations, although unsuccessfully so, such as in the French Facebook case, where an arbitrator was unsuccessfully challenged because he was a Facebook friend with the counsel of one of the parties.[17] Another arbitrator was challenged because he sat on the same conference panel as a counsel. Trickier are situations where an arbitrator has some relation to a minority shareholder of one of the parties. He witnessed such a situation that led to a debate to what extent also a minority shareholder may still have an influence on the party.

In sum, in-house counsel recognize several difficulties, *first* of all, to discover any potential issue early on when it can still be resolved informally; *second* to react to the pressure of management once the proceedings lead or seem to lead to a negative outcome; and *third* to apply the appropriate judgment in assessing the chances of a challenge given the difficulty of defining the relevant threshold. They all underline the fundamental importance of letting the parties choose their arbitrators, and this implies constant vigilance to ensure independence and impartiality at the same time.

16. DFSC 142 III 521 of September 7, 2016, *see* Akikol, Chapter 8 in this volume.
17. *Tecso v. Neoelectra*, Cour d'Appel, Paris, Case No. 09/28537, March 10, 2011.

CHAPTER 3

Statement on Selected Topics in International Arbitration from the User's Perspective

Ulrich Hagel & James Menz

1. ARBITRATOR INDEPENDENCE AND IMPARTIALITY

As users, we consider the independence and impartiality of arbitrators an indispensable element of fair arbitration. The importance of the integrity of the arbitral process cannot be overstated. Arbitration as a private and largely self-policed dispute resolution mechanism fundamentally rests on trust: that a neutral panel of decision makers will carefully review the disputes and adjudicate the factual and legal questions purely on their merits and without predisposition to either party. Moreover, one key reason why parties, at least for cross-border contracts, have favored arbitration is to avoid the proverbial "home-court advantage." Arbitrator independence and impartiality are thus part of arbitration's very *raison-d'etre*.

We have observed that in practice and when it comes to party-appointed arbitrators, less sophisticated users sometimes care less about independence or even overtly favor a "partial" advocate. The better view, and one espoused by many sophisticated users, is that party-appointed arbitrators, too, should be strictly independent and impartial. These arbitrators tend to be much more effective in meeting the appointing party's legitimate expectation that its position be heard and understood by the other members of the tribunal. At the end of the day, when it comes to influencing in a three-member tribunal, a strictly neutral wing will carry more weight than someone perceived as partial or biased.

Users and their counsel are rightly expected to pay careful attention to potential conflicts when selecting arbitrators. "Missing" a conflict, for example, because of faulty databases, can significantly disrupt an arbitration proceeding when the conflict is discovered later.

However, users also expect arbitrators to be full and frank in their disclosure. Without disclosure, an informed choice is impossible. Disclosure, especially at the time of appointment, has a strong disinfecting effect: given that arbitration is a private mechanism and that in arbitration, like in state court litigation, justice must be *seen to be done*, users tend to be suspicious of undisclosed circumstances even when they may be harmless. This is particularly true because domestic and international arbitration circles, inevitably, continue to have an air of "clubbiness" in which arbitrators and counsel change hats, and there are multiple contacts across professionals and social venues. Against that background, in our view, prospective arbitrators are too reluctant to be full and frank in their disclosure for fear of incurring an objection or a challenge. As the IBA Guidelines on Conflicts of Interest in International Arbitration aptly state: "It is ... essential to reaffirm that the fact of requiring disclosure—or of an arbitrator making a disclosure—does not imply the existence of doubts as to the impartiality or independence of the arbitrator. Indeed, the standard for disclosure differs from the standard for challenge." Arbitrators should take a long-term view: it is better to err on the side of over-disclosure and perhaps risk losing an appointment than to under-disclose and thereby risk, at best, the parties' faith in the arbitrator's integrity or, at worst, the fate of the arbitral award.

The flip side of expecting broad disclosures from prospective arbitrators is that parties should not raise objections over innocuous relationships or for purely tactical reasons and that institutions should not grant objections or challenges lightly. In practice, parties and institutions (at least at the appointing stage) could do better in both respects.

However, even the IBA's sophisticated "traffic light systems" or enhanced disclosure obligations like those introduced by the International Chamber of Commerce (ICC) in 2019 do not capture key informal relationships and characteristics that may affect the conduct or the outcome of an arbitration. These include questions such as which arbitrators appoint, or are appointed by, other arbitrators or counsel, which arbitrators have sat together frequently, and which counsel regularly appears before which arbitrator. Current disclosure rules naturally also cannot capture key characteristics, such as whether arbitrators tend to be more "legally dogmatic" or "business-oriented," or their procedural or even psychological dispositions. Due to the public nature of the proceedings and the availability of published awards and judgments, data on these aspects is much more widely available in the investment arbitration context or in some state court systems, where studying prospective arbitrators and judges has become a key exercise in litigation due diligence. The lack of information on prospective arbitrators, and the somewhat arcane reliance on internal and external networks to gather "bits and pieces" of intelligence, is a drawback in commercial arbitration. As users, we would therefore welcome more transparency initiatives, such as the modest steps taken by the ICC and the Vienna International Arbitration Centre in publishing information on arbitral tribunals.

2. EXPECTATIONS OF DIFFERENT MEMBERS OF A THREE-MEMBER ARBITRAL TRIBUNAL

Users expect all arbitrators to be neutral, open-minded and have a judicial temperament. In addition to excellent legal qualifications, arbitrators must be business savvy. Most cases turn on the facts and require an appreciation of business reality, commercial expectations and sometimes extensive technical details. Arbitrators should be curious to learn, willing to ask questions and be prepared to spend the time necessary to understand the details of a case. When choosing arbitration over litigation, we, as in-house counsel, often explain to our management that arbitrators will act more diligently than a busy, generalist state court judge. Arbitrators should live up to that promise.

A key user expectation is for arbitrators to be effective case managers. This is, first and foremost, the chairperson's responsibility as the overall steward of the process. Case management skills have become highly significant, especially as procedural rules and soft law have expanded, and cases have become more complex. This includes the ability to manage the co-arbitrators, to keep the proceedings on schedule, to respond to and efficiently resolve procedural disputes, and—where the parties so desire—to facilitate settlements. IT and technological skills, and understanding of data protection and IT security issues, are increasingly indispensable.

3. HOW IMPORTANT IS A PARTY'S RIGHT TO APPOINT AN ARBITRATOR?

While the question is focused on the party-appointed arbitrator in three-member tribunals, our answer applies to some extent also to chairpersons and to sole arbitrators. That is because the parties' right jointly to nominate the chairperson or the sole arbitrator reflects one of the central advantages of arbitration, namely the ability to select the decision maker (directly, or, even in the event a joint appointment fails, indirectly by way of choosing a trusted arbitral institution).

The parties' right to appoint arbitrators is of critical importance to users. The great promise of arbitration is that, as a creature of contract, it offers a flexible, custom-tailored dispute resolution mechanism in which the parties can determine not only the procedural rules but also the identity of the neutrals—unlike in state court, where they usually face randomly assigned judges. Parties can select the arbitrator most suitable for the dispute, taking into consideration issues like required areas of expertise, the applicable law, language skills, and other characteristics. (Therefore, and because they unnecessarily interfere with party autonomy, we tend to be skeptical of arbitral institutions that limit the choice of arbitrators to closed lists.)

Beyond the ability to ensure that the panel consists of arbitrators with the right set of qualifications and characteristics, the right to appoint arbitrators also enhances "buy-in" into the process as a whole. Given the effective absence of appeals and the very limited amount of state controls over arbitral proceedings, companies that refer multi-million-dollar disputes to three private individuals necessarily place a significant amount of trust in them. The ability to directly nominate at least one member of the tribunal, and to participate in the nomination of the chair, enhances this trust. It provides a degree of control over the process and augments the legitimacy of the outcome, which was (also) reached by someone whom the winning or losing party itself elevated to his or her position. Moreover, one of the wing arbitrator's key tasks is to ensure that the nominating party's position and arguments are understood and heard by the other members of the tribunal. The right to appoint an arbitrator permits the party to select the individual best suited for that task.

The right to appoint is also important because arbitral institutions' record of substitute appointments is mixed. While experienced arbitral institutions certainly try their best and wield considerable platforms, their candidate pools are almost inevitably skewed toward their particular geographic locale (with the possible exception of truly international institutions like the ICC), and their choices are the result of what users perceive as rather opaque selection processes that may reflect extraneous considerations not directly relevant to the parties or their case.

Finally, in light of the critical importance of the right to nominate arbitrators, sometimes we are disappointed by the way law firms recommend arbitrators. A recommendation should be tailor-made: why is this candidate best suited for this particular role in this particular dispute, taking into account (where applicable) the identity of the first wing or the two-wing arbitrators? Too often, we observe law firms repeatedly recommending the same (few) arbitrators in a variety of very different disputes or explaining the recommendation in generic terms such as "experience" or "competence."

4. WHEN AND WHY SHOULD AN ARBITRATOR BE OBJECTED AGAINST/CHALLENGED?

We will focus our answer on a lack of independence or impartiality, recognizing that challenges may also take place for additional reasons.

Users tend to approach both challenges and objections with restraint. Challenges will occur sometime after the arbitral tribunal has been constituted. Unless they have nothing to lose, companies will be wary of launching a challenge if they cannot be reasonably certain that they will prevail (because otherwise, the company having launched the unsuccessful challenge must expect the challenged arbitrator to harbor a grudge).

Objections take place during the appointment process. As such, they are less disruptive and have a higher rate of "success," also because prospective arbitrators may withdraw over an expected or actual objection and/or because arbitral institutions are more accommodating of objections. Nevertheless, they should not be resorted to lightly because they interfere with a party's right to select its arbitrator.

In some sense, objections and challenges reflect a breakdown in the system because they ought not to become necessary: if the circumstances affecting the arbitrator's independence or impartiality are sufficiently serious, the arbitrator on her own initiative should refuse the appointment or step down from the case; and if they are not, the party ought not to launch the objection or challenge. The fact that objections and challenges in commercial arbitration are relatively unusual probably indicates that the system overall works well.

One key challenge for users is to discover relationships and other potential grounds for timely challenges. The rules usually impose short deadlines, and accordingly, arbitrator due diligence is an important aspect for in-house and outside counsel alike.

Significant soft law and jurisprudential developments have taken place in the area of arbitrators working for large law firms and "double-hatting," i.e., arbitrators who, from time to time, also work as counsel. This includes the issue of attribution across offices in international law firms, which featured in the 2014 revisions of the IBA Guidelines on Conflicts of Interest. With some notable exceptions,[1] recent court judgments in various significant jurisdictions appear to reflect a trend toward more strict disclosure requirements,[2] which we welcome.

As a general matter, as a user, we are skeptical of the various instruments that attorneys at large law firms have employed to remedy concerns over arbitrator conflicts of interest. These may include advance waivers whose scope is sometimes unacceptably broad and whose general purpose can run contrary to the spirit of the ongoing disclosure requirements contained in arbitral rules. Some international law firms purport to limit their conflict checks to certain countries or to impose materiality thresholds, especially in cases with parties with multiple affiliates. Given the importance of the issues at stake for companies in arbitration, and in light of technological advances and office realities, our skepticism also extends to "Chinese walls" or similar purported safeguards to isolate files or attorneys.

To some extent, the above-mentioned practices reflect an attempt by prospective arbitrators from large law firms to have their cake and eat it, too. That is not to say that there are not many fine attorneys from these firms who make excellent arbitrators. However, there is a reason why over the past ten years, arbitrator boutiques have emerged, which in addition to reducing conflicts, also permit arbitrators to focus more on specialized industries or areas of the law. As a user, we welcome this development only because it broadens the pool and avoids some of the thorny debates briefly described above.

1. DFSC 4A_663/2018 of May 27, 2019.
2. Cour d'appel de Paris decision in *Socit Saad Buzwair Automotive Co c/ Socit Audi Volkswagen Middle East FZE LLC*, No. 16/09386 (March 27, 2018); English Court of Appeal decision in *Halliburton Company v. Chubb Bermuda Insurance Ltd*, [2018] EWCA Civ 817; Austrian Supreme Court decision in Docket 18 ONc 1/19w (May 15, 2019); U.S. 9th Circuit Court decision in Monster Energy, 940 F.3d 1130 (2019).

PANEL 2 Practical Experience: The View from Major Institutions

CHAPTER 4

Conflicts of Interest under the SIAC Rules

Claudia Annacker

1. THRESHOLD FOR DISCLOSURE?

In the exercise of its appointment functions under the Singapore International Arbitration Centre's (SIAC) Rules 2016 ('**SIAC Rules**') and in ad hoc arbitrations, SIAC's practice is to approach a prospective arbitrator with a briefing to set out the nature of the dispute, the identity of the parties and their representatives, a non-exhaustive list of all related parties involved or potentially involved in the arbitration, the sum in dispute and corresponding fee cap, and the terms of appointment.

All prospective arbitrators (including emergency arbitrators, as appropriate) are required to complete, sign and return to SIAC the Code of Ethics[1] before appointment or confirmation.

The SIAC Code of Ethics requires all prospective arbitrators to make any disclosures as to availability and conflicts, in particular:

- the details of any potential time-constraint in the next twelve months;
- all facts or circumstances that may give rise to justifiable doubts as to the arbitrator's impartiality or independence; and
- any past or present close personal relationship or business relationship, whether direct or indirect, with any party to the dispute, or any representative of a party, or any person known to be a potentially important witness in the arbitration.

Paragraph 3 of the Code of Ethics further explains '**impartiality**' and '**independence**' as follows:

1. https://www.siac.org.sg/our-rules/code-of-ethics-for-an-arbitrator.

- **impartiality**: partiality arises when an arbitrator favours one of the parties or where the arbitrator is prejudiced in relation to the subject matter of the dispute;
- **independence**: dependence arises from relationships between an arbitrator and one of the parties, or with someone closely connected with one of the parties; and
- any close personal relationship or current direct or indirect business relationship between an arbitrator and a party, or any representative of a party, or with a person who is known to be a potentially important witness, will normally give rise to justifiable doubts as to a prospective arbitrator's impartiality or independence. Past business relationships will only give rise to justifiable doubts if they are of such magnitude or nature as to be likely to affect a prospective arbitrator's judgment. The arbitrator should decline to accept an appointment in such circumstances unless the parties agree in writing that the arbitrator may proceed.

In cases where an external funder is involved, the SIAC Practice Note on Arbitrator Conduct in Cases Involving External Funding[2] (PN – 01/17, 31 March 2017) additionally applies. This Practice Note requires that arbitrators in an arbitration involving an external funder disclose any circumstances that may give rise to justifiable doubts as to their impartiality or independence, including any relationship, whether direct or indirect, with an external funder.

The duty to disclose is also found in the following instruments, which are applicable to any SIAC-administered arbitration:

- SIAC Rules: Rules 13.3 and 13.4, and paragraph 5 of Schedule 1 of the SIAC Rules provide that all prospective arbitrators are required to disclose to the parties and to the Registrar of the Court of Arbitration of SIAC ('**Registrar**') any circumstances that may give rise to justifiable doubts as to impartiality or independence;[3] and
- SIAC Practice Note for Administered Cases (2 January 2014): Paragraph 9 provides that any potential candidate for appointment must make a full declaration of independence and impartiality, and disclose to the parties and to the Registrar any fact, circumstance, or relationship which could give rise to justifiable doubts as to the arbitrator's independence and impartiality.[4]

For arbitrations seated in Singapore (including ad hoc arbitrations), the Arbitration Act (Cap. 10)[5] ('**AA**') and the International Arbitration Act (Cap. 143A)[6] ('**IAA**') additionally applies. The duty to disclose is contained in the following sections of the AA and IAA:

---

2. http://www.siac.org.sg/images/stories/articles/rules/Third%20Party%20Funding%20Practice%20Note%2031%20March%202017.pdf.
3. https://www.siac.org.sg/our-rules/rules/siac-rules-2016#siac.
4. https://www.siac.org.sg/our-rules/practice-notes/practice-note-for-administered-cases.
5. https://sso.agc.gov.sg/Act/AA2001.
6. https://www.siac.org.sg/our-rules/international-arbitration-act.

- **AA**: Section 14 requires the disclosure of any circumstances likely to give rise to justifiable doubts as to the arbitrator's impartiality or independence.
- **IAA**: Article 12 of Model Law requires the disclosure of any circumstances likely to give rise to justifiable doubts as to the arbitrator's impartiality or independence.

In all cases, after confirmation or appointment, the arbitrator continues to be under the duty to disclose throughout the proceedings. The threshold for disclosure is the same for a sole arbitrator, co-arbitrator or presiding arbitrator.

2. PROCEDURE FOR OBJECTIONS/CHALLENGES

2.1. Objections

Under Rule 9.3 of the SIAC Rules,[7] any arbitrator nominated by the parties, or by any third party including by the arbitrators already appointed, will be subject to confirmation by the President of the Court of Arbitration of SIAC ('**President**') at his discretion. In this regard, any agreement on an 'appointment' is deemed to be a nomination which is subject to this same confirmation.

SIAC will generally give effect to joint nominations for a sole arbitrator or presiding arbitrator subject to submission of the Code of Ethics (and the presence of any countervailing circumstances such as non-waivable conflicts or an arbitrator who would be wholly inappropriate for a dispute). In the case of a party-nominated co-arbitrator where the counterparty objects to a disclosure, SIAC will invite comments from the parties and the nominated arbitrator in order to determine whether the nomination ought to be confirmed. Subject to the particular circumstances of any objection, SIAC will generally confirm most party-nominated arbitrators and let any objections be resolved through the challenge process.

The treatment is slightly different for institutional appointments of a sole arbitrator or presiding arbitrator. In these cases, SIAC will consider any objection very carefully by a party to a disclosure of sufficient weight (e.g., 'Orange List') and may proceed with an alternate candidate who is unburdened by any disclosures. The ethos of SIAC's appointment process is that all appointments must be 'lily white'.

2.2. Challenges

Under Rule 14 of the SIAC Rules, an arbitrator may be challenged for, broadly, two grounds. First, if circumstances exist that give rise to justifiable doubts as to the arbitrator's impartiality or independence. Second, if the arbitrator does not possess any requisite qualification on which the parties have agreed. In accordance with Rule 14.2,

7. Rule 9.3 of the SIAC Rules.

a party may challenge an arbitrator nominated by it only for reasons of which it becomes aware after the appointment has been made.[8]

An arbitrator may also be challenged for a refusal or failure to perform his/her functions in accordance with the SIAC Rules or within prescribed time limits, or in the event of a de jure or de facto impossibility by an arbitrator to perform his/her functions. The President also has the power to remove an arbitrator on his own volition under Rule 17.3 upon consultation with the parties and the members of the tribunal, including the arbitrator to be removed (or if the tribunal has not yet been constituted, any appointed arbitrator).

The SIAC procedure prescribes strict timelines on a challenge in order to avoid tactical challenges to disrupt the proceedings. There is no automatic stay of the proceedings for challenges, and the Registrar will determine whether to suspend the proceedings based on the circumstances of the case. Finally, in order to promote transparency, all decisions on challenges must be reasoned.

A party-nominated arbitrator may only be challenged by the party which nominated him or her for reasons which the party becomes aware of after the appointment has been made.

Due to SIAC's rigorous appointment process, from the many hundreds of appointments, SIAC received only six challenges between 2016 and 2018. Out of these six challenges, five were rejected, and only one was accepted.

Limitation:[9] A party intending to challenge an arbitrator is to file a Notice of Challenge (NOC) with the Registrar within fourteen days after receipt of the notice of appointment of the arbitrator or fourteen days after circumstances giving rise to justifiable doubts as to the arbitrator's impartiality or independence became known (or should have been reasonably known) to the party.

Filing a challenge: The NOC must state the reasons for the challenge, and the moving party is required to serve the NOC on the other party and all members of the tribunal (including the challenged arbitrator), or if prior to the constitution of the tribunal, to any appointed arbitrators.[10] The party making the challenge is required to pay a non-refundable Challenge Fee of SGD 8,000 (exclusive of GST).

Steps after receipt of NOC: Under the SIAC Rules, the Registrar may, if appropriate, suspend the proceedings pending the decision on the challenge.[11] In the event that the Registrar does not suspend the proceedings, the challenged arbitrator is entitled to continue to participate in the arbitration pending determination of the challenge by the SIAC Court of Arbitration ('SIAC Court').[12]

Agreement to remove or withdraw: If the other party agrees to the challenge, the SIAC Court will remove the challenged arbitrator. The challenged arbitrator also has the option to withdraw from office.[13] Neither of these options implies acceptance of the validity of the grounds for the challenge.

8. Rule 14.2 of the SIAC Rules.
9. Rule 15.1 of the SIAC Rules.
10. Rule 15.2 of the SIAC Rules.
11. Rule 15.4 of the SIAC Rules.
12. *Ibid.*
13. Rule 15.5 of the SIAC Rules.

Decision-making body: In cases where the other party does not agree to the removal or if the arbitrator does not voluntarily withdraw from office within seven days from receipt of thc NOC, the SIAC Court decides the challenge.[14] In such a case, the SIAC Court may invite comments from the parties, the challenged arbitrator and other members of the tribunal.[15]

Decision:[16] A decision on a challenge under the SIAC Rules must be reasoned unless otherwise agreed by the parties. Some of these reasoned decisions by the SIAC Court have spanned in excess of fifty pages in particularly complex challenge cases. The SIAC Rules provide that the decision of the SIAC Court is final and not subject to appeal (subject to resort at the supervisory court (*see*, *e.g.*, Article 13(3) of the Model Law)).

The SIAC Court has generally relied on the following instruments/documents to determine the applicable criteria for the challenge:

- the standards prescribed under the SIAC Rules;
- the standards prescribed under the applicable lex arbitri;
- international soft law; and
- previous decisions of the SIAC Court on challenges to arbitrators.

Next steps after removal: If the SIAC Court accepts the challenge, a substitute arbitrator is appointed.[17] If the SIAC Court rejects the challenge, the challenged arbitrator continues with the arbitration.[18]

If the sole arbitrator or presiding arbitrator is challenged and replaced, any hearings held previously must be repeated unless otherwise agreed by the parties. If any other arbitrator is replaced, any hearings held previously may be repeated at the discretion of the tribunal after consulting with the parties.[19]

3. CRITERIA FOR APPOINTING ARBITRATORS

Under the SIAC framework, the President (which includes any Vice President and the Registrar) makes or confirms all arbitrator appointments upon receipt of the briefing from the SIAC Secretariat. The President may consult with two members of the SIAC Court on any appointment.[20]

The majority of SIAC appointments are made from the **SIAC Panel of Arbitrators** ('**SIAC Panel**').[21] The SIAC Panel is comprised of more than 500 arbitrators from over 40 jurisdictions. SIAC also maintains a specialist IP Panel of Arbitrators and a non-published 'Reserve Panel' for arbitrators who do not yet meet the minimum

14. Rule 16.1 of the SIAC Rules.
15. *Ibid.*
16. Rule 16.4 of the SIAC Rules.
17. Rule 16.2 of the SIAC Rules.
18. Rule 16.3 of the SIAC Rules.
19. Rule 18 of the SIAC Rules.
20. Paragraph 6 of the SIAC Practice Note for Administered Cases (2 January 2014).
21. https://www.siac.org.sg/our-arbitrators/siac-panel.

standards of admission to the SIAC Panel. The SIAC Panel is an 'open panel', and parties are free to nominate an arbitrator of their choice.

SIAC closely monitors the performance of its arbitrators and has also entered into an arrangement with Arbitrator Intelligence whereby users are encouraged to provide anonymised, confidential feedback on the performance of arbitrators in SIAC arbitrations. To this end, SIAC endeavours to make appointments with a view to achieving the efficient and expeditious resolution of disputes.

SIAC has a growing body of institutional knowledge and may take into account any of the following factors when making appointments:

- **Agreed qualifications and proposals**: SIAC will look to give effect to any agreed qualifications and additionally consider any proposals put forward by the parties.
- **Arbitrator's experience and track record**: SIAC will review the relevant experience of the arbitrator and analyse the performance of the arbitrator in previous SIAC arbitrations.
- **Complexity**: The factual and legal complexity of the dispute will guide the appointment of an arbitrator.
- **Sector**: SIAC considers the nature of the dispute to appoint an arbitrator who has the necessary sectoral experience. SIAC receives cases across a range of sectors including, *inter alia*, international trade, corporate and commercial, construction/engineering, energy, maritime/shipping, and technology.
- **Seat and governing law**: SIAC will consider a prospective arbitrator's experience with arbitrations applying the *lex arbitri* and the governing law of the contract. SIAC will seek to appoint an arbitrator qualified in the relevant jurisdiction or trained in the underlying common law or civil law system.
- **Diversity**: In 2018, of the 175 arbitrators appointed by SIAC, sixty (34.3%) were female arbitrators. SIAC also prioritises the appointment of arbitrators from diverse backgrounds, including arbitrators from emerging jurisdictions, ethnically diverse arbitrators, and younger arbitrators.
- **Quantum**: SIAC operates on an ad valorem system whereby arbitrators' fees are subject to a maximum cap based on the sum in dispute. SIAC will generally look to match the seniority of the arbitrator with the sum in dispute. For lower value cases, SIAC will sometimes request that the arbitrator agree to bear any travel expenses to broaden the geographic reach of SIAC's appointments.
- **Availability**: SIAC considers the availability and manageability of a prospective arbitrator's current caseload. By selecting arbitrators who are able to conduct arbitrations with efficiency and expedition, the median duration of a SIAC arbitration is 11.7 months (as per SIAC's Cost and Duration Study).[22]

22. https://www.siac.org.sg/images/stories/press_release/SIAC%20Releases%20Costs%20and%20Duration%20Study_10%20Oct%202016.pdf.

- **Composition of the tribunal**: When SIAC is called upon to appoint an arbitrator in a three-member tribunal, SIAC will consider factors such as the nationality of the parties and the other arbitrators, seniority and standing of the tribunal, breadth and depth of experience among the arbitrators, and the overall cohesiveness of the tribunal.

CHAPTER 5

The View from the LCIA on Conflicts of Interest

Jamie Harrison

It is reassuring, having heard my fellow panellists, that there is a great deal of overlap between their approach and the approach that the London Court of International Arbitration (LCIA) takes in these matters. This is an area which the LCIA regards, first and foremost, as the responsibility of the arbitrator, but it is also something that comes within the jurisdiction of the LCIA court.

The LCIA Notes for Arbitrators[1] set out the approach that the LCIA takes (note 2.6):

> Parties to arbitrations are entitled to expect of the process a just, well-reasoned and enforceable award. To that end, they are entitled to expect arbitrators: to disclose possible conflicts of interest at the outset; to avoid putting themselves in a position where conflicts will arise during the course of the proceedings; to conduct the arbitration fairly, in a timely manner and with careful regard to due process; to maintain the confidentiality of the arbitration; and to reach their decision in an impartial manner.

1. THRESHOLD AND DISCLOSURE

The starting point is LCIA Article 5.3-5.5 which sets out the duty to disclose before appointment and, in particular under Article 5.4, that all arbitrators are required to sign a declaration of any circumstances currently known to them that are likely to give rise 'in the mind of any party to any justifiable doubts as to his or her impartiality or independence'. Each candidate is then provided with a Statement of Independence

1. https://www.lcia.org/adr-services/lcia-notes-for-arbitrators.aspx.

which he or she is required to complete with the help of the Notes for Arbitrators. The Notes for Arbitrators set out the threshold that the LCIA expects arbitrators to meet:

> In completing their statements of independence, arbitrators should take into account, amongst other things, the existence and nature of any past or present relationships, direct or indirect, with any of the parties or their counsel. Any doubt as to whether a relationship should be disclosed must be resolved in favour of disclosure … . There is a continuing obligation on all arbitrators immediately to disclose any further circumstance of which they become aware at any time during the course of the arbitration, which might give rise to conflicts.

The Statement of Independence requests the prospective arbitrator to delete one of two statements that is not applicable and contains the following health warning: 'which of the declarations you delete will be determined after you have taken into account inter alia the existence and nature of any past or present relationships, direct or indirect, with any of the parties or their counsel. Any doubts should be resolved in favour of disclosure'. The two statements that the arbitrator is asked to consider in this context are: 'I am impartial and independent of each of the parties and I intend to remain so. There are no circumstances currently known to me likely to give rise in the mind of any party to a justifiable doubt as to my impartiality or independence.' The second option points out: 'I am impartial and independent of each of the parties and I intend to remain so while I wish to disclose certain circumstances for the consideration of the LCIA court prior to my appointment, whether or not any such circumstance is likely to give the rise in the mind of any party to any justifiable doubts as to my impartiality or independence. Other than such circumstances here disclosed by me, there are no circumstances currently known to me likely to give rise in the mind of any party to any justifiable doubts as to my impartiality or independence.' You will note the continuing obligation to disclose, which is stressed at all times. We also request prospective arbitrators to give confirmation of their availability, which we regard as a key element of their disclosure at this early stage.

2. INCIDENCE OF CHALLENGES

The number of challenges made to arbitrators in LCIA arbitrations is low – indeed, the 2019 figures reveal even fewer challenges than the previous year.

In LCIA arbitrations, seven challenges were made in 2019, of which five were rejected, and two are pending since the end of 2019. Proportionately, there is also a drop in the total number of challenges when compared to the number of new cases commenced in 2019 – there were seven challenges out of 346 new cases, whereas in 2018, there were six challenges in 233 new cases. The number of challenges in each year over the past five years as a percentage of arbitrations commenced in that year is just 2%.

Set out below are the LCIA's numbers for the last four reported years. These relate to cases where parties have chosen the LCIA rules and do not contain cases where we administer a UNCITRAL arbitration. It is also important to note that the LCIA regards a challenge made before arbitrators are appointed as objections to a nomination rather than a formal challenge. Objections on the basis of pre-appointment disclosures were made in ten cases. The LCIA proceeded with the appointment in four of those cases.

Year	*No of Challenges in LCIA Arbitrations*	*Upheld*	*Rejected*	*Not Decided (Withdrawn/Resigned/ Superseded/Pending)*
2016	6	1 (partially)	3	2
2017	6	0	5	1
2018	6	0	4	2
2019	7	0	5	2

This record is impressive because the challenge process is robust. We believe that the ability and the practice of the LCIA to publish details of the challenges and reasons for them is part of the reason why we receive so few challenges, as parties contemplating a challenge can see how such challenges are reviewed and indeed what constitutes a frivolous challenge. Challenges are published on the website, and I invite you to look at them there.[2]

We find that in over half of the challenged decisions, the challenging party presented a procedural decision contrary to their interests as evidence of bias. Those sorts of challenges are much more common than allegations of conflict of interest.

3. PROCESS OF CHALLENGES

The process is regulated in LCIA Article 10. Under the LCIA rules, essentially, the initial review of the challenge is undertaken by the Registrar, who refers it to the President or Vice-President of the LCIA Court. In complex cases, this can also be to a division of three members of the LCIA Court. It is worth noting that the member of the LCIA Court to whom the challenge is referred will have played no part in the appointment of the arbitrator in question.

The timetable is set out in LCIA Article 10.4, which provides that the 'LCIA Court may revoke any arbitrator's appointment … upon a written Challenge by any party if … circumstances exist that give rise to justifiable doubts as to that arbitrator's impartiality and independence.'

Pursuant to Article 10.3, the challenging party must deliver a written statement of the reasons for its challenge within fourteen days of the formation of the Tribunal or within fourteen days of becoming aware of any ground of challenge.

Once a challenge is filed, the LCIA Court will offer a reasonable opportunity for other parties and for the challenged arbitrator to respond, but not to the other arbitrators (Article 10.4).

2. https://www.lcia.org/challenge-decision-database.aspx, currently containing thirty-two decis ions of 2010-2017, out of which twenty-five were rejected and seven fully or partially upheld the challenge.

If all other parties agree in writing to the challenge within fourteen days of receipt of the written statement, then the arbitrator's appointment shall be revoked (and no reasons will be given). In the absence of such agreement, the LCIA Court will decide the challenge, and if upheld, will revoke the appointment. The decision is made in writing with reasons, and the Registrar is tasked with sending a copy to all parties (Article 10.6).

4. CONCLUSION

The LCIA Rules provide for a comprehensive disclosure process pre-appointment, which leads to very few formal challenges to Arbitrators later in the proceedings. The evidence suggests that very few of the limited number of challenges that are made have merit and that the LCIA's commitment to publishing challenge awards deters others from making them.

The LCIA has yet to publish details of the number and result of Challenges for 2020 but expects that the trends noted in this chapter will be maintained. The LCIA Rules 2020 came into effect on 1 October 2020, and there were no changes to the LCIA Rules 2014, which impact the issues discussed in this chapter.

CHAPTER 6

SCAI's Approach to Conflicts of Interest

*Gabrielle Nater-Bass**

1. INTRODUCTION

The purpose of this article is to provide insights into the issue of conflicts of interest from the point of view of the Swiss Chambers' Arbitration Institution (SCAI).[1] This article shall discuss the legal and practical approach of SCAI to the disclosure obligations of potential arbitrators (below section 3), the appointment and confirmation of arbitrators, particularly in the face of disclosures (below section 4) and to the challenges of arbitrators (below section 5). Before presenting SCAI's approach to these issues, the author will give a summary overview of the organization of the SCAI Arbitration Court (Court) to the extent it is relevant to the issues discussed (below section 2).

2. ORGANIZATION OF THE SCAI ARBITRATION COURT

Arbitration proceedings under the Swiss Rules of International Arbitration (Swiss Rules) are administrated by the Court and the SCAI Secretariat (Secretariat). The Court's main task is to develop a common practice for efficient and consistent conduct of all arbitration proceedings. The Court has adopted Internal Rules of the Arbitration Court (Internal Rules, the current edition entered into force on January 1, 2020). The

* This chapter is based on the author's presentation at the ASA Annual Conference on February 7, 2020. The author would like to thank Dilber Devitre and Okan Uzun, associates at Homburger, for their assistance with this article.

1. SCAI has been converted to Swiss Arbitration Centre Ltd as of June 1, 2021 under the leadership of ASA. The Swiss Rules have been revised by the same time. The revised provisions are included in the Appendix below. Further, *see* https://swissarbitration.org.

Internal Rules define the organization, the composition and the tasks of the main bodies of the Court and the Secretariat.

Besides the Full Court, which currently consists of twenty-six members and meets in regular plenary sessions, the Court has three main bodies that deal with case administration. These are:

(1) the Case Administration Committee, which is composed of one to four Court member(s) acting as "rapporteurs" to the case (*see below*);
(2) the Court Special Committee, which is composed in general of four Court members plus the President, Vice-Presidents and Secretary (i.e., eight members in total); and
(3) the President of the Court and two Vice-Presidents.[2]

All these bodies play a role in the appointment, challenge and removal of arbitrators.

For each case under the Swiss Rules, a Case Administration Committee consisting of a "rapporteur" and, if the circumstances so justify, a vice-rapporteur and up to two additional Court members is formed to assist the Secretariat in its administrative tasks. As per Article 3 of the Internal Rules, the Case Administration Committee may take any decisions within the powers of the Court, which are not expressly delegated to the Court Special Committee or the President or any Vice-President. This includes, in particular, the confirmation and appointment of arbitrators under Articles 5-8 of the Swiss Rules.

Decisions concerning the appointment of arbitrators in certain circumstances, as well as the challenge, removal and revocation of arbitrators as per Articles 5(3), 11, 12, and 13(2) of the Swiss Rules, fall into the competence of the Court Special Committee,[3] while the President and the Vice-President are, among others, the authorities designated to appoint and deal with the challenge and removal of an emergency arbitrator under Article 43 of the Swiss Rules.[4]

3. SCAI'S APPROACH TO DISCLOSURE OBLIGATIONS OF POTENTIAL ARBITRATORS

While Shakespeare may have been preoccupied with the existential question of "to be or not to be," a modern-day dilemma for many potential arbitrators can be framed in similar terms: "To disclose or not to disclose"—that is the question.

2. For more detailed information, *see* "Internal Rules of the Arbitration Court of the Swiss Chambers' Arbitration Institution" (www.swissarbitration.org).
3. Article 4 Internal Rules.
4. Article 6 Internal Rules.

3.1. The Threshold Found in the Swiss Rules Concerning the Disclosure Obligations of Potential Arbitrators

As found in several other arbitration rules, the Swiss Rules impose an obligation of independence and impartiality on arbitrators, both at the time of their appointment and throughout the proceedings. Article 9(1) of the Swiss Rules provides that "[a]ny arbitrator conducting an arbitration under the Swiss Rules shall remain at all times impartial and independent of the parties." In support of such independence and impartiality obligations, Article 9(2) of the Swiss Rules requires all arbitrators to disclose "any circumstances likely to give rise to justifiable doubts as to their impartiality or independence."[5]

The thresholds for disclosure found in the Swiss Rules, therefore, are of a rather general nature and follow the standards set in international commercial arbitration.

3.2. The Court's Practice to Solicit and Deal with Disclosures

In practice, potential arbitrators that have been approached for appointment under the Swiss Rules must fill out a standard form entitled "Consent to Appointment and Statement of Impartiality and Independence." Either the arbitrators indicate on this form that they have nothing to disclose, or in the opposite scenario, they must submit the disclosures they wish to make on a separate sheet to the parties and the Court. The relevant text reads as follows:

5. Article 9(2) of the Swiss Rules reads in full: "Prospective Arbitrators shall disclose to those who approach them in connection with a possible appointment any circumstances likely to give rise to justifiable doubts as to their impartiality or independence. An arbitrator, once designated or appointed, shall disclose such circumstances to the parties, unless they have already been so informed."

Consent to Appointment and Statement of Impartiality and Independence
Case No 2

IMPARTIALITY AND INDEPENDENCE

☐ **Nothing to disclose:** I declare that I am, and shall remain, impartial and independent. To the best of my knowledge, and having made due enquiry, there are no facts or circumstances, past or present, likely to give rise to justifiable doubts as to my impartiality or independence.

☐ **Acceptance with disclosure:** I declare that I am, and shall remain, impartial and independent. However, in accordance with Article 9(2) of the Swiss Rules, I wish to disclose to the Swiss Chambers' Arbitration Institution and to all parties, the matters **on the separate sheet.** To the best of my belief, these circumstances do not impair my impartiality or independence.

I will declare to the Court and all the parties, for the entire duration of the arbitration, any future fact that could give rise to justifiable doubts as to my impartiality or independence.

The Court does not rely entirely and solely on the information provided by the arbitrators. If the Court is privy to information that the arbitrator has not disclosed certain facts, which—in the Court's opinion—should have been disclosed, the Court will encourage the arbitrator to disclose that information.

The Court adopts a fully transparent approach concerning both disclosures and objections thereto. Any disclosures made by an arbitrator are transmitted to all parties involved. Likewise, any reactions to the disclosures made by the parties in the form of objections to the appointment are also communicated to all involved, including the arbitrator who made the disclosure. All concerned parties are then given the opportunity to comment.

In case of extraordinary disclosures made by an arbitrator, the Case Administrative Committee may ask the concerned arbitrator additional questions in order to solicit further information.

4. SCAI'S APPROACH TO APPOINTMENT/CONFIRMATION OF ARBITRATORS

Once potential disclosures have been solicited, the Court is confronted with the task of deciding whether or not to appoint or confirm an arbitrator that has made disclosures.

4.1. The Threshold Found in the Swiss Rules Concerning the Appointment or Confirmation of Arbitrators

Arbitrators are either appointed directly by the Court in situations set forth in the Swiss Rules (Articles 5-8 of the Swiss Rules), or the arbitrator is being designated by the parties or the co-arbitrators, in which case, as per Article 5(1) of the Swiss Rules, the arbitrator must be confirmed by the Court. Article 5(1) of the Swiss Rules specifies that the Court has no obligation to give reasons if it decides not to confirm an arbitrator.[6] This begs the question of how the Court deals with disclosures made by potential arbitrators when deciding whether to appoint them or confirm their appointment.

4.2. The Court's Practice in Case of Disclosures

When deciding whether or not to confirm an arbitrator who has made a disclosure, the Court often uses the IBA Guidelines on Conflicts of Interest in International Arbitration 2014 (the IBA Guidelines) as a non-binding reference.

The threshold as for the appointment applied by the Court in practice is usually higher in institutional appointments and in cases where nonparticipating respondents are involved. In such cases, the Court is more likely to take a cautious approach and not to appoint the arbitrator. Conversely, the threshold applied by the Court is lower when confirming arbitrators designated by the parties or the co-arbitrators. The threshold is the highest in the case of an institutional appointment of a sole arbitrator.

If the parties still favor the confirmation of a given arbitrator notwithstanding the fact that the arbitrator has made a disclosure, then the Court would usually confirm the appointment of the arbitrator unless the disclosed facts fall within the nonwaivable red list of the IBA Guidelines. In this case, the Court would reject the designation of the arbitrator. In line with Article 5(1) of the Swiss Rules, the Court generally does not communicate reasons for its decision when deciding not to confirm an arbitrator.

5. SCAI'S APPROACH TO CHALLENGE OF ARBITRATORS

Puns aside, it would be no exaggeration to say that one of the most challenging tasks of the Court is dealing with the challenge of arbitrators.

5.1. The Threshold Found in the Swiss Rules Concerning the Challenge of Arbitrators

The threshold for challenges under the Swiss Rules is found in Article 10(1), which provides that "[a]ny arbitrator may be challenged if circumstances exist that give rise to justifiable doubts as to the arbitrator's impartiality or independence." Article 10(1) thus reflects the disclosure obligations of arbitrators found in Article 9(1) of the Swiss Rules described above. Article 10(2) contains an exception to a party's right to challenge its own arbitrator by providing that "[a] party may challenge the arbitrator designated by it only for reasons of which it becomes aware after the appointment has

6. Article 5(1) of the Swiss Rules reads as follows: "All designations of an arbitrator made by the parties or the arbitrators are subject to confirmation of the Court, upon which the appointments shall become effective. The Court has no obligation to give reasons when it does not confirm an arbitrator."

been made." This provision reinforces the party's obligation to undertake due diligence vis-à-vis its own arbitrator prior to his/her appointment.

It is also worth mentioning that as per Article 1(4) of the Swiss Rules, by submitting their dispute to the Swiss Rules, "the parties confer on the Court, to the fullest extent permitted under the law applicable to the arbitration, all of the powers required for the purpose of supervising the arbitral proceedings ... including the power ... to decide on the challenge of an arbitrator on grounds not provided for in these Rules." Thus, in addition to the grounds for challenge explicitly set out in Articles 9 and 10 of the Swiss Rules, the parties may agree on specific qualifications for arbitrators, which, if not respected, might lead to a challenge.

5.2. The Procedure for Challenges under the Swiss Rules

The procedure for challenges is laid down in Article 11 of the Swiss Rules.

A party intending to challenge an arbitrator must send a notice of challenge to the Secretariat within fifteen days "after the circumstances giving rise to the challenge became known to that party" (Article 11(1) of the Swiss Rules). The Court is not involved in the initial stages of the challenge procedure. First, the notice of challenge is sent to the Secretariat that communicates it to the arbitrator concerned and the other parties involved. Within fifteen days of receipt of such notice, the arbitrator may decide to withdraw, or the other party(ies) may agree to the challenge (Article 11(2) of the Swiss Rules). In these circumstances, the procedure ends without a decision of the Court. The Court is then called upon to replace the arbitrator according to Article 13 of the Swiss Rules. Hence, it is only if the arbitrator does not withdraw of his or her own free will or the party(ies) do not agree on the challenge that the Court must decide on the challenge.

5.3. The Court's Practice When Faced with the Challenge of an Arbitrator

If the challenged arbitrator does not withdraw of his or her own free will or if the parties do not agree on the challenge, then the challenged arbitrator, as well as all the parties and the other arbitrators, are set a deadline within which they can comment on the challenge. The comments of the parties and the other arbitrators are made available to the challenged arbitrator.

When deciding upon the challenge, the Court again often uses the IBA Guidelines as a non-binding reference. It should come as no surprise that the Court's practice concerning the threshold to accept a challenge is the same as for the appointment or the confirmation of an arbitrator. The decision of the Court is final, and in this case too, the Court does not have to and normally does not give reasons for its decision (Article 11(3) of the Swiss Rules). However, the Court recently rendered its first reasoned decision on a challenge.[7]

7. *Cf.* section 5.5.2.

5.4. Statistics

As mentioned above, the competent body within the Court that deals with challenges (except in the case of an emergency arbitration) is the Court Special Committee. From 2013 (after the new Swiss Rules were enacted in 2012) until 2019, the Court Special Committee was called upon to decide on nine cases of challenges to arbitrators. The challenge was upheld only in one case. In the eight other cases, the challenge was denied. This translates into an 89% rejection rate.

As mentioned above, since the Court is only called upon to intervene in the event the challenged arbitrator does not withdraw, or all the parties do not accept the challenge, these statistics only concern the cases where the Court was asked to render a decision.

Despite the often discussed trend that the number of challenges in international arbitration is increasing, SCAI's statistics portray the opposite. The statistics show a decline in challenges. Between 2013 and 2014, over two years, seven notices of challenges were filed (3.5 per year), whereas one of them was upheld. On the other hand, only three notices were filed in the subsequent five years from 2015 onwards up to 2019, and all of them were rejected by the Court.

5.5. Categories

From the cases under review, the challenges can be classified into one of the three following categories:

(1) professional relationships of the arbitrator;
(2) personal relationships of the arbitrator; and
(3) perceived bias due to orders | actions of the arbitrator.

Since SCAI arbitration proceedings and decisions rendered by the Court are confidential as per Article 44(1) of the Swiss Rules and Article 10 of the Internal Rules, the following sections contain an abstract summary of the most prominent cases showcasing SCAI's approach to challenges.

5.5.1. *Professional Relationships of the Arbitrator*

The only case where the Court upheld a challenge concerned a situation involving an alleged professional relationship of the arbitrator. In this case, dating back to 2013, the respondent challenged the arbitrator nominated by the claimant due to concerns about the arbitrator's potential partiality "for lack of independence, impartiality and his incorrect statement of independence." More specifically, the respondent pointed out that the webpage of the law firm of the challenged arbitrator mentioned the claimant's group, and particularly the family owning that group, among the high-profile clients of the law firm. The respondent's challenge to the claimant's arbitrator was upheld by the Court.

In other cases, the alleged professional relationship between the arbitrator and a party put forward by the challenging party was not considered sufficient or sufficiently proven for the challenge to succeed. In another case, also dating back to 2013, the respondent challenged the sole arbitrator who had been appointed by the Court, citing an alleged "conflict of interest" resulting from a previous involvement of the sole arbitrator in another case. However, since this previous involvement was as counsel of a third party in an unrelated dispute which was *a fortiori* not against the respondent but against another company in which the respondent had a minority shareholding, the challenge was dismissed.

In both these cases, the Court used the IBA Guidelines as a non-binding reference when deciding upon the challenges.

5.5.2. Personal Relationships of the Arbitrator

An interesting case of challenge concerning the personal relationship of the arbitrator with the parties was raised in 2017. This is the only case where the Court Special Committee decided to provide reasons for its decision.

The party seeking the challenge of the presiding arbitrator alleged that the presiding arbitrator had failed to disclose a close personal relationship with a partner of the opposing counsel's law firm and some professional relationships with the firm. In the first Statement of Independence filled out in 2014, the presiding arbitrator had, however, indicated that there are "private contacts with another partner of the Counsel of the Claimant." No questions were raised at the time by the challenging party. The professional relationships with the opposing counsel's law firm were also publicly available information at the time of appointment.

In subsequent disclosures, almost three years later, upon related requests by the challenging party, the presiding arbitrator explained that these relationships involved joint family vacations and dinners. In its challenge, the party seeking the challenge stated that the presiding arbitrator had failed to disclose these facts and the professional relationships, which, if disclosed, would have given rise to justifiable doubts as to the presiding arbitrator's impartiality and independence. The Court agreed that the presiding arbitrator's initial disclosures were partly incomplete or could have been substantiated in more detail. However, it dismissed the challenge because it concluded that the party seeking the challenge was under a duty to investigate and inquire when the presiding arbitrator had first disclosed private contacts with a partner in the opposing counsel's law firm before accepting the appointment. Furthermore, the Court also dismissed the challenge because the challenging party had waited almost three years to raise a challenge, almost until the time when the arbitral tribunal was about to render its award.

Another case relating to the personal relationship of an arbitrator occurred in 2014. The respondent challenged the sole arbitrator appointed by the Court on the ground that the sole arbitrator had the same nationality, spoke the same language and came from the same town as the claimant. The Court did not find these facts to constitute a sufficient reason for a challenge.

In a subsequent case of the same year, a challenge was based on a "serious dispute" that had allegedly arisen between the co-arbitrator designated by the claimant and the respondent's counsel, who had been on opposing sides in a previous arbitration that was unrelated to the arbitration at hand. The Court found that such personal animosity between the co-arbitrator and one of the counsel was based on subjective sensations of the applicant and thus did not warrant a challenge.

5.5.3. *Perceived Bias Due to Orders or Actions of the Arbitrator*

An illustrative and interesting case of a challenge concerning perceived bias to the actions of the arbitrator arose in 2014. In this case, the claimant filed a notice of challenge based on the written statement that the presiding arbitrator had previously filed following his own removal request. According to the claimant, the arbitrator had manifested in that letter a personal opinion on the arbitration at hand. Moreover, the arbitrator had stopped all the work as soon as the request for removal had been filed. The Court did not comment on the merits of the challenge but found the challenge to be time-barred. Article 11(1) of the Swiss Rules provides that the applicant shall file the challenge within fifteen days after the circumstances giving rise to the challenge became known to it. According to the Court, the deadline for the challenge started to run when the challenging party learned of the arbitrator's written statement in the framework of the removal proceedings and not only once the decision rejecting the request for removal was notified to it. This means that even if a decision on the request for removal is still pending, the notice period for a possible challenge will not be extended. Further, the Court Special Committee noted that the Swiss Rules do not provide any guidance with respect to the impact of a challenge on the arbitral proceedings. The arbitrator may proceed with the arbitration but is not obliged to do so. Hence, the fact that the arbitrator had stopped working was not a valid ground for a challenge.

6. CONCLUSION AND OUTLOOK

SCAI's approach to conflict of interests is in line with general standards. Recent trends such as increased transparency, better accountability and clearer guidelines have also influenced SCAI's approach and form an integral part of its outlook on this issue for the future. Thereby SCAI is committed to preserving a certain pragmatism when dealing with issues of disclosure as well as the confirmation, appointment and challenge of arbitrators without reneging on keeping up a high standard of integrity of its proceedings.

Panel 3 Practical Experience: The View from State Courts

CHAPTER 7

The View from the State Courts on Conflicts of Interest: Introduction

Felix Dasser

Arbitration is, as we know, a *creature of contract*. There is no private arbitration unless the parties at some time signed up to it. Consequently, the arbitration community has to listen to what current and potential future parties, the users of our arbitration services, want. This is difficult enough as the users are not a uniform mass, and their needs and requests not always as clear as we would wish. Still, the users do provide some crucial guidance, as we heard this morning.

Then again, arbitration is not just a creature of contract. It is also a *creature of countries*. Arbitration as a means of settling disputes with the full force of law only exists by leave of the states. State law provides the framework within which arbitration can and does exist. So, no matter what the users want, no matter what the institutions say, in the end, the states have the last word and thus also on the issue of conflicts of interests.

Any local idiosyncrasy on independence and impartiality could sink an arbitration that happens to come within reach of a particular jurisdiction. That concerns not only challenges and appeals but also recognition and enforcement.

On the global level, international conventions may have an impact. The by far most important one, the **New York Convention of 1958** (NYC),[1] is surprisingly silent on the issue of independence and impartiality, essentially leaving the issue to state law. In practice, courts tend to address the issue under the *ultima ratio* ground of public policy (Article V(2)(b) NYC,[2] sometimes also under Article V(1)(d) NYC), which refers to the arbitration agreement as well as to the country of origin, by stating:

1. United Nations Convention on the Recognition and Enforcement of Foreign Arbitral Awards, New York 1958.
2. Reinmar Wolff, NEW YORK CONVENTION. COMMENTARY, in Article V, n. 530 et seqq. (Reinmar Wolff ed., C. H. Beck/Hart/Nomos, Munich 2012); Ulrich Haas/Heiner Kahlert, *New York Convention* in

(d) The composition of the arbitral authority or the arbitral procedure was not in accordance with the agreement of the parties, or, failing such agreement, was not in accordance with the law of the country where the arbitration took place;[3]

It is also argued that bias could fall under Article V(1)(b) NYC, as a biased arbitrator in effect prevents a party from presenting its case.[4] While this view seems rather far-fetched, it highlights the lack of a proper provision addressing independence and impartiality. Public policy is, of course, a convenient stopgap for all kinds of mishaps, but only intended for the most outrageous cases and granting broad, if not too broad, discretion to the court. The public policy ground does not provide a well-defined test and thus not enough predictability.

Far more important, therefore, is the **UNCITRAL Model Law on International Commercial Arbitration 1985/2006**. Its Article 12 sets a nowadays common standard for challenges and, related thereto, for disclosure obligations of (prospective) arbitrators by referring to 'circumstances ... that give rise to justifiable doubts as to his [or her] impartiality or independence':

Article 12. Grounds for challenge

(1) When a person is approached in connection with his possible appointment as an arbitrator, he shall disclose any circumstances likely to give rise to justifiable doubts as to his impartiality or independence. An arbitrator, from the time of his appointment and throughout the arbitral proceedings, shall without delay disclose any such circumstances to the parties unless they have already been informed of them by him.

(2) An arbitrator may be challenged only if circumstances exist that give rise to justifiable doubts as to his impartiality or independence, or if he does not possess qualifications agreed to by the parties. A party may challenge an arbitrator appointed by him, or in whose appointment he has participated, only for reasons of which he becomes aware after the appointment has been made.

This provision was inspired by Articles 9 and 10 of the UNCITRAL Arbitration Rules of 1976.[5] In addition, it clarifies that the arbitrator's duty of disclosure continues during the whole proceedings, leaving open, however, to what extent, if at all, the arbitrator has a duty to investigate. Article 12 does not specify what circumstances could give rise to justifiable doubts. The Analytical Commentary by the UNCITRAL Secretariat consciously avoids providing any example, noting that a 'general formula'

PRACTITIONER'S HANDBOOK ON INTERNATIONAL COMMERCIAL ARBITRATION, n. 21.495, (Frank-Bernd Weigand/Antje Baumann eds., 3rd ed., Oxford University Press, Oxford 2019); Albert Jan van den Berg, THE NEW YORK ARBITRATION CONVENTION OF 1958, 377 et seqq. (Kluwer 1981).

3. Christian Borris/Rudolf Hennecke, in NEW YORK CONVENTION. COMMENTARY, Article V n. 293 et seqq. (Wolff ed., *supra* n. 2); Haas/Kahlert, *supra* n. 2, n. 21.451.
4. Van den Berg, *supra* n. 2, 302. Article V(1)(b) reads: '(b) The party against whom the award is invoked was not given proper notice of the appointment of the arbitrator or of the arbitration proceedings or was otherwise unable to present his case.'
5. Marianne Roth, *UNCITRAL Model Law on International Commercial Arbitration*, in Weigand/Baumann, *supra* n. 2, no. 20.214/217. The text of the relevant provisions in the revised 2010/2013 version of the UNCITRAL Arbitration Rules was, in turn, modelled on Article 12 of the Model Law, *see* the Appendix of this book.

'seems preferable to listing all possible connections and other relevant situations'.[6] Apparently, the drafters expected wider acceptance of this provision if they kept it on this general level; and that was how it turned out.[7]

One of the jurisdictions that adopted Article 12 *verbatim* is **Germany**.[8] Not surprisingly, German commentators grapple with the vagueness of the test: 'Filling out the general condition of impartiality and independence in a comprehensive manner remains difficult. Because of the lack of generally applicable standards in the literature and jurisprudence, the legislator has left the concrete decision on these characteristics to the judges.'[9]

At the other end of the spectrum, we might find **India**. India adopted the Model Law in 1996, but in 2015 added schedules that largely copy the IBA Conflicts Guidelines[10] by listing specific scenarios that require disclosure as well as scenarios that render an arbitrator ineligible.[11]

The UNCITRAL Model Law is only that – a model law. States may or may not adopt it; they may or may not amend provisions. Nonetheless, the UNCITRAL Model Law led to a breakthrough in the harmonization of arbitration laws throughout the world. It has been described as one of the 'principal pillars in the worldwide system of arbitral justice'.[12] To date, eighty-five states (with a total of 118 jurisdictions) have adopted the Model Law so far.[13]

Owing not least to the success of the UNCITRAL Model Law, there is, at first sight, a global standard for conflicts of interest: 'justifiable doubts as to his [or her] impartiality or independence'. What that means in practice might be another matter. It is doubtful whether all courts in all those 116 jurisdictions share the same understanding of what justifiable doubts or even what independence and impartiality means. Arguably, the present panel could gather representatives of various Model Law jurisdictions and still have quite a lively debate. Even if there is consensus as to the interpretation and application of Article 12, we are far from a global standard.

Strikingly, many important arbitration jurisdictions have not adopted the Model Law: jurisdictions such as England, France, New York, Sweden, or Switzerland have their own independent arbitration laws and typically not because they have not come around to adapt their traditional laws to the Model Law.[14] Rather, these relevant arbitration jurisdictions consciously chose not to adopt the Model Law. Almost all of them have, in the meantime, amended their laws, paying little heed to the Model Law.

6. Analytical Commentary on Draft Text of a Model Law on International Commercial Arbitration. Report of the Secretary-General, A/CN.9/264, 25 March 1985, Article 12 no. 4.
7. Roth, *supra* n. 5, no. 20.216.
8. *See* § 1036 German Code of Civil Procedure, in force since 1998.
9. Patricia Nacimiento/Amelie Abt, in ARBITRATION IN GERMANY. THE MODEL LAW IN PRACTICE, § 1036 ZPO no. 29 (Böckstiegel/Kröll/Nacimiento eds, 2nd ed. Kluwer 2014).
10. IBA Guidelines on Conflicts of Interest in International Arbitration 2014 (first version 2004).
11. The Arbitration and Conciliation (Amendment) Act, 2015, Fifth and Seventh Schedules.
12. Timothy Lemay and Corinne Montineri, *Review of the Model Law's Implementation after Twenty-Five Years*, in THE UNCITRAL MODEL LAW AFTER 25 YEARS, 4 (Frédéric Bachand and Fabien Gélinas eds., Juris 2013).
13. https://uncitral.un.org/en/texts/arbitration/modellaw/commercial_arbitration/status.
14. *See* Felix Dasser, *'Soft Law' in International Commercial Arbitration*, in RECUEIL DES COURS 402, 385-596, paras 101 et seqq. (2019).

A typical example is **Switzerland**: Chapter 12 on International Arbitration of the Swiss Private International Law Act was drafted partly in parallel with the UNCITRAL Model Law. The Swiss drafting commenced earlier and ended later – not really surprising given the time-proven leisurely pace of Swiss legislation. The legislator could still have considered the UNCITRAL Model Law but decided not to, given the established arbitration tradition in Switzerland. Even as we speak, the Swiss legislator is revising Chapter 12.[15] Both at the level of Government and Parliament, the UNCITRAL Model Law was simply not an issue. The governmental report to Parliament accompanying the revision bill does mention the UNCITRAL Model Law a few times, but not once to support a change of Swiss law.[16]

I understand that the Swiss approach has been largely shared by other jurisdictions, such as England and France. In **England**, the 1996 Arbitration Act was drafted with limited regard to the UNCITRAL Model Law with the exception of the structure and language that would make the Arbitration Act more accessible to foreigners than a typical English statute.[17] In **France**, the recent 2011 revision of the French arbitration law moved French law even farther away from the Model Law than its 1981 revision. The official report of the Justice Ministry to the 2011 revision did not even mention the Model Law.[18]

Consequently, we cannot expect uniformity among the major arbitration venues on the topic of conflicts of interest of arbitrators. The good news is that there is some uniformity. As the reports from the panellists will show, all of the jurisdictions represented apply the standard of independence and impartiality. That is, however, where the consensus ends. The four jurisdictions, England, France, Switzerland and the US, at least judging from the wording of the statutes, adhere to different thresholds.

While the UNCITRAL Model Law requires the now ubiquitous dual threshold of impartiality and independence, the English Arbitration Act 1996 only mentions impartiality, eschewing independence,[19] and the Swiss International Private Law Act, on the other hand, mentions independence, but not impartiality.[20] The US Federal Arbitration Act only allows vacating an award in case of 'evident partiality or corruption' of the arbitrator.[21] Of the four jurisdictions represented on the panel today, only the French

15. In the meantime, the Swiss Parliament has enacted the revised Chapter 12 on 19 June 2020. The revision entered into force on 1 January 2021.
16. Botschaft zur Änderung des Bundesgesetzes über das Internationale Privatrecht (12. Kapitel: Internationale Schiedsgerichtsbarkeit), Bundesblatt 2018, 7163 et seqq. (24 October 2018).
17. *Departmental Advisory Committee on Arbitration Law, A Report on the UNCITRAL Model Law on International Commercial Arbitration*, HMSO, London 1989; SARA LEMBO, THE 1996 UK ARBITRATION ACT AND THE UNCITRAL MODEL LAW – A CONTEMPORARY ANALYSIS, 34 et seqq. (2010); Johan Steyn, *England's Response to the UNCITRAL Model Law of Arbitration*, ARBITRATION INTERNATIONAL 10, 1 et seqq. (1994).
18. Ministère de la justice et des libertés, 'Rapport au Premier ministre relatif au décret n° 2011-48 du 13 janvier 2011 portant réforme de l'arbitrage', Journal officiel de la République Française, texte 8 sur 177, (2011); *see also* Emmanuel Gaillard and Pierre de Lapasse, *Le nouveau droit français de l'arbitrage interne et international*, RECUEIL DALLOZ 2011 n° 3.
19. Section 24(1)(a) Arbitration Act 1996.
20. Article 180(1)(c) Swiss Private International Law Act. With the current revision, impartiality is being added to the wording.
21. Section 10(a)(2) US Federal Arbitration Act.

statute lists both independence and impartiality.[22] Does the different wording matter? Is it possible that major arbitration jurisdictions of the world cannot even agree on a common test of bias? Or is it all the same? Is 'independence and impartiality' just a hendiadys, a figure of twins? Is one part of the other, as the English legislator considered?[23] Or are they two different concepts, independence being objective while impartiality denoting the subjective state of mind?[24]

To find out, we need to go where the music is playing, on the level of the case law. As with Article 12 of the Model Law, the statutes of the non-Model Law jurisdictions provide only so much guidance. Case law determine the practical thresholds.

This panel investigates the topic by focusing on *four specific questions*:

(1) What is the threshold for independence and impartiality?
(2) Is there a specific threshold for disclosure?
(3) What is the relevance of the IBA Conflicts Guidelines and other private instruments?
(4) Is there a duty of parties to investigate?

To the extent that data are available, the panellists also addressed how successful challenges in court are and on what grounds.

Each panellist focuses on one of these topics from the perspective of his or her home jurisdiction. Diana Akikol will start with the first topic from a Swiss perspective, followed by Laurence Shore on disclosure standards from a US perspective, Paula Hodges on the IBA Conflicts Guidelines from an English perspective, and Laurent Gouiffès on duty to investigate from a French perspective.

All of them will, however, also address other aspects of the general topic to the extent that the local jurisdiction provides particular insights. A case in point are '[...], most notably the **IBA Conflicts Guidelines**'. They were conceived to foster global standards and thus further predictability to the benefit of parties and arbitrators alike. They are regularly consulted by parties and arbitrators and also regularly invoked by parties in challenge proceedings. The English courts have repeatedly been asked to consider the IBA Conflicts Guidelines. The *Halliburton* case discussed by Paula Hodges is a prime example. There have been others.[25] The Swiss courts also were repeatedly asked to take into account or apply one or the other rule of the Guidelines as discussed by Diana Akikol in her paper. As it turns out, state courts acknowledge the eminence of the Guidelines but take care to emphasize their non-binding character.[26] The Swiss Federal Supreme Court calls them 'a useful working tool' but denies them any normativity as the only decisive factors are the 'circumstances of the specific case'.[27]

22. Article 1456(2) French Code of Civil Procedure.
23. As explained by Paula Hodges, the English legislator consciously omitted independence as a separate threshold as they considered it to be included in the threshold of impartiality (Hodges, Chapter 10).
24. On this, *see* Gouiffès, Chapter 9.
25. *See* Hodges, Chapter 10.
26. *See also* the comparative law analysis in Dasser, *supra*, Chapter 2 on the acceptance of the IBA Guidelines by courts.
27. DFSC 142 III 521 of 7 September 2016, cons. 3.1.2. *See* Akikol, Chapter 8; M. Leemann, *Challenging International Arbitration Awards in Switzerland on the Ground of a Lack of*

Sometimes courts explicitly depart from the IBA Guidelines, as in the English Commercial Court case *W Limited v. M SDN BHD*. There, Knowles J. criticized the IBA Guidelines for shifting the focus of the parties away from 'case-specific judgment' to abstract rules. He held that the case that clearly fell under the Non-Waivable Red List of the Guidelines did not justify the disqualification of the arbitrator under the specific circumstances.[28]

On the other hand, several recent free trade agreements explicitly refer to the IBA Conflicts Guidelines as the relevant threshold, and India, as mentioned before, implicitly refers to the Guidelines by basically copying their Red and Orange Lists, suggesting increasing recognition by state legislators.[29]

If the IBA Conflicts Guidelines do not (or not yet) offer sufficient predictability of law,[30] what does? Or is there simply no predictability? Arguably, bias is also a matter of 'I know it when I see it' in the famous words of Justice Potter Stewart,[31] but different people may well see different things.

In the area of investor-state dispute settlement (ISDS), these issues are particularly controversial and provoke numerous challenges. The ICSID and UNCITRAL are working on a code of conduct for arbitrators that has in the meantime been published for public consultation.[32] The draft code provides some more detailed guidelines concerning the test of independence and impartiality (Article 4 of the draft) and disclosure obligations (Article 5 of the draft).

Independence and impartiality are not digital concepts, but continua where there is more grey than black or white. What shade of grey is too grey? Is common sense any guideline, or are individual and cultural differences too big to provide a sense that is common to at least a large majority of arbitration practitioners as well as judges? Is the standard of justifiable doubts strictly objective, an 'objective standard based on a reasonable evaluation of the evidence by a third party,[33] or do the subjective beliefs and the cultural background of a party also need to be considered? Is the threshold the same or different for party-appointed arbitrators and for sole or presiding arbitrators? Are the

---

Independence and Impartiality of an Arbitrator, ASA Bulletin 29, 10 et seqq., 14 (2011). For a similar decision in the U.S. Ninth Circuit, *see* Shore, Chapter 11 (*New Regency v. Nippon Herald Films*, 501 F.3d 1101, 9th Cir. 2007).

28. *W Limited v. M SDN BHD*, 2 March 2016, [2016] EWHC 422 (Comm), per Knowles CBE J., n. 37.
29. *See* the Comprehensive Economic and Trade Agreement between the EU and Canada (CETA) of 30 October 2016 in Article 8.30(1); the Agreement between the United States of America, the United Mexican States, and Canada (USMCA) of 30 November 2018 in Article 14.D.6; and the Comprehensive and Progressive Agreement for Trans-Pacific Partnership (CPTPP) of 8 March 2018, in Article 3(e) of the Code of Conduct for Investor-State Dispute Settlement under Chapter 9 Section B; *see* the Appendix below for the relevant wording.
30. Further on this issue, *see* the comparative analysis by Dasser, *supra*, 518 et seqq.
31. *Jacobellis v. Ohio*, 378 U.S. 184 (1964), J. Potter Stewart concurring.
32. Draft Code of Conduct for Adjudicators in Investor-State Dispute Settlement, https://icsid.worldbank.org/en/Documents/Draft_Code_Conduct_Adjudicators_ISDS.pdf; *see* Cosmo Sanderson & Tom Jones, *ICSID and UNCITRAL unveil draft conduct code*, GAR 1 May 2020.
33. Suez, *Sociedad General de Aguas de Barcelona S.A. v. The Argentine Republic* (ICSID Cases Nos ARB/03/17 and ARB/03/19), Decision of the ICSID Administrative Council on the Proposal for the Disqualification of a Member of the Arbitral Tribunal, para. 39 (22 October 2007).

thresholds for a challenge and for disclosure the same or different?[34] What exactly are the consequences of a breach of the duty to disclose?[35] Could the arbitrator be held liable for sunk costs?[36] Do the arbitrators have a duty to investigate whether there is a conflict? Are the parties considered to have waived a challenge if they could have known about a potential conflict but did not sufficiently investigate and thus failed to challenge in time? And, most importantly or not, does friendship on Facebook disqualify an arbitrator?[37]

We may not be able to provide final answers to all questions, but the panellists will give it a least a good try to shed some light.

34. *See* the *Halliburton* case discussed by Hodges, Chapter 10, where the Court of Appeal held that the arbitrator should have disclosed certain circumstances, but that he could not be removed and the Supreme Court confirmed.
35. In the US, the answer to this and other questions will depend upon the pertinent Circuit, *see* Shore, Chapter 11.
36. *See* Gouiffès, Chapter 9 for such a case in France.
37. At least for the French Cour de cassation, 'friendship' on social media does not justify a challenge, *see* Gouiffès, Chapter 9.

CHAPTER 8

The View from the Swiss Courts on Conflicts of Interest, Disclosure, Objection, and Challenges*

Diana Akikol

1. INTRODUCTION

The guarantee of an independent and impartial tribunal lies at the core of the right to a fair process. The Swiss Act of International Arbitration, Chapter 12 (Articles 176-194) of the Federal Private International Law Act of 18 December 1987 (PILA), provides three means to ensure that arbitrators decide the case submitted to them with an unbiased, open mind.

Article 180(1)(c) of the PILA allows for an interlocutory challenge of an arbitrator during an ongoing arbitration 'if circumstances exist that give rise to justifiable doubts as to his independence'.[1] Although this provision only mentions independence, it also

* This chapter was prepared prior to the ASA Annual Conference held on 7 February 2020 and reflects the status of case law and doctrine as at 31 December 2019. At the time, the Swiss law of international arbitration was under revision. The revised law entered into force on 1 January 2021. Where relevant, the new provisions are mentioned in footnotes herein. I have furthermore included a new landmark ruling of the Swiss Federal Tribunal (the 'Supreme Court' or the 'Court') in section 5 below, which was handed down shortly before this article went to press.

I am grateful to Jake Lowther, Magnusson, Stockholm, for his review of this article and valuable comments.

Throughout this article, masculine forms (he/his/him) are used for simplicity only and are to be considered to refer to all genders, except when referring to a particular person.

Supreme Court decisions that were published in the official Court Reporter ('DFSC') as of 1954 are available on the Court's website (www.bger.ch). This website also offers access to most of the decisions rendered since 1 January 2000 and all final decisions made since 1 January 2007, including those which have not been designated for publication in the Court Reporter.

1. In addition to this statutory basis for a challenge, the parties may invoke grounds for disqualification arising from the specific terms of their agreement to arbitrate: an arbitrator may be

guarantees an arbitrator's impartiality.[2] However, pursuant to Article 180(2) of the PILA, parties may challenge an arbitrator appointed by them, or in whose appointment they have participated, only for reasons of which they became aware after the appointment.[3] As a further restriction, the same provision requires the challenging party to inform the tribunal and the other party of the grounds for challenge 'without delay'.[4] Article 180(3) of the PILA provides the courts at the seat of the tribunal with the authority to make a final decision on the challenge insofar as the parties have not agreed upon the procedure.[5]

Under Article 190(2)(a) of the PILA, a party may request the annulment of the award 'if the sole arbitrator was not properly appointed or if the arbitral tribunal was not properly constituted'. An annulment on this basis is especially warranted if there are grounds for challenge within the meaning of Article 180(1)(c) of the PILA against one or several arbitrators who made the award.[6] Accordingly, the threshold for a challenge to an arbitrator at the award annulment stage is the same as that applied to challenges raised during the arbitration. Pursuant to Article 191 of the PILA, the Supreme Court has exclusive authority to decide on challenges to international awards made in Switzerland. If an argument under Article 190(2)(a) of the PILA is successfully made out, the Court may not only annul the award but also order the removal of the arbitrator(s) concerned.[7] However, a challenge to the award under Article 190(2)(a) of the PILA is excluded insofar as the courts at the seat of the tribunal have already decided on a challenge brought against the arbitrator(s).[8] Moreover, as an overarching

challenged if he does not meet the qualifications agreed upon by the parties or if a ground for challenge exists under the rules of arbitration agreed upon by the parties, *see* Article 180(1)(a) and (b) of the PILA.

2. DFSC 136 III 605 of 29 October 2010, para. 3.3.1 (for more details, *see* section 2.2 below). This case law is now reflected in Article 180(1)(c) of the revised PILA ('if circumstances exist that give rise to justifiable doubts as to his independence or his impartiality').
3. Article 12(2), second sentence, of the 2006 UNCITRAL Model Law includes an essentially identical restriction.
4. This wording has been deleted from the text of Article 180(2) of the PILA in the revised Chapter 12. A new Article 180a, para. 1, of the PILA provides for a thirty-day time limit to challenge an arbitrator, unless the parties have agreed otherwise.
5. In practice, this default provision only applies to ad hoc arbitrations, as the rules of all major arbitral institutions include a procedure for the challenge of arbitrators and confer the decision-making authority on an administrative body. The revised Chapter 12 of the PILA includes a new Article 180a on the challenge procedure, including the right to obtain a final decision from the local courts. Article 180(3) of the PILA has therefore been repealed.
6. *See, e.g.*, DFSC 118 II 359 of 18 August 1992, para. 3c. The term 'arbitral tribunal' within the meaning of Article 190(2)(a) of the PILA refers to the tribunal that actually made the challenged award; the plea of an irregular constitution of the tribunal is inadmissible insofar as it is directed against a previous composition of the tribunal (DFSC 118 II 359 of 18 August 1992, para. 3a). In DFSC 139 III 511 of 13 November 2013, the Court confirmed that the plea of Article 190(2)(a) of the PILA is available not only in the event of a violation of the guarantee of an independent and impartial tribunal, but also if the tribunal was constituted in violation of an agreement made by the parties (e.g., regarding the number of arbitrators, qualifications required of the arbitrators or the procedure for their nomination).
7. DFSC 136 III 605 of 29 October 2010, para. 3.3.4.
8. A challenge decision made by a lower court based on Article 180(3) of the PILA (now Article 180a, para. 2, of the revised PILA) may not be appealed to the Supreme Court and a party may not seek an indirect review of such decision when challenging an award (DFSC 138 III 270 of 2 May 2012, confirmation of the Court's case law).

principle of the Swiss legal system, the duty to act in good faith requires a party to raise any objection to an arbitrator promptly during the arbitration, failing which the right to challenge the award will be deemed to have been waived.[9] The annulment of the award is thus a remedy of last resort, which is only open to parties who have unsuccessfully raised an objection or challenge before an institutional (or otherwise private) body or who were unable to discover the facts giving rise to a challenge before the award was made.[10] Additionally, in such cases, the aggrieved party must challenge the first award (*see* Article 190(3) of the PILA) and may not keep the objection to the composition of the tribunal in reserve for a challenge to any subsequent award.[11]

Finally, if a party discovers circumstances giving rise to justifiable doubts as to an arbitrator's independence or impartiality after the expiry of the time limit for filing a challenge to the award pursuant to Article 190(2)(a) of the PILA, such party may request the revocation of the award.[12] This third remedy further strengthens the parties' right to an award made by an independent and impartial tribunal.

9. *See* section 5 below.
10. There is no direct appeal to the Supreme Court against a challenge decision made by an institutional body, such as the ICC International Court of Arbitration (*see* Article 14(3) of the 2017 and 2021 ICC Rules); however, such decisions are subject to an indirect review by the Court in the context of an appeal brought against the award (DFSC 138 III 270 of 2 May 2012, para. 2.2.1; DFSC 128 III 330 of 3 July 2002, para. 2.2; DFSC 118 II 359 of 18 August 1992, para. 3b).
11. *See* DFSC 138 III 270 of 2 May 2012 (confirmation of the Court's case law).
12. According to the Supreme Court's case law, which has filled a gap in the previous law, a party may request the revocation (called 'revision') of an arbitral award in certain cases where the award is tainted by particularly serious flaws (*see* DFSC 118 II 199 of 11 March 1992, para. 2). The sole judicial authority to revoke an award is the Supreme Court. If the Court allows an application for revocation of an award, the Court does not decide on the merits of the dispute itself but refers the case back to the arbitral tribunal that made the award, or to a new arbitral tribunal to be constituted in accordance with the applicable rules (DFSC 142 III 521 of 7 September 2016, para. 2.1 and DFSC 134 III 286 of 14 March 2008, para. 2). In 2016, the Court expressed the view that a revocation of the award should also be possible if a party discovers grounds for the challenge of an arbitrator after the time limit for filing an action for annulment based on Article 190(2)(a) of the PILA has expired, provided that the applicant was unable to discover the grounds for the challenge during the arbitration by acting with the diligence required in the circumstances. However, the Court ultimately left this question undecided, as it considered it appropriate to leave the matter for decision by the legislator as part of the then ongoing revision of Chapter 12 of the PILA (DFSC 142 III 521 of 7 September 2016, para. 2 and, more particularly, para. 2.3.5). In a recent decision, the Court has now answered the question in the affirmative (DFSC 4A_413/2019 of 28 October 2019, para. 4.2; *see* for more details on this ruling section 5 below). The revised Chapter 12 of the PILA, enacted on 1 January 2021, includes a new Article 190a which expressly provides for the revocation of an award, including in cases where a party was unable to discover grounds for challenge of an arbitrator before the arbitral proceedings were terminated and no other remedy is available. A request for revocation must be filed within ninety days from the discovery of the grounds for challenge and no later than ten years from the day on which the award became final and binding.

2. THE THRESHOLD FOR CHALLENGE

2.1. The Constitutional Basis

In Switzerland, the right to an independent and impartial tribunal is guaranteed by Article 30(1) of the Federal Constitution of 1999. The grounds for challenge provided in Articles 180(1)(c) and 190(2)(a) of the PILA must be interpreted in light of the principles developed in the Supreme Court's case law based on this 'higher ranking norm'.[13]

Under Article 30(1) of the Constitution and Article 6 No. 1 of the European Convention on Human Rights, which are substantially identical on this particular point,[14] any person whose case is to be decided in judicial proceedings is entitled to have their case heard by a court of competent jurisdiction established by law, which must be impartial and independent of the parties. The Supreme Court has consistently held that arbitrators, like judges in a court of law, must present sufficient guarantees of independence and impartiality.[15] The rationale for this requirement is based on the rule that once notified to the parties, an arbitral award has the same legal effects in terms of res judicata and enforceability as a judgment made by a Swiss court. This rule is only justified if arbitrators are held to the same standards of independence and impartiality as judges.[16]

However, the Court acknowledges the need to consider the specific features of arbitration, and especially those of international arbitration, when examining whether the circumstances of a given case call for the disqualification of an arbitrator. This is because the world of international arbitration is small, and it is therefore inevitable that, after a few years of practice in this field, the arbitrators, often themselves practising lawyers, will have had occasion to collaborate with one another or with a party's counsel in other proceedings. For those involved in arbitration, such relationships arise more often than for state court judges as a result of economic and professional necessity. As a consequence, such relationships may not readily be considered grounds for challenge.[17]

It follows from the above that the constitutional principles developed by the Court in respect to the independence and impartiality of judges only apply *mutatis mutandis* to determine whether an arbitrator must be removed.[18]

---

13. *See* DFSC 136 III 605 of 29 October 2010, para. 3.3.1. The guarantees of Article 30(1) of the Constitution are substantially identical to the ones previously provided by Article 58 of the Constitution of 1874 (*see* DFSC 131 I 113 of 3 May 2005, para. 3.4). Thus, the cases decided by the Court based on Article 58 of the old Constitution remain good law.
14. *See, e.g.*, DFSC 135 I 14 of 6 October 2008, para. 2.
15. DFSC 136 III 605 of 29 October 2010, para. 3.2.1; DFSC 125 I 389 of 26 July 1999, para. 4a; and DFSC 119 II 271 of 15 March 1993, para. 3b and the references there. The requirements of independence and impartiality also apply to tribunal-appointed experts (DFSC 126 III 249 of 28 April 2000, para. 3c).
16. *See* DFSC 92 I 271, para. 4 and, for more recent decisions, DFSC 135 I 14 of 6 October 2008, para. 2; DFSC 4P_208/2004 of 14 December 2004, para. 4.1; and DFSC 4P_168/1999 of 17 February 2000, para. 2a.
17. DFSC 129 III 445 of 27 May 2003, para. 3.3.3.
18. *See* DFSC 4P_196/2003 of 7 January 2004, para. 3.1.

2.2. The Relevant Test

According to the Court's case law, Article 30(1) of the Constitution allows either party to challenge 'an arbitrator whose position or conduct is such as to cause doubts as to his or her independence or impartiality'.[19] This guarantee, which applies irrespective of the applicable procedural rules,[20] is meant to avoid any influence of circumstances outside the subject matter of the arbitration on the decision to the benefit or detriment of a party.[21]

In a landmark ruling made on 29 October 2010 in *Valverde Belmonte v. Italian National Olympic Committee,* the Court acknowledged that its case law does not make a strict distinction between independence and impartiality but tends to see both concepts as part of a wider notion of impartiality. In line with more recent decisions, the Court referred to 'objective impartiality', which means independence, and 'subjective impartiality'.[22]

The *Valverde Belmonte* decision makes it clear that party-appointed arbitrators are held to the same standards of independence and impartiality as the president of the tribunal or a sole arbitrator.[23] In the same judgment, the Court rejected the idea that arbitrators sitting on a panel of the Court of Arbitration for Sport (CAS) in Lausanne are

19. *See, e.g.*, DFSC 136 III 605 of 29 October 2010, para. 3.2.1. A decision made in 1992 refers to 'serious doubts' as to the arbitrator's independence (DFSC 118 II 359 of 18 August 1992, para. 3c). This wording is not employed in more recent decisions. Nevertheless, as will be discussed below, the Court continues to impose a high threshold for the challenge of arbitrators.
20. DFSC 5A_701/2017 of 14 May 2018, para. 4.3.
21. *See* DFSC 136 III 605 of 29 October 2010, para. 3.2.1 and DFSC 129 III 445 of 27 May 2003, para. 3.3.3.
22. *See* DFSC 136 III 605 of 29 October 2010, para. 3.2.1; DFSC 4A_586/2008 of 12 June 2009, para. 3.1.1; DFSC 4A_539/2008 of 19 February 2009, para. 3.2; and DFSC 4A_506/2007 of 20 March 2008, para. 3.1.1.
23. DFSC 136 III 605 of 29 October 2010. Before the PILA was enacted, the Court considered all arbitrators to be bound by the same standards of independence and impartiality (*see* DFSC 105 Ia 247 of 14 November 1979). Under the aegis of the PILA, it remained unclear for some time whether party-appointed arbitrators must be as independent and impartial as the president or a sole arbitrator. This uncertainty arose because the legislator had deliberately decided against including a reference to impartiality in Article 180(1)(c) of the PILA. In an officially reported decision of 1992, the question was left undecided (DFSC 118 II 359 of 18 August 1992, para. 3c). By contrast, in two unpublished judgments issued in 1994 and 1998, the Court held that the degree of impartiality required from the tribunal was not the same for all arbitrators. In later decisions, the issue was again left open (*see* DFSC 136 III 605 of 29 October 2010, para. 3.3.1, referring to DFSC 4P.224/1997 of 8 February 1998, para. 3a and DFSC 4P.292/1993 of 30 June 1994, para. 4). In the *Valverde Belmonte* ruling, the Court unequivocally dismissed the idea that an arbitrator appointed by a party would not be required to be as independent and impartial as the presiding arbitrator. Although mindful of the fact that 'absolute independence of all arbitrators is an ideal which will seldom accord with reality', the Court held that '[t]he idea that an arbitrator within an arbitral tribunal may be little more than counsel for the party having appointed him must be resolutely discarded, failing which arbitration will be jeopardised as an institution'. In reaching this conclusion, the Court, *inter alia,* referred to the fact that the IBA Guidelines on Conflicts of Interest in International Arbitration adhere to a monolithic concept of independence that applies to all arbitrators (DFSC 136 III 605 of 29 October 2010, para. 3.3.1). As mentioned above (*supra* n. 2), Article 180(1)(c) of the revised Chapter 12 PILA incorporates this case law by including an express reference to the requirement of impartiality.

bound by stricter standards of independence and impartiality than commercial arbitrators.[24]

The relevant test to determine whether an arbitrator must be removed can be summarised as follows:

(1) An arbitrator must withdraw not only when it is established that he is actually biased (as an inner disposition can seldom be proved), but it will suffice that circumstances exist which give rise to an appearance of bias and the apprehension that the arbitrator might act in a biased manner.[25]
(2) The Court applies an objective, two-pronged test: a challenge will only be successful if it is based on specific (objective) facts and if, in addition, such facts create an appearance of bias from an objective and reasonable perspective. Purely subjective perceptions of a party are not decisive.[26] Whether this test is met is, to a large extent, a matter of judgment for the court or body called upon to decide on the challenge.[27]
(3) There are no 'absolute' grounds for challenge; rather, the relevant test is whether, considering all established factual and procedural circumstances of a given case, there is an appearance of bias. As previously stated,[28] when examining allegations of bias, regard must be had to the specific features of arbitration. In assessing whether a conflict of interest exists, the parties may also be assisted by the IBA Guidelines on Conflicts of Interest in International Arbitration ('IBA Guidelines' or 'Guidelines').[29]
(4) Impartiality is presumed until proven otherwise.[30] The Court's case law is based on the assumption that arbitrators are capable of deciding the dispute

24. The Court is mindful that sports arbitration under the CAS rules involves particular features, such as a closed list of arbitrators, which reduces the parties' choice of arbitrators and may explain why CAS arbitrators have had previous contact with sports organisations, specialist lawyers and other experts in sports law. According to the Court's case law, these particularities cannot be disregarded when assessing a CAS arbitrator's independence and impartiality, although they do not per se justify applying lower standards than in commercial arbitration. In the *Valverde Belmonte* decision, the Court clarified that, conversely, it will not apply stricter standards when deciding on a challenge brought against a CAS arbitrator. Rather, the arbitrator's compliance with the requirements of independence and impartiality must be examined with reference to the same standards as those applied in commercial arbitration (*see* DFSC 136 III 605 of 29 October 2010, para. 3.3.3).
25. DFSC 136 III 605 of 29 October 2010, para. 3.2.1.
26. *See* DFSC 111 Ia 259 of 8 November 1985, para. 3a and DFSC 92 I 271, para. 5. *See also* DFSC 142 III 521 of 7 September 2016, para. 3.1.1 and 3.3.3 ('from the point of view of a reasonable third party'); DFSC 136 III 605 of 29 October 2010, para. 3.2.1; DFSC 129 III 445 of 27 May 2003, paras 3.3.3 and 4.2.2.2; and DFSC 117 Ia 182 of 21 August 1991, para. 3b.
27. *See* DFSC 111 Ia 259 of 8 November 1985, para. 3a; *see also* DFSC 4P.156/2000 of 3 November 2000, para. 2.
28. *See* section 2.1.
29. DFSC 142 III 521 of 7 September 2016, para. 3.1.2 and the references there. For further details, *see* section 4 below.
30. *See* DFSC 136 III 605 of 29 October 2010, para. 3.2.1 and DFSC 129 III 445 of 27 May 2003, para. 3.3.3.

submitted to them with an open mind.[31] The challenging party bears the burden of properly substantiating and proving its allegations. The decided cases show that the Court is not prepared to consider mere speculations or otherwise vague allegations.

(5) The standards of independence and impartiality are 'formal' guarantees, meaning that, if they are found to be violated, the award will be annulled, irrespective of whether the lack of independence or impartiality had an impact on the outcome of the decision. The challenging party is not required to demonstrate that the award would have been different had the tribunal been properly constituted.[32]

2.3. Case Groups and Principles

The Supreme Court has handed down numerous decisions on the independence and impartiality required of judges and arbitrators, in which it has further refined the applicable standards by developing a number of constitutional principles. Overall, the decided cases show a rather restrictive approach to allegations of bias, particularly when a challenge is based on an arbitrator's conduct rather than his professional or social ties with a party or a party's counsel.[33] The following sections provide a non-exhaustive review of the principles established by the Court in respect to a number of case groups.

2.3.1. Interest in the Outcome of the Dispute

It is a long-standing principle of Swiss case law that no one can be a judge or arbitrator in their own case or in a case they represent.[34] For example, the administrator of a bankrupt estate may not act as a judge in a dispute involving the estate.[35]

In general, an arbitrator must withdraw if he has a personal interest in the dispute, whether it be a direct or indirect interest.[36] Such interest can be of a financial or non-financial nature, and it may either concern the arbitrator's legal or factual domain. For example, an arbitrator has a personal interest in the case if he is an intervening party, a joint creditor or debtor, a guarantor or the owner of assets provided

31. *See* DFSC 136 III 605 of 29 October 2010 in the matter *Valverde Belmonte*, para. 3.4.4, *in fine* and DFSC 129 III 445 of 27 May 2003, para. 4.2.2.2, *in fine* and the references there.
32. DFSC 136 III 605 of 29 October 2010, para. 3.3.2.
33. *See* DFSC 4A_458/2009 of 10 June 2010, para. 3.3.3.2 and DFSC 4A_236/2017 of 24 November 2017, para. 3.3 (stating that, although it is conceivable that an arbitrator's conduct in the proceedings may cast doubt on his or her independence and impartiality, the Court will apply a strict standard in assessing allegations of bias).
34. *See* DFSC 33 I 143 of 31 January 1907, para. 2. This case law is in line with the situations described in item 1.1 of the IBA Guideline's Non-Waivable Red List.
35. *See* DFSC 33 I 143 of 31 January 1907, para. 2 and DFSC 38 I 91 of 26 October 1966, 95-96.
36. *See* DFSC 4A_162/2010 of 22 June 2010, para. 2.2. In general, an indirect but 'close' interest in the outcome of the case is sufficient to create an appearance of bias (*see* DFSC 111 Ia 72 of 14 March 1985, para. 2a).

as security for a party's debt, or if the arbitrator holds a significant stake in a company which is a party to the dispute.[37]

In 2010, the Court granted a challenge against a sole arbitrator who was vice-director of a company that had granted the claimant a loan to overcome liquidity problems incurred in connection with the transaction in dispute. The fact that, as a board member, the arbitrator was under a duty to safeguard the company's interests and had financial responsibility was sufficient to create a personal, indirect interest in the outcome of the case, even though he was not a significant shareholder.[38]

2.3.2. Relationship with a Party

An arbitrator's independence and impartiality are compromised by the existence of close links (in French: *liens étroits*) with a party to the proceedings.[39]

It is settled case law that an arbitrator is conflicted if he has an ongoing attorney-client relationship with a party or if he has repeatedly represented or advised a party in the past or shortly before the award was made.[40] This applies irrespective of whether the past or present legal services are related to the dispute and regardless of any other circumstances.[41] However, a single closed case does not normally create an appearance of bias.[42] A past activity for a party may only constitute grounds for challenge if it can be assumed that, at the time of the arbitration, a relationship of an economic or emotional nature remains in place that affects the arbitrator's freedom to make decisions.[43]

The chances of succeeding with a challenge against an arbitrator on account of a past professional relationship with a party depend on the type, the timing and other aspects of the services involved. In *Valverde Belmonte*, the athlete challenged one of the CAS arbitrators on the grounds that he had acted for one of the parties to the proceedings, the World Anti-Doping Agency (WADA), on two previous occasions. The Court found that the arbitrator had been involved in just two isolated missions for WADA, both of which ended several years before the start of the arbitration. In both

37. *See* DFSC 4A_162/2010 of 22 June 2010, para. 2.2 (domestic arbitration).
38. *Ibid.*, para. 2.3.
39. DFSC 4A_586/2008 of 12 June 2009, para. 3.1.2.
40. *See* DFSC 135 I 14 of 6 October 2008, para. 4.1 and 4.3, concerning the situation of lawyers who occasionally sit as judges on the bench of a Swiss state court. This case law also applies to arbitration, *see* DFSC 4A_598/2014 of 14 January 2015, para. 2.2.1-2.2.2.
41. *See* DFSC 4A_598/2014 of 14 January 2015, para. 2.2.1, with reference to DFSC 140 III 221 of 20 May 2014, para. 3.1.
42. *See* DFSC 116 Ia 485 of 20 December 1990, para. 3b (concerning challenges to two judges in an administrative court).
43. *See* DFSC 4P.188/2001 of 15 October 2001, para. 2d. Overall, this case law appears to be in line with the approach taken by the IBA Guidelines, which draw a distinction between an arbitrator's ongoing professional relationship with a party and past services in an unrelated matter. While the first situation is included in item 2.3.1 of the Waivable Red List ('currently represents or advises one of the parties') and thus bars the arbitrator from acting unless specifically accepted by the parties, previous services for one of the parties in an unrelated matter are covered in point 3.1.1 of the Orange List and therefore do not necessarily lead to the disqualification of the arbitrator concerned.

cases, the arbitrator had acted as an independent expert and was not bound by instructions from WADA in the performance of his missions. Moreover, it was not established that he had received any remuneration other than a reimbursement of expenses. In these circumstances, the athlete's argument that the arbitrator's relationship with WADA was comparable to that of a lawyer and client was rejected.[44]

An arbitrator also appears biased if he acts, or has recently acted, as counsel against one of the parties in an unrelated matter.[45] In the Court's view, it is a fact that parties often transfer their negative feelings towards the opposing party to their legal representative and that many parties, therefore, see the other party's counsel as their opponent.[46]

A friendship or enmity between a judge (or arbitrator) and a party to the dispute may only create an appearance of bias if it is of a certain intensity. In general, this threshold will not be met if a judge and one of the parties live in the same neighbourhood or know each other from university, military service or regular contacts in a professional context.[47] In line with these principles, the Court found that, in the absence of additional circumstances, the fact that a judge was a party's Facebook 'friend' was insufficient to warrant her removal.[48]

By contrast, in 1966, the Court confirmed the removal of a party-appointed arbitrator whose spouse was an associate in the law firm of the appointing party's counsel, although the spouse was not involved in the dispute.[49]

2.3.3. *Relationship with Counsel*

The Court accepts that an arbitrator may also be conflicted if he has a close relationship (in French: *relation étroite*) with a party's counsel. However, because in such cases, the link to the party is only indirect, the Court applies a higher threshold in its assessment of allegations of bias.[50]

According to the case law, an amicable relationship between an arbitrator and a party's counsel (e.g., a relationship on a first-name basis or mutual recommendations to potential clients) is, in principle, insufficient to create grounds for challenge.[51]

44. DFSC 136 III 605 of 29 October 2010, para. 3.4.4.
45. DFSC 135 I 14 of 6 October 2008 (relating to a challenge against a state court judge); *see also* DFSC 139 III 120 of 26 February 2013, para. 3.2.1 and 3.2.2.
46. *See* DFSC 135 I 14 of 6 October 2008, para. 4.3.
47. *See* DFSC 5A_701/2017 of 14 May 2018, para. 4.3.
48. *See* DFSC 5A_701/2017 of 14 May 2018, para. 4.5.
49. DFSC 92 I 271 of 26 October 1966, para. 5. The IBA Guidelines consider this scenario in item 3.3.5 of their Orange List ('A close family member of the arbitrator is a partner or employee of the law firm representing one of the parties, but is not assisting with the dispute').
50. DFSC 4A_586/2008 of 12 June 2009, para. 3.1.2.
51. DFSC 129 III 445 of 27 May 2003, para. 4.2.2.2 and the references there; DFSC 4A_586/2008 of 12 June 2009, para. 3.1.2 (domestic arbitration); DFSC 4P.105/2006 of 4 August 2006, para. 4. *See also* DFSC 1P.99/2000 of 20 March 2000, para. 3b, where the Court observed that the grounds for challenge concern first and foremost the relationship between the judge and the parties. Given that counsel do not represent their own interests in the proceedings but the interests of their client, a judge may, as a rule, not be considered biased for the sole reason that he maintains an amicable or otherwise closer relationship with a party's counsel.

Similarly, the Court considered the fact that two out of three arbitrators and a party's counsel were members of the same association to be unproblematic in the absence of additional circumstances that might have led to a different assessment of the situation.[52]

Likewise, the fact that an arbitrator and a party's counsel sat on a tribunal in a different, unrelated matter is, in and of itself, insufficient to justify the arbitrator's removal.[53] This also applies if the other matter is still pending at the time of the arbitration. Moreover, the arbitrator is not obligated to disclose such fact to the parties.[54]

In a judgment rendered in 1998, the Court did not exclude the possibility that two partners in the same firm who share expenses but not profits may be involved in the same matter, one as arbitrator and the other as counsel. In the Court's view, lawyers acting as arbitrators can be expected to be able to distinguish between their professional relationships and the neutrality required of them as arbitrators.[55] However, in view of the current trend towards stricter standards of independence and impartiality in international arbitration, it is questionable whether the Court would still hold the same view today.

In a recent ad hoc arbitration, the court at the seat of the arbitration, acting as appointing authority, confirmed the nomination of an arbitrator who had worked for three years at the same law firm as the nominating party's counsel.[56]

2.3.4. *Relationship Between an Arbitrator's Law Firm and a Party's Affiliate*

According to the published case law, the members of a law firm are seen as one identity.[57] The same uniform approach applies to some extent to the companies of a corporate group.[58] However, the Court is mindful that a strict application of these principles to both law firms and corporate groups would lead to multiple conflicts and may not always be justified in the circumstances. Therefore, in a decision of 27 May 2019, the Court clarified that a past or current relationship between an arbitrator's law firm and a party to the arbitration, or an affiliate of one of the parties, does not per se constitute a conflict. Rather, it must be examined case by case whether the relationship

52. DFSC 4A_586/2008 of 12 June 2009, para. 3.1.2, with reference to DFSC 4A_506/2007 of 20 March 2008, para. 3.3.2.
53. *See* DFSC 129 III 445 of 27 May 2003, para. 4.2.2.2; DFSC 4P.105/2006 of 4 August 2006, para. 4.
54. *See* DFSC 4P.105/2006 of 4 August 2006, para. 4.
55. *See* DFSC 4A_586/2008 of 12 June 2008, para. 4.2.2.2, referring to the unpublished DFSC 4P.224/1997 of 9 February 1998, para. 3. By contrast, item 3.3.2 of the Guidelines' Orange List mentions as an example of a potential conflict the situation that an arbitrator and a party's counsel are members of the same barristers' chambers.
56. *See* DFSC 4A_292/2019 of 16 October 2019, para. Ba.
57. DFSC 140 III 221 of 20 May 2014, para. 4.3.1 and DFSC 139 III 433 of 27 August 2013, para. 2.1.5.
58. DFSC 139 III 433 of 27 August 2013, para. 2.1.6.

creates an appearance of bias. The Court found this approach to be in line with General Standard 6(a) of the IBA Guidelines.[59]

2.3.5. *Relationship with Another Person Interested in the Outcome of the Dispute*

The case law accepts that grounds for challenge may also stem from an arbitrator's relationship with a person or entity that is not a party to the dispute but otherwise interested in, or related to, the case. For example, a conflict may result from the fact that the arbitrator served as counsel for a witness whose testimony might be material to the outcome of the case.[60]

In a judgment relating to a criminal matter, the Court granted a challenge against a lawyer sitting as a judge because one of his clients (a bank) had a considerable financial interest in a matter related to the criminal proceedings.[61]

In 1998, the Court upheld a challenge against a court judgment because one of the judges, 'X', was acting as counsel for an unrelated party in parallel proceedings, which turned on the same legal issue as the one determined in the challenged decision. The Court found that there was a manifest appearance of bias, as the challenged decision essentially adopted the position advocated by X on behalf of his client in the parallel dispute and could be expected to serve as persuasive authority in those proceedings. The Court considered it unrealistic to assume that a judge would, in such circumstances, be capable of disregarding the interests of the party represented by him in the parallel proceedings.[62]

2.3.6. *Previous Involvement in the Dispute or in Settlement Discussions*

It is well established that an appearance of bias may also result from the fact that an arbitrator had prior involvement in the case. An accumulation of roles in the same dispute may only be accepted if the arbitrator has not, in his previous role, already expressed an opinion on certain issues in such a manner that the outcome of the decision appears to be sealed. Whether this is the case depends on the particular circumstances of the individual case.[63]

In a judgment rendered on 10 June 2010 in the matter *Adrian Mutu v. Chelsea Football Club*, the Court saw no grounds for challenge in the fact that the co-arbitrator

59. DFSC 4A_663/2018 of 27 May 2019, para. 3.5. Pursuant to the General Standard 6(a) of the Guidelines, the 'arbitrator is in principle considered to bear the identity of his or her law firm, but when considering the relevance of facts or circumstances to determine whether a potential conflict of interest exists, or whether disclosure should be made, the activities of an arbitrator's law firm, if any, and the relationship of the arbitrator with the law firm, should be considered in each individual case' and the 'fact that the activities of the arbitrator's firm involve one of the parties shall not necessarily constitute a source of such conflict, or a reason for disclosure'.
60. *See* a decision made on 16 September 1988, published in 1 ASA Bull., 80-82 (1989).
61. DFSC 116 Ia 135 of 3 August 1990, para. 3c.
62. DFSC 124 I 121 of 9 April 1998, para. 3c.
63. *See* DFSC 133 I 89 of 7 November 2006, para. 3.2 and the references there.

nominated by Chelsea had previously chaired a CAS panel in the same matter, which found Mr Mutu to be in unilateral breach of contract. The Court reasoned that the second arbitration dealt with a different issue (i.e., the amount of damages due) and that the first award did not give rise to the belief that the arbitrators had prejudged this issue.[64]

The criterion of whether the outcome of the decision appears to be open also applies when an arbitrator has been involved in settlement discussions between the parties. From the Swiss perspective, such involvement is not per se sufficient to create an appearance of bias. Rather, the arbitrator may only be challenged if, in particular circumstances, his involvement in settlement discussions gives rise to justifiable doubts as to his impartiality. This would be the case if, for example, the arbitrator considers a certain fact established before the taking of evidence is completed, or if he has made up his mind on certain issues of a factual or legal nature in a manner that casts doubt on his ability to come to a different conclusion later in the proceedings.[65]

The tribunal members may not be challenged if their award is annulled and the matter is remanded back to the same tribunal for a new decision (as is the case under the Swiss award annulment regime). The fact that the tribunal is called upon to correct its own mistakes is not incompatible with the requirements of independence and impartiality. Rather, tribunals are expected to decide on a remanded matter in an objective and unbiased manner, even more so as they are bound by the considerations set out in the Supreme Court's annulment decision.[66]

2.3.7. Previously Expressed Legal Opinion

No apparent bias is normally established if an arbitrator has previously expressed an opinion on legal issues that also arise in the arbitration.[67] The situation was different in the case *Swiss Pilots Association v. Swiss International Air Lines AG* ('Swissair'), as one of the arbitrators, prior to his appointment, had published an article expressing the view that a first award made by the then constituted tribunal was 'grossly incorrect'. When he was later appointed as a replacement for Swissair's arbitrator, who had resigned, the claimant successfully challenged him in court on the ground of an apparent bias. In a decision made in 2006, the Supreme Court upheld the arbitrator's removal, sharing the lower courts' view that the arbitrator had criticised the first award in a manner that gave rise to the apprehension that he had already made up his mind on the questions in dispute.[68]

64. *See* DFSC 4A_458/2009 of 10 June 2010, para. 3.3.3.2.
65. *See* DFSC 131 I 113 of 3 May 2005, para. 3.6 (relating to state court proceedings).
66. *See* DFSC 113 Ia 407 of 17 November 1987, para. 2b.
67. *See* DFSC 133 I 89 of 7 November 2006, para. 3.3. *See also* item 4.1.1 on the Green List of the IBA Guidelines ('The arbitrator has previously expressed a legal opinion (such as in a law review article or public lecture) concerning an issue that also arises in the arbitration (but this opinion is not focused on the case)').
68. *See* DFSC 133 I 89 of 7 November 2006, para. 3.5 and para. 3.7.

2.3.8. *Conduct and Decisions of the Arbitrator*

As previously mentioned,[69] an arbitrator's conduct in the arbitration will rarely give rise to justifiable doubts as to his impartiality. Most importantly, the Court has consistently held that procedural measures, irrespective of whether they are correct or flawed, do not, as such, give rise to justifiable doubts as to an arbitrator's impartiality.[70] Procedural mistakes or an erroneous decision on the merits can only create an appearance of bias if the errors made are particularly serious or repeated and constitute a blatant violation of the arbitrator's duties.[71] To date, there are no reported decisions in which such a challenge was upheld.

However, in a recent decision granting a request for revocation of an award, the Court has for the first time removed an arbitrator on the grounds that his conduct outside the arbitration (i.e., the publication of certain messages on his public Twitter account) had created an appearance of bias.[72]

3. THE THRESHOLD FOR DISCLOSURE

The Supreme Court confirmed as early as 1985 that a prospective arbitrator has a pre-contractual duty and, once appointed, a contractual duty to inform the parties of any facts that may be grounds for challenge, at least if he or she has reason to believe that such facts are unknown to the party who might seek to rely on them.[73]

Unlike the ICC Rules and the IBA Guidelines, which provide a subjective threshold for disclosure based on what could be considered grounds for challenge 'in the eyes of the parties',[74] the 1985 decision appears to set out an objective test.

---

69. Section 2.3 (introduction) above.
70. *See* DFSC 111 Ia 259 of 8 November 1985, para. 3b/aa; DFSC 4A_505/2017 of 4 July 2018, para. 4.2.2; DFSC 4A_236/2017 of 24 November 2017, para. 3.3; DFSC 4A_704/2015 of 16 February 2017, para. 3.1.
71. *See* DFSC 115 Ia 400 of 20 December 1989, para. 3b; DFSC 4A_704/2015 of 16 February 2017, para. 3.1; DFSC 4A_348/2009 of 6 January 2010, para. 3.3.3; DFSC 4A_539/2008 of 19 February 2009, para. 3.3.2. The reason for this strict approach to challenges for allegedly flawed arbitral decisions is two-fold. First, the Court is mindful of the fact that an adjudicator's role involves deciding issues which are often controversial or a matter of discretion. A decision made as part of a normal exercise of this role, even if it were to be substantially flawed, is therefore insufficient to create an appearance of bias. Second, the Court has made it clear that the procedure for the challenge of an arbitrator may not serve the purpose of examining alleged procedural mistakes or substantive errors of the arbitrator, for such pleas are to be raised in a potential annulment procedure (*see* DFSC 115 Ia 400 of 20 December 1989, para. 3b).
72. *See* DFSC 147 III 65 of 28 October 2019 in the matter *Sun Yang v. WADA and Fédération Internationale de Natation (FINA)* and, for more details, section 5 below.
73. *See* DFSC 111 Ia 72 of 14 March 1985, para. 2c ('des faits pouvant être tenus pour un motif de récusation'). A new Article 179(6) of the revised PILA now imposes an express duty on any prospective or appointed arbitrator to disclose immediately 'the existence of circumstances that might raise reasonable doubts about his or her independence or impartiality'. This is in line with a similar provision for domestic arbitrations (Article 363 of the Swiss Code of Civil Procedure), which in turn was inspired by Article 12(1) of the UNCITRAL Model Law.
74. Pursuant to Article 11(2) of the 2017 and 2021 ICC Rules, a prospective arbitrator shall disclose 'any facts or circumstances which might be of such a nature as to call into question the arbitrator's independence in the eyes of the parties, as well as any doubts that could give rise to

However, the 1985 ruling qualifies this objective threshold based on the arbitrator's understanding as to whether the relevant facts are known to the party concerned. In 2012, the Court confirmed that the duty of disclosure only extends to facts which the arbitrator has reason to believe are unknown to the party that might invoke them.[75]

As illustrated by a 2006 decision, there is no duty to disclose facts that are insufficient to justify a challenge in light of the principles developed in the Court's case law.[76]

A 2001 decision suggests that a breach of the duty to disclose relevant facts does not, as such, amount to a reason for disqualification. Instead, the question is whether the undisclosed facts create an appearance of bias.[77] However, as another decision shows, non-disclosure may be taken into account as an aggravating factor in such an assessment.[78] Conversely, the fact that the arbitrator disclosed the relevant facts in a timely manner may be seen as an element confirming his independence and impartiality.[79]

4. THE RELEVANCE OF THE IBA CONFLICTS OF INTEREST GUIDELINES

The Supreme Court first mentioned the IBA Guidelines in a judgment issued on 20 March 2008. According to this decision, the parties may, *inter alia*, refer to the IBA Guidelines to verify the independence of their arbitrators. The Court acknowledged that the Guidelines, although not legally binding, constitute a 'valuable working tool', which is likely to contribute to the harmonisation and unification of the standards applied in international arbitration to deal with conflicts of interest and to influence the practice of arbitral institutions and the courts. However, the Court pointed out that the particular circumstances of a given case will always be determinative when deciding on a challenge.[80]

In the 2008 decision, the fact that two CAS arbitrators and the counsel of one of the parties were members of the same sports-related association was found to be insufficient to create an appearance of bias. The Court relied on item 4.4.1 of the Guidelines' Green List in support of this finding but noted that, on this point, the Guidelines merely expressed the principles laid down in the Court's case law.[81]

---

reasonable doubts as to the arbitrator's impartiality'. Similarly, General Standard (3)(a) of the IBA Guidelines requires the arbitrator to disclose such facts or circumstances that 'may, in the eyes of the parties, give rise to doubts as to the arbitrator's impartiality or independence'.

75. DFSC 4A_110/2012 of 9 October 2012, para. 2.2.2 ('Semblable devoir n'existe, d'ailleurs, qu'à l'égard des faits dont l'arbitre a des raisons de penser qu'ils ne sont pas connus de la partie qui pourrait s'en prévaloir (ATF 111 Ia 72 c. 2c i.f., p. 76)').
76. DFSC 4P.105/2006 of 4 August 2006, para. 4.
77. *See* DFSC 4P.188/2001 of 15 October 2001, para. 2f.
78. *See* DFSC 4A_162/2010 of 22 June 2010, para. 2.3 *in fine.*
79. *See* DFSC 136 III 605 of 29 October 2010, para. 3.4.4.
80. DFSC 4A_506/2007 of 20 March 2008, para. 3.3.2.2. This was confirmed in a decision published in the official court reporter: DFSC 142 III 521 of 7 September 2016, para. 3.1.2.
81. DFSC 4A_506/2007 of 20 March 2008, para. 3.3.2.2.

Over the past twelve years, the Guidelines have repeatedly been mentioned by the Court. For example, in *Valverde Belmonte*, the Court relied on, among other sources, the IBA Guidelines to conclude that party-nominated arbitrators are held to the same standards of independence and impartiality as the president or a sole arbitrator.[82] As already mentioned,[83] in a 2019 decision, the Court invoked General Standard 6(a) of the Guidelines in support of the case law principle that a past or present relationship between an arbitrator's law firm and a party to the dispute, or an affiliate of one of the parties, does not necessarily create an appearance of bias.[84]

In other cases, the parties invoked practical examples from the Guidelines' application lists in submissions before the Court.[85] In most of these cases, the Court examined in detail whether any of the examples invoked by the parties were analogous to the case before it. In doing so, the Court has contributed to the interpretation of the Guidelines.

For example, in a decision made in 2016, the Court was called to interpret the term 'the arbitrator's law firm' within the meaning of the Guidelines. The respondent in the arbitration applied for revocation of the award,[86] arguing that the sole arbitrator, a partner in a Zurich-based law firm that is a member of the CMS network of law firms, appeared to be conflicted because a CMS firm based in Germany had advised a sister company of the claimant in another matter while the arbitration was pending. In support of the request, the respondent relied on several examples in the Guidelines' Red List and Orange List. The Court observed that, although the CMS members operate a joint website on which they emphasise the cooperation between them, they are separate legal entities that do not share any revenue. In these circumstances, the German firm could not, in the Court's view, be considered 'the arbitrator's law firm'. Instead, the sole arbitrator's case fell within the scope of item 4.2.1 of the Green List and did not constitute grounds for challenge.[87] However, the Court did not end its analysis there but went on to examine whether the circumstances of the case from the perspective of a reasonable observer warranted the removal of the arbitrator (which it found not to be the case).[88]

In a decision issued in 2019, the Court broke new ground as it referred for the first time to the IBA Guidelines on Party Representation in International Arbitration of 25 May 2013. The respondent had challenged the claimant's arbitrator before the arbitral tribunal arguing, *inter alia*, that an invoice of the claimant's counsel filed as part of the

82. DFSC 136 III 605 of 29 October 2010, para. 3.3.1.
83. *See* section 2.3.4 above.
84. DFSC 4A_663/2018 of 27 May 2019, para. 3.5.
85. *See* DFSC 142 III 521 of 7 September 2016, para. 3.2.1 (application for revocation of the award); DFSC 136 III 605 of 29 October 2010, para. 3.4.4; DFSC 4A_110/2012 of 9 October 2012, para. 2.2.1; DFSC 4A_458/2009 of 10 June 2010, para. 3.3.1-3.3.3; DFSC 4A_258/2009 of 11 January 2010, para. 3.1.2; and DFSC 4A_292/2019 of 16 October 2019, para. 3.2.
86. On the possibility of requesting the revocation ('revision') of an award, *see* section 1 above and *supra* n. 12.
87. DFSC 142 III 521 of 7 September 2016, para. 3.2-3.3. Item 4.2.1 of the Guidelines' Green List mentions the scenario that a 'firm, in association or in alliance with the arbitrator's law firm, but that does not share significant fees or other revenues with the arbitrator's law firm, renders services to one of the parties, or an affiliate of one of the parties, in an unrelated matter'.
88. DFSC 142 III 521 of 7 September 2016, para. 3.3.3.

claimant's cost submission revealed that the arbitrator and the claimant's counsel had discussed questions on the applicable law over the phone. The tribunal dismissed the challenge in the award, whereupon the respondent brought an action for annulment before the Supreme Court. In the respondent's view, item 4.4.1 of the Conflicts Guidelines made it clear that unilateral contacts between an arbitrator and one of the parties were acceptable only if made *prior* to the appointment,[89] whereas the challenged arbitrator had contacted the claimant's counsel *after* the appointment. The Court accepted the tribunal's explanation that the phone call in question was made to ascertain whether the agreement in dispute contained a choice of law clause and that this enquiry served the purpose of selecting a suitable chairperson. Moreover, the call was made with the agreement of the other co-arbitrator and the chairman, once appointed, was informed of the call. In these circumstances, the Court dismissed the challenge, citing, *inter alia*, Section 8(b) of the IBA Guidelines on Party Representation, which provides that a party representative may communicate with a *prospective or appointed* party-nominated arbitrator for the purpose of selecting the presiding arbitrator.[90] This decision confirms that the Court is open to to incorporate new soft law in international arbitration in its decision-making process where appropriate, thus providing a dynamic and up-to-date body of case law.

As shown by the aforementioned decisions, the IBA Guidelines have come to play an important role in the Court's decision-making process since they were first mentioned in a judgment dated 20 March 2008. However, it is worth noting that in the cases decided so far, the Court has referred to the Guidelines merely to confirm decisions reached based on its own case law. To date, there has been no case in which the solutions indicated by the Guidelines differed from the principles laid down in the Court's case law. Thus, it is doubtful whether these Guidelines have played a normative role.[91] The Court has indeed made it clear that the circumstances of each individual case, as well as the principles laid down in its case law, will always remain decisive when determining whether an arbitrator appears to be conflicted.[92]

---

89. Item 4.4.1 on the Guidelines' Green List reads as follows: 'The arbitrator has had an initial contact with a party, or an affiliate of a party (or their counsel) prior to appointment, if this contact is limited to the arbitrator's availability and qualifications to serve, or to the names of possible candidates for a chairperson, and did not address the merits or procedural aspects of the dispute, other than to provide the arbitrator with a basic understanding of the case.'
90. *See* DFSC 4A_292/2019 of 16 October 2019, para. 3.4. Under No. 8 of the IBA Guidelines on Party Representation of 25 May 2013, it is not improper for a Party Representative to have *ex-parte* communications in, *inter alia*, the following circumstances: '(a) A Party Representative may communicate with a prospective Party-Nominated Arbitrator to determine his or her expertise, experience, ability, availability, willingness and the existence of potential conflicts of interest; (b) A Party Representative may communicate with a prospective or appointed Party-Nominated Arbitrator for the purpose of the selection of the Presiding Arbitrator.'
91. *See* Felix Dasser, *'Soft Law' in International Commercial Arbitration*, in COLLECTED COURSES OF THE HAGUE ACADEMY OF INTERNATIONAL LAW, VOLUME 402, para. 359 (2019).
92. *See* DFSC 4A_458/2009 of 10 June 2010, para. 3.3.3.1 ('les circonstances du cas concret, tout comme la jurisprudence du Tribunal fédéral en la matière, resteront toujours décisives pour trancher la question du conflit d'intérêts'); DFSC 4A_506/2007 of 20 March 2008, para. 3.3.2.2.

5. THE DUTY OF PARTIES TO INVESTIGATE POTENTIAL CONFLICTS

It is a firmly established principle of Swiss case law that grounds for challenging an arbitrator must be raised as soon as a party becomes aware of them.[93] By virtue of this principle, the right to challenge the composition of the arbitral tribunal lapses and can thus no longer be heard at the award annulment stage if the party concerned does not assert it immediately, as a party cannot keep its objections in reserve and invoke them only in the event that the award goes against it.[94]

This case law also applies to requests for revocation of an award based on an arbitrator's alleged bias.[95] Such requests are only admissible if the applicant was unable to discover the grounds for the challenge during the arbitration by acting with the diligence required in the circumstances.[96]

The said principle applies to both grounds for challenge that were actually known to a party and to those of which the party concerned would have been aware had it acted with the requisite due diligence.[97] In other words, each party is under a duty to conduct the investigations necessary to ensure that the tribunal members present sufficient guarantees of independence and impartiality.[98] A party may thus not simply rely on the declaration of independence provided by an arbitrator but can be expected to make further investigations or direct enquiries with the arbitrator.[99]

---

93. A party intending to challenge an appointed arbitrator may be expected to act in accordance with the applicable procedural rules and within the time limit set under those rules (e.g., in DFSC 4P.196/2003 of 7 January 2004, the petitioner's right to request the annulment of the award on the grounds of an irregular composition of the tribunal was found to be forfeited, because the petitioner had failed to submit a challenge against the arbitrator concerned within the thirty-day time limit granted by the applicable ICC Rules). The Court has extended this principle to prospective arbitrators: if a party has been expressly invited to comment on the envisaged composition of the arbitral tribunal and to state any objection to a nominated arbitrator within the time limit granted, its silence may be understood as acceptance or any objection raised at a later point may be deemed to have been forfeited due to the party's contradictory behaviour (*see* DFSC 130 III 66 of 21 November 2003, para. 4.3; DFSC 4A_620/2012 of 29 May 2013, para. 3.6). As already mentioned (*see supra* n. 4), Article 180a, para. 1 of the revised PILA now provides for a thirty-day time limit to challenge an arbitrator unless the parties have agreed otherwise.
94. *See* DFSC 4A_506/2007 of 20 March 2008, para. 3.1.2 and the references there. This principle was first developed for proceedings before state authorities (*see*, instead of many, DFSC 116 Ia 485 of 20 December 1990 para. 2c and DFSC 124 I 121 para. 2) and then extended to arbitration proceedings (*see, e.g.*, DFSC 136 III 605 of 29 October 2010, para. 3.2.2; DFSC 130 III 66 of 21 November 2003, para. 4.3; DFSC 129 III 445 of 27 May 2003, para. 3.1; DFSC 4P.263/2002 of 10 June 2003, para. 6.1; DFSC 4A_506/2007 of 20 March 2008, para. 3.1.2; and DFSC 4P.188/2001 of 15 October 2001, para. 2b).
95. *See* DFSC 4A_234/2008 of 14 August 2008, para. 2.2.1 and DFSC 4A_528/2007 of 4 April 2008, para. 2.5.1.
96. *See supra* n. 12 and the references there.
97. *See* DFSC 136 III 605 of 29 October 2010, para. 3.2.2; DFSC 129 III 445 of 27 May 2003, para. 4.2.2.1; and DFSC 4A_506/2007 of 20 March 2008, para. 3.1.2.
98. *See* DFSC 129 III 445 of 27 May 2003, para. 4.2.2.1; DFSC 4P.188/2001 of 15 October 2001, para. 2c.
99. *See* DFSC 4A_506/2007 of 20 March 2008, para. 3.2.

A number of decided cases suggest that the duty to investigate potential arbitrator conflicts (referred to as 'duty of curiosity', in French: *devoir de curiosité*[100]) applies at least in high-stakes matters between parties who are on a level playing field and could not be unaware of the importance of the choice of arbitrators.[101] A recent landmark decision makes it clear that the duty as such applies in all cases, but its scope depends on the specific circumstances.[102]

In award annulment proceedings, the Court has set a high threshold in assessing whether the party challenging the composition of the tribunal could have raised this plea during the arbitration.

For example, in *X. v. Union Cycliste Internationale (UCI) et al.*, an athlete challenged a CAS award, arguing that the arbitrator appointed by the UCI had failed to disclose that he had, within less than a year, been nominated by the UCI in at least five other CAS arbitrations which turned on the same question of law, i.e., financial sanctions based on Article 326 of the UCI's anti-doping regulations. In a much-criticised judgment rendered in 2012, the Supreme Court dismissed the challenge as time-barred. The Court found that the athlete's counsel knew about at least two other CAS arbitrations in which the UCI had appointed the same arbitrator. At the hearing held in the athlete's case, his counsel had indeed asked the UCI-appointed arbitrator whether he considered himself to have a sufficiently open mind to hear the parties' case, notwithstanding the fact that the UCI had appointed him in two other cases involving financial sanctions based on Article 326 of the UCI's anti-doping regulations. The Court, in essence, held that this question did not go far enough. In the Court's view, it would have been necessary to formally question the arbitrator in clear terms, during the hearing, on how many times exactly he had been appointed by the UCI as an arbitrator on a CAS panel.[103]

I agree that a legal representative's knowledge must be attributed to the party he or she represents and that counsel can be expected to question an arbitrator on potential grounds for challenge early in the process. This approach is sound and necessary to prevent the use of abusive tactics. However, the 'duty of curiosity' should not be interpreted in a manner that renders meaningless the arbitrator's duty to disclose potential conflicts. In the present case, the arbitrator concerned was best placed to identify the number of prior or parallel appointments by the UCI, and it was therefore not obvious why the burden of clarification should lie with the parties. Rather, one might have expected the Court to scrutinise the arbitrator's conduct and shed light on whether and to what extent he should have disclosed the repeat appointments. The Court should not shy away from admonishing arbitrators for withholding relevant information from a party, even if it concludes that the composition of the tribunal can no longer be challenged for lack of a timely objection.

100. DFSC 136 III 605 of 29 October 2010, para. 3.4.2.
101. *See* DFSC 129 III 445 of 27 May 2003, para. 4.2.2.1 and DFSC 4A_506/2007 of 20 March 2008, para. 3.2.
102. *See Sun Yang v. WADA and Fédération Internationale de Natation (FINA)*, DFSC 147 III 65 of 28 October 2019, para. 6.5. This decision is further discussed below.
103. *See* DFSC 4A_110/2012 of 9 October 2012, para. 2.2.2.

A number of decisions suggest that in arbitrations conducted before the CAS, the parties may generally be expected to be aware of information published on the CAS website.[104] Similarly, in a decision relating to a CAS arbitration involving WADA, the Court found that the athlete should have been aware of information stated in a report published on WADA's website.[105]

The very fact that a party was able to uncover relevant facts during the thirty-day time limit for filing an action for annulment of the award may raise doubts as to whether such facts could not have been discovered earlier in time.[106]

Depending on the circumstances, the degree of diligence required of a party may go beyond a duty to consult public information, as such information may indeed prompt a need to conduct further investigations. This is illustrated by the already mentioned 2008 decision relating to a challenge against a CAS award brought on the basis that the panel chair, the co-arbitrator nominated by the respondent and the respondent's counsel were all members of the same association.[107] As the information published on the CAS website with regard to the tribunal chair expressly indicated his role in the said association, the Court found that the claimant should have made enquiries as to whether the co-arbitrators and the other party's counsel were perhaps also members of the association. Alternatively, this question could, in the Court's view, also have been directly raised with the arbitrators.[108] In my view, this decision overstretches the duty to investigate potential arbitrator conflicts. A party should not be required to search for circumstances that are not readily apparent based on public information.

Shortly before the publication of this article, the Court issued a landmark decision in the matter *Sun Yang v. WADA and Fédération Internationale de Natation (FINA)*, which makes it clear that the duty of curiosity has its limits.[109] By an award dated 28 February 2020, a CAS panel chaired by Italian Judge Franco Frattini unanimously determined that Chinese swimmer Sun Yang had violated Article 2.5 of the FINA Doping Control Rules by his conduct during an anti-doping control and decided to suspend the athlete for a period of eight years. On 28 April 2020, within the statutory thirty-day time limit,[110] Mr Yang challenged the CAS award pursuant to Article 190 of the PILA (on the grounds that are not of interest here). On 15 June 2020, after the expiry of the said time limit, he applied for revocation of the award,[111] requesting the Supreme Court to annul the award and replace the president of the CAS panel.

In support of his application for revocation of the CAS award, Mr Yang claimed that he had learned from an article dated 15 May 2020, posted by a journalist on the website xxx.com, that Mr Franco Frattini had repeatedly published unacceptable

104. *See* DFSC 129 III 445 of 27 May 2003, para. 4.2.2.1; DFSC 4A_506/2007 of 20 March 2008, para. 3.2 and DFSC 4A_110/2012 of 9 October 2012, para. 2.2.2.
105. *See* DFSC 136 III 605 of 29 October 2010, para. 3.4.2.
106. *See* DFSC 4P.188/2001 of 15 October 2001, para. 2c and DFSC 4A_506/2007 of 20 March 2008, para. 3.2.
107. *See* section 4 above.
108. *See* DFSC 4A_506/2007 of 20 March 2008, para. 3.2.
109. *See* DFSC 147 III 65 of 28 October 2019.
110. *See* Article 100(1) of the Supreme Court Act dated 17 June 2005.
111. *See* on this remedy section 1 and *supra* n. 12.

comments on his Twitter account with regard to Chinese nationals in 2018 and 2019, i.e., both before and during the CAS proceedings, which raised legitimate doubts as to Mr Frattini's impartiality in the present dispute involving a Chinese athlete.[112] According to Mr Yang, his counsel conducted a Google search on Mr Frattini when he was appointed as panel chair on 1 May 2019. Mr Yang explained that none of the tweets in question appeared when his counsel entered the words 'Franco + Frattini', 'Franco + Frattini + sport', or 'Franco + Frattini + Court of Arbitration for Sport' into the Google search engine.[113]

The CAS and WADA took the view that Mr Yang could and should have discovered the tweets in question during the arbitration had he acted with the care required by the circumstances. The CAS argued, *inter alia*, that it was not sufficient to enter only the arbitrator's name in the Google search engine; a further occurrence should be added to establish a possible link between the arbitrator and another person or entity. Therefore, Mr Yang's counsel should have used, for example, the words 'Frattini' and 'China', which would have been sufficient to make some of the tweets appear on the first page of the list of search results produced by Google.[114] WADA pointed out that by entering the arbitrator's first name and surname, with or without inverted commas, in the Google search engine, his Twitter account appears on the first page of the search results. According to WADA, Mr Yang could legitimately be expected to browse Mr Frattini's Twitter account, which is public and thus accessible to all, by performing, at the very least, a simple search using a search engine. He should indeed have examined the 'leading social networks such as Facebook, Twitter, Instagram'.[115]

The Supreme Court observed that it had never defined the exact scope of the duty of curiosity and that the contours of this duty are indeed difficult to define, as they depend on the circumstances of each specific case. For the first time, the Court has now clarified that the duty of curiosity is not unlimited. The parties to an arbitration can certainly be expected to conduct an investigation on the internet by using the main search engines and consulting sources that are likely to provide information as to a possible risk of bias on the part of an arbitrator, such as the websites of those involved in the arbitration (arbitral institution, parties, counsel and their law firms, as well as the arbitrators and their firms, etc.). However, a party cannot be expected to perform a systematic and thorough screening of all available sources relating to an arbitrator. Thus, the mere fact that an item of information is freely accessible on the internet does not *ipso facto* mean that a party who was not aware of it has failed in its duty of curiosity. In this respect, the circumstances of the specific case will always remain decisive.[116]

In the present case, Mr Frattini's Twitter account appeared among the first results when his first name and surname was entered into the Google search engine. By contrast, it was not established that such a search would have made it possible to

112. The content of said tweets is reproduced at para. 5.1 of the Court's decision (*see supra* n. 109).
113. *See* DFSC 4A_413/2019 of 28 October 2019, para. 6.2 (excluded from official publication in DFSC 147 III 65).
114. *Ibid.*, para. 6.3.
115. *Ibid.*, para. 6.4.
116. *Ibid.*, para. 6.5.

display the controversial tweets. The Court found that Mr Yang could not be criticised for not including the word 'China' in the Google search, as this would have been meant that he should have speculated from the outset on a possible lack of impartiality on the part of the arbitrator based on the nationality criterion, although there was nothing to suggest that Mr Frattini might have preconceived ideas about athletes of Chinese origin. As to the question of whether a party can be expected to search the leading social networks, the decision gives no clear-cut answer. The Court did not exclude that a party may be required to examine various social networks but stressed that it might be appropriate not to be too demanding in this respect so as to avoid very extensive, if not unlimited, time-consuming investigations. In Mr Yang's case, there was no need to examine this question further as, in the Court's view, he had shown the attention required by the circumstances when conducting a Google search on Mr Frattini. Notably, the Court also held that a party cannot be required to continue its internet searches throughout the arbitration, let alone scan the messages published by the arbitrators on social networks during the proceedings.[117] On the merits, the Court granted the request for revocation of the CAS award and ordered the removal of Mr Frattini as panel chair, as some of the controversial tweets were considered inadmissible and giving rise to an appearance of bias.[118]

This judgment is to be welcomed. Whilst previous decisions have, in my view, gone too far in the interpretation of the parties' duty to investigate potential grounds for challenge of an arbitrator, the *Sun Yang* ruling adopts a balanced and nuanced approach by making it clear that the scope of this duty depends on the individual circumstances and may not generally go so far as to require the parties to screen systematically and thoroughly all information accessible on the internet relating to an arbitrator, let alone to continue to do so during the arbitration.

6. THE SUCCESS RATE OF CHALLENGES IN COURT

As shown by Prof. Felix Dasser in his statistical analyses of the decisions handed down by the Supreme Court since the enactment of the PILA on 1 January 1989, the chances of an international award made in Switzerland being set aside are low. In commercial arbitration, only approximately 7% of all challenges brought under Article 190 of the PILA and decided on the merits in the period 1989-2019 were (at least partly) successful.[119]

117. *Ibid.*, para. 6.5.
118. *Ibid.*, para. 7.9.
119. *See* the first empirical study for the years 1989-2005 in Dasser, *International Arbitration and Setting Aside Proceedings in Switzerland: A Statistical Analysis*, 25 ASA BULL. 3, 444-472 (452-453) (2007), and the figures provided in subsequent updates: 28 ASA BULL. 1, 82-100 (86) (2010); 32 ASA BULL. 3, 460-466 (463) (2014); 34 ASA BULL. 2, 280-300 (283-284) (2016); 36 ASA BULL. 2, 276-294 (280) (2018); and 39 ASA BULL. 1, 2021, 7-41 (15-16).

The data further reveals that an improper constitution of the tribunal was the least frequently invoked reason for the annulment of an award.[120] In absolute figures, only one (out of 54) challenges on the grounds of an improper constitution of the tribunal have been granted by the Court since the PILA was enacted more than thirty years ago, which corresponds to a success rate of only 1.8%.[121] The chances of succeeding with a challenge to an award based on Article 190(2)(a) of the PILA, therefore, appear to be considerably lower than for challenges on other grounds.

What is more, it appears that the only successful challenge under Article 190(2)(a) of the PILA was not about an apparent lack of independence or impartiality but concerned other errors made in the constitution of the arbitral tribunal. To the best of our knowledge, there is no reported decision annulling an award on the grounds of an arbitrator bias. However, as mentioned above, in a recent decision concerning a request for revocation of a CAS award, the Court removed an arbitrator because certain messages published by him on his Twitter account had given rise to an appearance of bias.[122]

The fact that Article 190(2)(a) of the PILA is one of the least used grounds for annulment of an award suggests that, in most cases, parties accept the composition of the tribunal, either because they see no grounds for challenge or because a party has decided not to raise an objection based on the facts disclosed by an arbitrator. In the few instances where a challenge was brought before the Supreme Court, the case either did not meet the substantive test for the removal of arbitrators, or the right to challenge the award was forfeit due to the challenging party's failure to raise a timely objection in the arbitration.

Moreover, many challenges fail for lack of substantiation or proof. The Court imposes high thresholds in this respect. For example, in a 2010 decision dealing with allegations of multiple appointments by the same party, the Court took the view that the party making the challenge should have specifically named the various arbitrations at issue by indicating their sequence and the parties involved. Furthermore, it would have been necessary to elaborate on which party had appointed the challenged arbitrator and on the relationship between said party and the arbitrator.[123] In my view, these requirements go too far, as it is for the arbitrator (not the parties) to shed light on previous appointments by a party.

Finally, it is important to note that the Court is bound by the findings of fact made in the challenged award when deciding whether the constitutional guarantee of an independent and impartial tribunal has been violated.[124] The Court may only review

120. *See* Dasser, 36 ASA Bull. 1, 20 (2021).
121. *Ibid.*
122. *See* DFSC 147 III 65 of 28 October 2019 in the matter *Sun Yang v. WADA and Fédération Internationale de Natation (FINA)* and, for more details, section 5 above.
123. *See* DFSC 4A_258/2009 of 11 January 2010, para. 3.1.2. *See also* DFSC 4A_110/2012 of 9 October 2012, para. 2.2.2.
124. Pursuant to Article 105(1) of the Supreme Court Act of 17 June 2015, the Court is required to base its decision on the facts established in the challenged decision. This rule also applies in award annulment proceedings (*see* Article 77(2) of the Supreme Court Act *e contrario*). The

the facts insofar as grounds for annulment pursuant to Article 190(2) of the PILA are established.[125] New facts and evidence may only be taken into account insofar as prompted by the award.[126]

In summary, a challenge to an arbitrator at the award annulment stage will rarely ever be successful due to a combination of substantive requirements and procedural hurdles.[127]

7. CONCLUSIONS

The threshold for arbitrator challenges is well established in the Supreme Court's case law and has been detailed in a number of principles for various case groups. However, there are no hard and fast rules. As ever, the circumstances of a given case will always be decisive when it comes to the question of whether an arbitrator should be removed. This approach is to be welcomed. There must be room for a balanced case-by-case analysis by the competent courts, with no overregulation by any abstract guidelines.

The decided cases show that allegations of potential bias are taken very seriously by the Court and examined in detail. Moreover, the landmark ruling in *Valverde Belmonte* has further strengthened the guarantee of independence and impartiality by imposing the same standards on all arbitrators and allowing the Court to order the removal of a seemingly biased arbitrator together with the annulment of the award. The same decision confirms that an award made by a tribunal that does not meet the guarantees of independence and impartiality will be annulled irrespective of whether its outcome would have been different had the tribunal been properly constituted.

Nevertheless, the Court's overall approach to arbitrator challenges is conservative and, in case of doubt, will be guided by the presumption that arbitrators are capable of deciding the dispute submitted to them with an independent mind. In the author's experience, the trust placed in arbitrators is justified.

---

facts and legal arguments relied on by an institutional body in a decision on a challenge to an arbitrator are deemed to be incorporated in the award (*see* Matthias Leemann, *Challenging International Arbitral Awards in Switzerland on the Ground of a Lack of Independence and Impartiality of an Arbitrator*, 29 ASA Bull. 11-32 (2011); DFSC 4A 234/2010 of 29 October 2010, para. 2.2). In cases where no reasons are given for the dismissal of a challenge by an institutional body, there are different possibilities for the Supreme Court to establish the factual basis for its decision on the challenge to the award (*see* Leemann, 22 et seq.). The Court has unfettered powers to determine whether, in light of the established facts, the constitutional guarantee of independence and impartiality has been violated (DFSC 92 I 271 of 26 October 1966, para. 4).

125. DFSC 133 II 139 of 19 February 2007, para. 5 and DFSC 129 III 727 of 16 October 2003, para. 5.2.2.
126. *See* Article 99 of the Supreme Court Act.
127. On the potential pitfalls of the procedure to enforce the right to an independent and impartial tribunal before the Supreme Court, *see* Leemann, *supra* n. 124.

CHAPTER 9

The View from the French Courts: Disclosures – Objections – Challenges: Clear Path or Jungle in Commercial Arbitrators' Conflicts of Interest?

*Laurent Gouiffès**

Despite there being relatively few instances of French Courts annulling awards due to conflicts of interest in international arbitration, this 'hot topic' has been debated at length in France over the past ten years, as the landmark *Tecnimont* case unfolded.

To mitigate the risk of conflicts of interest, legislation imposes a duty of disclosure on arbitrators and allows parties to submit objections and challenges. Setting the rules on conflicts of interest is, therefore, a matter of striking a balance between protecting the arbitral process from unnecessary disruption by the parties and preserving the parties' trust in that process.

This balance is achieved by international instruments[1] and domestic laws on arbitrators' disclosure obligations (section 1), the parties' ability to request an arbitrator's recusal (section 2) and consequences at the ultimate annulment stage (section 3) and beyond (section 4). This chapter explores the position of the French law on these issues.

* The views expressed herein are solely those of the author and do not represent the views of Hogan Lovells or its clients.

1. Such as the INTERNATIONAL BAR ASSOCIATION GUIDELINES ON CONFLICTS OF INTEREST, dated 23 October 2014. To our knowledge, and contrary to some other jurisdictions, the French courts have not so far made any explicit reference to the IBA guidelines.

1. DISCLOSURE

In order for an arbitrator to comply with his or her disclosure obligations, French law requires that s/he disclose any circumstance that may affect his/her independence or impartiality (section 1.1.). This requirement has been construed broadly by the French Courts (section 1.2.).

1.1. An Arbitrator Must Disclose Any Circumstance That May Affect His/Her Independence or Impartiality

The arbitrator's duty to disclose circumstances that may affect his/her impartiality or independence is set out in Article 1456(2) of the French Code of Civil Procedure,[2] which provides that: '[b]efore accepting a mandate, an arbitrator shall disclose any circumstance that may affect his or her independence or impartiality. He or she shall also disclose promptly any such circumstance that may arise after accepting the mandate'.[3]

In general, the arbitrator's disclosure takes the form of a declaration of independence, listing any circumstance that may affect his/her independence or impartiality, sometimes including a copy of the arbitrator's resume. Should any disclosable element arise at a subsequent stage, the arbitrator will be expected to update his/her initial disclosure.[4]

Although independence and impartiality are often grouped together, it is generally understood that these are two different concepts.

Independence is objective in nature, amounting to the absence of a material or intellectual link between the arbitrator and parties. It may include, for example, frequent appointments of a particular arbitrator by one of the parties or by a law firm, the subordinate relationship between an arbitrator and one of the parties, or current and former business relationships between arbitrators and the parties.[5]

Impartiality is subjective in nature, consisting of the absence of any bias held by the arbitrator towards the parties or the dispute. It may include situations where an arbitrator previously sat on a case bearing on similar or identical facts to those at hand; when an arbitrator is simultaneously sitting in a case relating to the ongoing case; or when the arbitrator has issued an opinion on all or at least a significant part of the ongoing case, prior to his or her appointment or nomination.[6]

2. Applicable to international arbitration pursuant to Article 1506(2) of the French Code of Civil Procedure.
3. Article 1456(2) of the French Code of Civil Procedure. The text of this article is relatively recent and implemented with the decree of 13 January 2011.
4. *Cour de cassation*, civ. 1, No. 14-26279 (16 December 2015).
5. Astrid Westphalen and Vincent Carriou, *The Arbitrators' duty to disclose and the parties' duty to investigate: what are the safeguard mechanisms to ensure the independence and impartiality of Arbitrators?*, IBLJ N°6, 543 (2018).
6. *Id.*

In order to identify what information should be disclosed, the arbitrator must determine whether such information would provoke reasonable doubt in the parties' minds as to the arbitrator's impartiality and independence.[7]

One of the main justifications for an arbitrator's duty to disclose is to put the parties in a position to request recusal, but more importantly, it is aimed at preserving the parties' confidence in the arbitral process, which in turn consolidates the legitimacy of the arbitral tribunal, thus avoiding any appearance of bias. This is one of the principles of justice recognized by the European Court of Human Rights, which considers that 'it is not enough that justice be done, it must be seen manifestly and undoubtedly to be done'.[8] This explains in particular why circumstances requiring disclosure are interpreted more broadly than the specific grounds for recusal. An arbitrator is not expected to only disclose events that may give rise to recusal; French Courts require arbitrators to disclose any circumstance for which an arbitrator may have a doubt about his or her independence or impartiality. We explore below the circumstances that may affect an arbitrator's independence or impartiality under French law.

1.2. French Courts Interpret Circumstances That May Affect an Arbitrator's Independence or Impartiality Broadly

The following sections look at the broad standard of disclosure set by the French Courts (section 1.2.1.) and the exception provided for knowable facts (*faits notoires*) (section 1.2.2.).

1.2.1. French Courts Interpret Circumstances to Be Disclosed by an Arbitrator Broadly

The debate surrounds arbitrators' disclosure obligations under French law crystallized in the *Tecnimont* case. The dispute entailed a request for the annulment of an arbitral award on the grounds that the President of the Arbitral Tribunal had produced an incomplete declaration of independence. It was alleged in particular that the arbitrator failed to mention that another department of his law firm had advised a subsidiary of one of the parties to the arbitration in separate litigation proceedings. Information about those links had been made publicly available on the website of one of the party's subsidiary.

The *Tecnimont* saga includes numerous decisions. Following the rendering of the arbitral award on 10 December 2007, annulment proceedings were initiated before the Paris Court of Appeal, which issued a decision on 12 February 2009.[9] This decision was

7. Paris Court of Appeal, 2 July 2013, Rev. Arb., 1033, note Henry (2013).
8. *See Micallef v. Malta*, 15 October 2009, European Court of Human Rights, Grand Chamber, Case No. 17056/06, para. 98 and *Martinie v. France*, 12 April 2006, European Court of Human Rights, Grand Chamber, Case No. 58675/00, para. 53, endorsing the famous statement of Lord Hewart in *R v. Sussex Justices, ex parte McCarthy* [1924] 1 KB 256, [1923] All ER Rep 233, 259.
9. Paris Court of Appeal, 12 February 2009, RG No. 07/22164.

then overturned by the *Cour de cassation* on 4 November 2010[10] and referred to the Reims Court of Appeal, which rendered its decision on 2 November 2011.[11] This decision was also overturned by the *Cour de cassation* on 25 June 2014[12] and sent back to the Paris Court of Appeal, which issued its decision on 12 April 2016.[13] A further challenge was brought again before the *Cour de cassation*, which finally settled the dispute on 19 December 2018.[14] The *Cour de cassation* rejected the annulment request by finding that given the knowable nature of the facts, the parties could easily have introduced a request for recusal within the thirty-day period set forth in the ICC rules, and since they had failed to do so, the arbitrator had not breached their disclosure duties.

Although the underlying decisions leading to the *Cour de cassation's* decision of 19 December 2018 were overturned, these overturns were only based on specific points, thus preserving the relevance of the Courts' rationale on the specific points we now turn to.

The first act of the saga led the Paris Court of Appeal in its decision of 12 February 2009 to weigh the arbitrator's *actual* independence or impartiality against his or her duty to disclose circumstances that could affect the parties' *perception* of the arbitrator's independence or impartiality.

In this first decision, the Paris Court of Appeal came to the conclusion that arbitrators were supposed to disclose circumstances likely to affect the parties' perception of the arbitrator's independence or impartiality. It was therefore irrelevant that the conflict of interest be material. To this end, the Court of Appeal insisted that an arbitrator could not invoke the worldwide dimension of the firm it belonged to, especially given that such law firms had internal conflicts-checks procedures. The Paris Court of Appeal required that arbitrators investigate potential conflicts of interest they would otherwise be unaware of, for example, where a lawyer in the arbitrator's firm advised one of the parties to the arbitration on an unrelated matter, even if the arbitrator was unaware of this business tie. Failure to disclose a conflict of interest is therefore not excused by lack of knowledge where an arbitrator does not perform reasonable enquiries.[15]

The second *Tecnimont* decision relevant for disclosure purposes is the Reims Court of Appeal decision dated 2 November 2011. Following the overturning of the Paris Court of Appeal decision of 12 February 2009 by the *Cour de cassation* on 4 November 2010,[16] the Reims Court of Appeal to which the decision had been referred decided to annul the award on the grounds that an arbitrator must 'reveal entirely both information that is strictly personal and information relating to his or her law firm,

10. *Cour de cassation*, civ. 1, 4 November 2010, No. 09-12716.
11. Reims Court of Appeal, 2 November 2011, RG No. 10/02888.
12. *Cour de cassation*, civ. 1, 25 June 2014, No. 11-26529.
13. Paris Court of Appeal, 12 April 2016, RG No. 14/14881.
14. *Cour de cassation*, civ. 1, 19 December 2018, No. 16-18349.
15. Paris Court of Appeal, 12 February 2009, RG No. 07/22164.
16. *Cour de cassation*, civ. 1, 4 November 2010, No. 09-12716.

regardless of his or her degree of association with the law firm'. It was immaterial that the arbitrator was only 'of counsel' and not a partner of the firm.[17]

In line with this broad interpretation of the arbitrator's duty to disclose, Courts have also developed consistent case law on an arbitrator's duty to disclose business ties. For example, in a case involving an arbitrator's systematic appointment by companies of the same group,[18] the *Cour de cassation* held that frequency and regularity of appointments over a long period of time, and in relation to similar contracts, gave rise to circumstances amounting to business ties requiring disclosure.[19] In another case, the *Cour de cassation* even went a step further by imposing a duty to disclose business ties involving third parties if these parties have an interest in the arbitration.[20]

As a result, while French Courts define circumstances that may affect independence or impartiality on a case by case basis, it can generally be said that their interpretation of circumstances that may affect his or her independence or impartiality is broad and favours full transparency.[21]

1.2.2. Knowable Facts Arising Before the Constitution of the Tribunal Are Not Subject to the Arbitrators' Disclosure Obligation

In contrast to this strict position, French case law provides an important exception to an arbitrators' disclosure obligation for knowable facts (*faits notoires*).[22]

This exception was confirmed in the last Court of Appeal decision of the *Tecnimont* saga dated 12 April 2016, which ultimately rejected the annulment request, on the grounds that the circumstances raised to show a perceived lack of independence or impartiality (i.e., the role of the arbitrator's law firm advising a subsidiary of one of the parties) were 'available on the internet' and therefore 'publicly and easily available'. As such, the circumstances were deemed knowable and not subject to disclosure.[23]

This decision was endorsed by the *Cour de cassation* on 19 December 2018, thus confirming that Article 1456(2) of the French Code of Civil Procedure had to be

17. Reims Court of Appeal, 2 November 2011, RG No. 10/02888.
18. In this instance, the arbitrator was appointed fifty-one times by the same party.
19. *Cour de cassation*, civ. 1, 20 October 2010, No. 09-068997.
20. *Cour de cassation*, civ. 1, 1 February 2012, No. 11-11084. In this instance, the company d'Expert was awarded a conciliation contract according to which it was mandated to improve the relationship between the company *Papeteries de Gascogne* and EDF. A dispute arose between the company *Papeteries de Gascogne* and the company d'Expert, in relation to the conciliation contract. The dispute was submitted to arbitration but the subsequent award was annulled as the Court found the arbitrator had failed to disclose he had often represented the EDF Company.
21. *See also* Auto Guadeloupe Investissements Paris, 14 October 2014, Rev. Arb., note M. Henry, 151 (2015) (dismissal by the *Cour de cassation* in a decision of 16 December 2015, n° 14-26279) and Volkswagen Paris, 27 March 2018, 2448, obs. Th. Clay (2018); *Gaz. Pal.* 24 July 2018, 19, obs. D. Bensaude; *Sem. Jur.* 16 December 2019, obs. J. Ortscheidt and C. Seraglini, 2331; Rev. Arb. 2019, 1st esp., note L.-C. Delanoy, 522; dismissal by the *Cour de cassation* in a decision of 3 October 2019, n° 18-15.756.
22. *Cour de cassation*, civ. 1, 16 December 2015, No. 14-26279.
23. *Cour de cassation*, civ. 1, 19 December 2018, No. 16-18349.

interpreted narrowly. It confirmed that the arbitrator's duty to 'disclose promptly any such circumstance that may arise after accepting the mandate' did not cover knowable circumstances.[24]

However, this notoriety exception has been limited by case law. French Courts have held that while a party's duty to look into the background of arbitrators before the beginning of arbitral proceedings excused an arbitrator's non-disclosure of knowable facts, such an exception could not apply once the arbitration began as the counsel were not bound to conduct research beyond this point.[25] If necessary, arbitrators are therefore expected to disclose knowable facts by updating their declaration throughout the entire arbitration proceedings.

This notoriety exception is strongly criticized by some authors who argue that it is not well defined given the vast amount of information that is now available on the internet but not necessarily accessible with a few 'clicks'.[26] If the arbitrator is unaware of the problematic circumstances, as, in *Tecnimont*, it must be that the circumstances are not so 'knowable'.[27]

Other circumstances which do not require disclosure by arbitrators according to French Courts include attending the same conferences as one of the parties,[28] the same dinner through a scientific club event – even if the dinner took place the day before to a hearing[29] – or more generally, disclosure of an arbitrator's political opinions.[30]

Ultimately, the arbitrator's duty to disclose is designed to put the parties in a position where they can properly decide whether to submit a request for recusal.

2. RECUSAL

Ensuring that the parties are adequately informed of circumstances on which they may claim recusal is also a way of fostering the parties' trust in the arbitral process. However, this right must not disrupt the arbitral procedure. The following sections look into procedural (section 2.1.) and substantive (section 2.2.) considerations relating to recusal.

2.1. Procedural Considerations

The recusal procedure is defined in Article 1456(3) of the French Code of Civil Procedure, which provides that: 'In the event of a dispute on whether or not the arbitrator should continue in his role, the issue is ruled upon by the person in charge of organizing the arbitration or, in that person's absence, by the supporting judge,

24. *Cour de cassation*, civ. 1, 19 December 2018, No. 16-18349.
25. *Cour de cassation*, civ. 1, 16 December 2015, No. 14-26279 and *Cour de cassation*, civ. 1, 3 October 2019, No. 18-15.756.
26. Thomas Clay, *Tecnimont, saison 5: La dissolution de l'obligation de révélation dans le devoir de réaction*, Cahiers de l'arbitrage – No. 2, 447 (1 July 2016).
27. *Id.*
28. *Cour de cassation*, civ. 1, 4 July 2012, No. 11-19.624.
29. Paris Court of Appeal, 14 October 2014, RG No. 13/14076.
30. *Cour de cassation*, civ. 1, 29 June 2011, No. 09-17346.

notified within one month following the disclosure or discovery of the contentious circumstances.'[31]

In most cases, as arbitrations are often administered by arbitral institutions, it will be incumbent on the institutions to rule on requests for recusal.[32] However, in instances of ad hoc international arbitrations where no institution administers the proceedings, recusal requests will be heard by a specialized judge at the *Tribunal de grande instance* (now *the Tribunal judiciaire* of Paris since 1 January 2020) known as the supporting judge (in French *juge d'appui*).

The time limit for submitting a claim for recusal is one month from disclosure or discovery of the contentious circumstances.[33] Beyond this point, a party's failure to request recusal is considered a waiver of that party's right to claim recusal, thus inviting the parties to submit their claims for recusal promptly and diligently once they have discovered the litigious circumstances.[34]

Importantly, the phrase 'discovery of the contentious circumstances' used by Article 1456(3) of the French Code of Civil Procedure has been interpreted to mean that the statute of limitations starts running from when a party had actual knowledge that a recusal claim could be brought.[35] In other words, the starting point of the statute of limitations is delayed until the day on which the parties can form an opinion about the arbitrator's impartiality or independence. Likewise, for arbitrator disclosures involving continued exchanges between the arbitrator and the parties, it should be considered that the starting point of the statute of limitations is the arbitrator's final statement.[36]

As an exception to the general statute of limitations standard – according to which time limitations run from when a party was aware or *should have been aware* of its right to bring a claim – French case law on recusal of arbitrators protects the parties' right to submit a claim for recusal, by finding that only actual knowledge of the right triggers the statute of limitations.[37]

This was made particularly clear by the *Cour de cassation's* decision of 3 October 2019, endorsing the Paris Court of Appeal's underlying decision dated 27 March 2018[38] on this very issue. It held that once the arbitral tribunal has been appointed and accepted their mission, the existence of a knowable fact likely to provoke a reasonable doubt in the parties' minds should be disclosed by the arbitrators. It also held that the parties were therefore not bound to investigate such circumstances beyond the date of

31. French Code of Civil Procedure, Article 1456(3).
32. For example, in International Chamber of Commerce ('ICC') administered arbitrations, the ICC Court of Arbitration will hear recusal requests, Article 14 of the ICC Rules.
33. Article 1456(3) of the French Code of Civil Procedure.
34. Article 1466 of the French Code of Civil Procedure: 'A party which, knowingly and without a legitimate reason, fails to object to an irregularity before the arbitral tribunal in a timely manner shall be deemed to have waived its right to avail itself of such irregularity.' On this point, *see, e.g.*, *Tribunal de grande instance* of Paris, 10 November 2011, RG No. 11/58755.
35. *Cour de cassation*, civ. 1, 25 June 2014, No. 11-26.529.
36. Marc Henry, *Le chant de la révélation: de profundis ou Gloria de l'arbitrage?*, Rev. Arb., 181 (2015).
37. *See, e.g.*, Article 2224 of the French Civil Code: 'Actions relating to personal rights or movable goods can be brought within five years from the day the holder of a right knew or should have known the facts enabling him to use his right.'
38. Paris Court of Appeal, 27 March 2018, RG No. 16-09386.

the constitution of the arbitral tribunal,[39] thus implying that awareness of such circumstances could not be expected of the parties.

2.2. Substantive Considerations

From a substantive point of view, French law considers an arbitrator's mandate as a jurisdictional mission and therefore applies the same grounds for recusal of arbitrators as it does for recusal of judges, all the while specifying that such grounds are not exhaustive.[40]

As per Article L. 111-6 of the French Code of Judicial Organization, an arbitrator's recusal may be sought: if the arbitrator or his/her partner has a personal stake in the dispute; if the arbitrator/partner is a creditor, debtor, presumed heir or donee of one of the parties; if the arbitrator/partner is a parent to or ally of one of the parties or partner up to the fourth degree inclusively; if there is a hierarchical relationship between the arbitrator/partner and one of the parties and his/her partner; or if there is a clear friendship or enmity between the judge and one of the parties.

With the development of social media and virtual friendships or connections on networks such as Facebook or Linkedin, the *Cour de cassation*, in a disciplinary proceeding before the Bar Council, has ruled that the term 'friendship' used by Article L. 111-6 of the French Code of Judicial Organization could not be interpreted to encompass 'friendship' on social media. It held that social media was, rather, a mere channel of communication between persons sharing the same interests, and in this case, the same profession.[41]

The threshold for showing an arbitrator's lack of independence or impartiality is whether the arbitrator is influenced by elements of a nature to provoke a reasonable doubt in the parties' minds. It follows that when arguing that an arbitrator lacks independence or impartiality, parties must show the existence of material or intellectual ties, or a situation of a nature to affect an arbitrator's judgment or to amount to a risk of bias towards one of the parties to the arbitration.

Importantly, the mere fact that grounds for recusal exist is not necessarily a bar to the arbitrator's mandate, as the parties are free to exercise their right to claim recusal or not.[42] In practice, although parties may require and expect the tribunal's impartiality and independence, they should exercise their right with caution. When submitting a claim for recusal, the parties run the risk that such a claim be dismissed, which might annoy the tribunal: 'when you strike at a king, you must kill him'.[43]

39. *Cour de cassation*, civ. 1, 3 October 2019, No. 18-15.756.
40. *Cour de cassation*, civ. 1, 28 April 1998, No. 96-18741.
41. *Cour de cassation*, civ. 1, 5 January 2017, No. 16-12394.
42. Paris Court of Appeal, 18 November 2004, RG No. 2002/19606.
43. From the US philosopher Ralph Waldo Emerson, quoted by Senator Orval Hansen in the Judicial Reform Act, 4 June 1969.

3. ANNULMENT

One of the direst consequences resulting from an arbitrator's lack of independence or impartiality is a finding by domestic courts that the arbitral award should be annulled for actual or perceived lack of independence or impartiality.

As discussed above, French Courts have a broad position on conflicts of interest and any lack or perceived lack of impartiality or independence will lead to the annulment of an award. The Paris Court of Appeal has set forth a firm line of case law on this, finding that:

> the arbitrator's independence is the essence of his jurisdiction in that he obtains, once appointed, the status of a judge, which by its nature excludes any relationships of dependence with the parties ... the circumstances invoked to challenge that independence must, on the basis of material or intellectual connections with one of the parties in dispute, be characteristic of a situation affecting that arbitrator's judgment and present a definite risk of bias with regard to one of the parties.[44]

The vast majority of annulment cases for lack of independence or impartiality are based on the specific ground of Article 1520(2) of the French Code of Civil Procedure, providing that an award may be annulled if 'the arbitral tribunal was not properly constituted'. In theory, arguments could also be made to seek an annulment on the grounds of a violation of due process or international public policy because of the fundamental nature of the prohibition of conflicts of interest; however, the use of these grounds is rare and does not represent the current trend in French courts.[45]

4. BEYOND ANNULMENT: CONSEQUENCES FOR ARBITRATORS

Beyond annulment, consequences can be very serious for arbitrators who have not appropriately disclosed circumstances that would provoke a reasonable doubt in the parties' minds as to the arbitrator's impartiality and independence. The following sections look into arbitrator immunity under French law (section 4.1.) and instances of arbitrator liability (section 4.2.).

4.1. The Extent of Arbitrator Immunity under French Law

A party seeking to hold an arbitrator liable for failing to appropriately disclose circumstances that would provoke a reasonable doubt in the parties' minds as to his or her impartiality and independence will be confronted with the principle of arbitral immunity.

The immunity of arbitrators is well established and broad under French law. It prevents parties to an arbitration from bringing claims related to the conduct of an

44. Paris Court of Appeal, 12 February 2009, RG No. 07/22164.
45. For an example of inaccurate disclosure from an arbitrator leading to a breach of international public policy, *see Cour de cassation*, civ. 1, 24 March 1998, No. 95-17285.

arbitration against their arbitrators. In line with the landmark *Azran* decision of 15 January 2015, the courts consider that owing to their judicial mandate, arbitrators benefit from judicial immunity, thus extending to arbitrators the immunity of judges deriving from Article L. 141-1 of the French Code of Judicial Organization.[46]

However, in setting this standard, the French Courts also explained the circumstances in which such immunity could be lifted, holding that an arbitrator was only liable for 'personal wrongdoings, which result in liability where they amount to wilful misconduct, fraud, gross negligence or denial of justice'.[47]

The Court also made clear that the mandate of arbitrators was 'both contractual and jurisdictional'. For this reason, some authors have considered that only matters relating to the jurisdictional mandate of an arbitrator could be covered by immunity.

On the contrary, matters pertaining to the contractual mission of an arbitrator, such as the arbitrator's duty to perform his or her obligations in good faith, to respect the procedural calendar, along with his or her duty of diligence and confidentiality, are contractual obligations.[48]

4.2. Instances of Arbitrator Liability Relating to Disclosure Issues

From a practical point of view – and assuming that disclosure obligations are a contractual rather than jurisdictional matter – an arbitrator's liability will depend on the type of contractual obligation at stake.[49]

French case law does not seem to make the duty of disclosure an obligation of results (in French, *obligation de résultat*), although commentators have argued that it would be adequate to consider that an arbitrator is bound by an enhanced best-efforts obligation in this respect.[50]

Under French law, the difference between a results and a best-efforts obligation lies in the fact that a person with an obligation of results commits to achieve a specified result, whereas a best-efforts obligation merely requires him or her to employ all necessary means to do so.

An arbitrator acting under an obligation of result will therefore be liable merely owing to non-performance, whereas an arbitrator acting under a best-efforts obligation will only be expected to compensate the damage caused by non-performance in the event of a breach on his part.[51] In other words, the arbitrator's compliance with his obligation will be monitored 'with more rigour' than if he were bound by a simple

46. *Cour de cassation*, civ. 1, 15 January 2015, No. 11-17196. *See also* Paris Court of Appeal, 21 May 2019, RG No. 17/12238.
47. *Cour de cassation*, civ. 1, 15 January 2015, No. 11-17196.
48. Eric Loquin, '*La dualité du régime de la responsabilité de l'arbitre*', La Semaine Juridique Edition Générale, 392-398 (2014, n° 8).
49. On the topic of the responsibility of the Arbitrator for lack of independence, *see* Thomas Clay, *La responsabilité de l'arbitre pour absence d'indépendence,* Electronic Bulletin of the European Court of Arbitration, 21-30 (2012, n° 2).
50. *Id.*
51. 'Rapport sur la Responsabilité des Arbitres, Rapport Ad'Hoc du Club des Juristes', 33 (2017).

best-efforts obligation.[52] This should prevent alleged, but ultimately false, conflicts of interest from being used as a basis for unjustified liability claims.

There have been very few instances of liability on such grounds before the French Courts. In one of those instances, the arbitrator was found liable for not disclosing he was hired by one of the parties on the day the award was rendered. Following the annulment of the award, the arbitrator was ordered to pay the damages resulting from the lack of award, the costs of the arbitration proceedings and the costs of the subsequent liability proceedings.[53]

5. CONCLUSION

French law on arbitrators' disclosure duties and its consequences at the annulment stage has crystalized over the last decade. The Courts have adopted a broad approach regarding circumstances to be disclosed, as arbitrators are expected to disclose any circumstance that would create a doubt in the parties' mind as to his or her independence or impartiality.

However, an important exception is provided for publicly and easily accessible facts (deemed knowable). French Courts consider that prior to the tribunal's constitution, it is for the parties to investigate potential conflicts of interest. However, this burden shifts once the tribunal is constituted. French Courts expect arbitrators to disclose any new circumstances that may arise following their appointment, including knowable facts.

From a practical perspective, this requires arbitrators to be extremely cautious throughout the arbitration proceedings, gathering constant updates on the activities of the firms they operate in.

52. *Id.*
53. Paris Court of Appeal (Raoul Duval), 12 October 1995, REV. ARB., 325 (1999), where the Court ordered the arbitrator to pay EUR 3,500 as damages resulting from the arbitration itself, EUR 3,800 as additional prejudice, and EUR 1,200 for costs of the proceedings. *See also* the *l'Oréal* case, Paris High Civil Court, 9 December 1992, REV. ARB., 483 (1996), obs. Philippe Fouchard; Paris, 30 June 1995, REV. ARB., 483 (1996), obs. Philippe Fouchard; Cour de Cassation, 2 December 1997, REV. ARB., note Marc Henry, 249 (1999).

CHAPTER 10

The View from the English Courts on Conflicts of Interest: *Halliburton* and Beyond

Paula Hodges QC

1. INTRODUCTION

At its heart, international arbitration is a process by which parties choose to submit their dispute to arbitrators, relying on a fair, neutral process followed by a just outcome. The private conduct of commercial arbitration means that there is no public hearing and, in the interests of finality, rights of appeal are very limited. There is usually no right to appeal on the basis of the merits of the award, and it can be very difficult to succeed with a challenge on the basis of procedural irregularity. This means that the behaviour of arbitrators and users' confidence in their ethical conduct is critical. Arbitrator impartiality is vital to this, and parties want effective regulation to protect the neutrality of the arbitral process. For instance, an overwhelming majority of respondents to the Queen Mary University of London Survey in 2018 expressed strong support for arbitrator independence and impartiality to be dealt with in institutional rules.[1]

The arbitration community has also sought to address this important issue by evolving the IBA Guidelines on Conflicts of Interest ('the IBA Guidelines'), which have arguably attained the status of soft law. The IBA Guidelines are widely cited by parties

1. The Queen Mary survey results for 2018 demonstrated that over 80% of those responding to the survey wanted arbitration rules to address standards of independence and impartiality for arbitrators. *See 2018 International Arbitration Survey: The Evolution of International Arbitration*, Queen Mary University of London, 34 (2018).

in international arbitration and are also extensively referred to by arbitral institutions[2] and courts in both civil law and common law countries[3] when deciding challenges to arbitrators' impartiality. These issues have recently received renewed attention in the wake of the controversy which followed the English Court of Appeal decision in *Halliburton* on arbitrator disclosure and apparent bias.[4]

This chapter will look at the threshold for independence and impartiality set by the English courts before turning to consider how the Courts have defined the obligation for arbitrators to disclose conflicts. The analysis will include reference to the recent *Halliburton* case and the challenges this has created, ending with an assessment of what may lie ahead.

2. THE THRESHOLD FOR INDEPENDENCE AND IMPARTIALITY FROM THE ENGLISH COURT PERSPECTIVE

The English Arbitration Act 1996 ('the Act') requires arbitrators to 'act fairly and impartially as between the parties', which is a duty set out in section 33 of the Act.[5] Under section 24 of the Act, parties to English-seated arbitrations have the right to apply to the Court to remove an arbitrator where circumstances exist which '*give rise to justifiable doubts*' as to the arbitrator's impartiality.[6] In assessing any potential allegation of arbitrator bias, the English Court applies an objective standard rather than assessing impartiality from the subjective viewpoint of the parties.

2. IBA Council, *The IBA Guidelines on Conflicts of Interests in International Arbitration* (2014) (https://www.ibanet.org/ENews_Archive/IBA_July_2008_ENews_ArbitrationMultipleLang.aspx). The LCIA refers to the IBA Guidelines in deciding arbitrator challenges. *For example, see* Thomas W. Walsh and Ruth Teitelbaum, *The LCIA Court Decisions on Challenges to Arbitrators: An Introduction*, ARBITRATION INTERNATIONAL, VOL. 27 ISSUE 3, 283-313 (2011). The ICC has reported that of cases between 1 July 2004 and 1 August 2009 where the ICC Court decided challenges to arbitrators or contested confirmation of arbitrators, the IBA Guidelines on Conflicts of Interest were referenced in 187 cases. In 106 of these cases, one or more articles of the IBA Guidelines on Conflicts of Interest were stated to cover the particular alleged conflict of interest. *See The IBA Guidelines on Conflicts of Interest in International Arbitration: The First Five Years 2004–2009*, Report of the IBA Conflicts of Interest Subcommittee, a subcommittee of the IBA Arbitration Committee; 4 Dispute Resolution International (May 2010, no. 1).
3. In the English courts, the IBA Guidelines on Conflicts of Interest were considered in *ASM Shipping Limited of India v. TTMI Limited of England* [2005] EWHC 2238 (Comm) and *A and Others v. B and X* [2011] EWHC 2345 (Comm). In the United States, cases include *Applied Industrial Materials Corp. v. Ovalar Makine Ticaret Ve Sanayi*, A.S. No. 05 CV 10540(RPP), 2006 WL 1816383 (S.D.N.Y. 2006) and *New Regency Productions, Inc. v. Nippon Herald Films*, 501 F.3d 1101 (9th Cir. 2007). The Swiss Supreme Court referred to the IBA Guidelines on Conflicts of Interest in a 2008 case. *See* Case Note on Swiss Supreme Court Decisions 4A_506/2007 of 20 March 2008 & 4A_528/2007 of 4 April 2008, ASA BULLETIN 3, 588, 589 (2008). *See also* the IBA Arbitration Guidelines and Rules Subcommittee, *Report on the reception of the IBA arbitration soft law products* (2016) (https://www.ibanet.org/Document/Default.aspx?DocumentUid=105D29A3-6261-4437-84E2-1C8637844BEB).
4. *Halliburton Company v. Chubb Bermuda Insurance Ltd* [2018] EWCA Civ 817. Since the time of writing, the Supreme Court has handed its decision in the appeal from the Court of Appeal Decision. The Supreme Court Decision is discussed in the Addendum to this chapter.
5. At section 33 English Arbitration Act 1996.
6. The test is found in section 24(1)(a) English Arbitration Act 1996.

Because England is not a UNCITRAL Model Law jurisdiction,[7] it is, perhaps, unsurprising that the test set out in the Act does not mirror the equivalent model law provision. The Model Law deals with arbitrator bias in Article 12, which allows for an arbitrator to be challenged where *'circumstances exist that give rise to justifiable doubts'* in relation to *'impartiality or independence'*.[8] It is noteworthy that while the Model Law refers to independence as well as impartiality, the English test only focuses on the requirement for impartiality. When the English arbitration legislation was formulated, independence was deliberately omitted as a separate ground for removal, on the basis that lack of independence was already covered by the impartiality ground because a lack of independence was seen as having the potential to give rise to a lack of impartiality. It was therefore decided that there was no need to include lack of independence as a separate category that would justify removal.[9] It was considered that if a lack of independence did not give rise to corresponding concerns in relation to an arbitrator's impartiality, the situation would not warrant the removal of that arbitrator. The DAC report also noted that there might well be cases where the parties would like their arbitrators to be familiar with a certain sector rather than being entirely independent.[10]

It seems likely that for all practical purposes, the difference between the Model Law test and the threshold in the English legislation is not material. Moreover, the English legislation is broadly in line with international norms, given that not all countries adopt the Model Law test. By way of comparison, the relevant Swiss arbitration legislation stipulates that an arbitrator may be challenged if circumstances exist that give rise to *'justifiable doubts as to his independence'*, but the section does not refer to impartiality.[11] While the United States Federal Arbitration Act ('FAA') does not include an express obligation for arbitrators to be either independent or impartial, the FAA provides that an award may be vacated when there is *'evident partiality'* on the part of the arbitrators.[12]

In practice, allegations of actual bias in arbitrators are rarely made in the English courts, and challenges brought on that ground have tended to have a low success rate. The vast majority of arbitrator challenges based on impartiality are therefore framed as an allegation of apparent bias. In these cases, the complaining party will often emphasise that it is not accusing the arbitrator of actual bias but that, objectively speaking, there is a risk of unconscious bias.[13] It is not surprising, therefore, that the English Court of Appeal has made it clear that applications to remove arbitrators under section 24 of the Act will be decided in relation to the current threshold for determining apparent bias under English law. The test for apparent bias is 'whether a fair-minded

7. The UK has not based its arbitration legislation on the UNCITRAL Model Law on International Commercial Arbitration (1985).
8. Article 12 of the UNCITRAL Model Law on International Commercial Arbitration (1985).
9. Departmental Advisory Committee on Arbitration, *DAC Report on Arbitration Bill 1996*, paras 101-104 (1996).
10. *Ibid.*
11. Article 180(c) Swiss Private International Law Statute ('PILA').
12. Section 10(a)(2) United States Federal Arbitration Act.
13. David Sutton, Judith Gill QC, Matthew Gearing QC, 'Russell on Arbitration', 24th ed., Sweet & Maxwell 4-111, 170 (2015).

and informed observer, having considered the facts, would conclude that there is a real possibility that the tribunal was biased'.[14] This test has been restated in the Court of Appeal's judgment in the *Halliburton* case.[15]

Before the *Halliburton* case, the test for apparent bias was not perceived as being problematic. The English courts have historically taken a pro-arbitration, non-interventionist approach and have been reluctant to interfere with the arbitral process on the basis of unsubstantiated objections to arbitrators.[16] In short, the apparent bias test has been applied robustly by the English courts to reject unmeritorious challenges. For example, in the case of *Amega Limited*, it was alleged that the arbitrator was biased because the arbitrator had proceeded with two preliminary hearings in the absence of the complaining party, formalised three directions orders against the wishes of that party and had also refused their application for a stay. While the complaining party argued that the hearings should not have gone ahead without them, they had been notified of the hearings and had chosen not to attend. There was nothing in the making of the procedural orders or refusal of a stay that suggested bias, and the application was accordingly rejected.[17]

Conversely, in the relatively rare case where the English courts have been presented with clear evidence of apparent bias on the part of an arbitrator, the courts have applied the fair-minded observer test and have removed the arbitrator in question. In 2016, the Court removed an arbitrator where the evidence demonstrated that the arbitrator had received 18% of their total appointments and 25% of their overall income from cases involving one of the parties.[18] While the party in question did not directly appoint the arbitrator, they had manipulated the appointment process by setting out required characteristics, in combination with their suggestion of the arbitrator in question and a list of those they regarded as inappropriate for appointment.[19] This relationship between the arbitrator and the relevant party was sufficient to demonstrate apparent bias, particularly when it was combined with the arbitrator's aggressive and evasive response to the complaining party's enquiries and inappropriate hostility at the arbitration hearing when these issues were raised.[20]

However, rather than this being a settled area of law, it has become apparent, following *Halliburton*, that there are uncertainties surrounding the application of this test for apparent bias in an arbitration context, hence the appeal to the Supreme Court for guidance.

14. This has been the accepted common law standard applying to arbitrators since the case of *Porter v. Magill* [2001] UKHL 67 [103].
15. *Halliburton* (*see supra* n. 4) [39].
16. *See* Al Trent, *'Who will rid me of this turbulent arbitrator?' Applications to Remove Arbitrators under English Law – Part 1: Apparent Bias* (2016) (http://arbitrationblog.kluwerarbitration.com/2016/08/15/who-will-rid-me-of-this-turbulent-arbitrator-applications-to-remove-arbitrators-under-english-law/?_ga=2.194730533.965368916.1576752127-1533985524.1565272616).
17. *Drs G and M v. Amega Limited* [2010] EWHC 2454 (TCC).
18. Keating Chambers, *Cofley Ltd v Anthony Bingham and Knowles Ltd* (2016) (http://www.keatingchambers.com/case-report/cofely-ltd-v-anthony-bingham-and-knowles-ltd-2016-ewhc-240-comm/).
19. *Cofely Limited v. Bingham & Knowles Limited* [2016] EWHC 240 (Comm) [107].
20. *Ibid.*, [110].

3. THE DUTY OF DISCLOSURE IN ENGLISH LAW

While English arbitration legislation itself does not state any particular requirements in relation to disclosure of potential conflicts of interest, the current standard for disclosure for arbitrators in English-seated arbitration is set out in the Court of Appeal judgment in *Halliburton*. The Court of Appeal stated that there was a duty on arbitrators to disclose to the parties circumstances of which they are aware that 'would or might lead the fair-minded and informed observer, having considered the facts, to conclude that there was a real possibility that the arbitrator was biased'. Under English law, the duty of disclosure applies only to those facts and circumstances already known to the arbitrator, and there is no duty of inquiry imposed on the arbitrator.

It is recognised that it may be difficult to ascertain at the outset of a particular case whether an issue is likely to be sufficiently significant to meet the apparent bias threshold. The Court of Appeal, therefore, recommended that disclosure should be made even when the issue is '*borderline*'. An important practical justification for the duty to disclose is that it is advantageous to deal with any potential issues early in the course of proceedings.[21] Accordingly, there is likely to be a duty to disclose even in relation to matters which are not ultimately sufficient to amount to apparent bias.[22] However, the threshold for disclosure should still be judged objectively. The Court of Appeal in *Halliburton* commented that while a more subjective approach 'may reflect good practice in international commercial arbitration ... the more certain standards of an objective observer apply to the issue of disclosure under English law'.[23]

Where there is an application for removal of an arbitrator for apparent bias, the Court will consider whether the issues in question should have been disclosed and will judge this in light of the position at the time the disclosure potentially fell to be made, rather than on how matters ultimately transpired.[24] If it is then determined that there has been a failure to disclose, the Court will consider the significance of the non-disclosure and will take the non-disclosure into account as a factor in considering the question of apparent bias itself. Failure to disclose may lead to the conclusion that the arbitrator has failed to display *'the badge of impartiality'* that every arbitrator should wear.[25] When an arbitrator has responded inappropriately to a suggestion that disclosure is required, this will be a further factor to be taken into account in relation to an allegation of apparent bias.[26]

It is, however, very important to note that a failure to disclose which does not give rise to justifiable doubts about an arbitrator's impartiality will not itself lead to an inference of apparent bias. The Court of Appeal judgment in *Halliburton* explained this

21. *Halliburton* (*see supra* n. 4), 60, 65.
22. As in *Almazeedi* in a litigation context, where the Cayman Islands' Court of Appeal decided that links between a party and a judge should have been disclosed, even though they would not have been sufficient to lead to a finding of apparent bias. *See* the Cayman Islands' Court of Appeal in *Wael Almazeedi v. Michael Penner and Stuart Sybermsa* (on this, *see Almazeedi v. Penner and another*, Privy Council [2018] UKPC 3).
23. *Halliburton* (*see supra* n. 4), 68.
24. *Ibid.*, 83.
25. *Ibid.*, 74.
26. *Halliburton* and *see, e.g.*, in *Cofely Limited* (*see supra* n. 19).

apparently contradictory state of affairs by saying that there must be *'something more'* than the relevant non-disclosure, but there is no elaboration in the judgment on what this means.[27] As will be discussed below, this is an aspect of the judgment that has elicited a significant amount of criticism.[28]

4. THE *HALLIBURTON* CASE

In December 2019, the English Supreme Court heard the appeal in *Halliburton*, which has been described as the most significant case in English arbitration since 2011.[29] The judgment is expected imminently. Halliburton had provided offshore services in relation to the Deepwater Horizon project in the Gulf of Mexico. Claims arising out of the Deepwater Horizon incident were made against Halliburton, and Halliburton, in turn, sought to claim compensation under its insurance policy with Chubb. Chubb declined to make payment, and, in January 2015, Halliburton commenced arbitration against Chubb under a Bermuda Form policy, which is governed by New York law, with an arbitration clause providing for London-seated ad hoc arbitration.

The parties to the arbitration could not agree on the selection of the presiding arbitrator, and an application was accordingly made to the English High Court. In June 2015, the Court appointed an arbitrator, M, to chair the tribunal. M was Chubb's preferred candidate, but Halliburton had objected to M on the basis that the policy was governed by New York law and M was an English lawyer. Before appointment, M had disclosed his previous appointment as arbitrator in relation to *'a number of arbitrations'* in which Chubb was a party. This included past *'appointments on behalf of Chubb'*,[30] although the exact number of these references and the timescale is not set out in the Court of Appeal judgment. M had also disclosed that he was currently acting as arbitrator in two ongoing references in which Chubb was involved.

After M took up appointment as chair in the arbitration between Halliburton and Chubb, he accepted appointment in two subsequent related arbitrations. In December 2015, he accepted appointment by Chubb as arbitrator in respect of a disputed claim under the liability cover Chubb had provided to another insured party, Transocean, also in relation to the Deepwater Horizon incident. In August 2016, M then accepted appointment by Transocean in relation to another claim Transocean was bringing against a different insurer. This claim also arose from the same incident and related to the same layer of insurance. M did not disclose the December 2015 or August 2016

27. *Halliburton* (*see supra* n. 4), 76.
28. Paul Stanley, *Halliburton Company v Chubb Bermuda Insurance*, 15 (https://s3-eu-west-2.amazonaws.com/sqe-essexcourt/wp-content/uploads/2018/05/08152814/hburton.pdf).
29. It has been suggested that *Halliburton* is the most important case in arbitration since *Jivraj v. Haswani* [2011] UKSC 40; *see also* Craig Tevendale, *Will Halliburton be the final word on apparent bias?* (https://globalarbitrationreview.com/article/1211113/will-halliburton-be-the-final-word-on-apparent-bias).
30. *Halliburton* (*see supra* n. 4), 11.

appointments to Halliburton,[31] but Halliburton discovered the existence of the two undisclosed arbitrations in November 2016.[32]

After discovering the additional appointments, Halliburton asked M to resign, but he stated that he felt unable to do so, given that he had been appointed by the court. The arbitrator argued that the cases did not raise the same or similar issues and that he had always been independent and impartial and would continue to be.[33] At this stage, Halliburton applied to the English courts for the removal of the arbitrator under section 24 of the Act.[34] The High Court rejected the application, and Halliburton appealed to the Court of Appeal.

The Court of Appeal concluded that while '*inside information and knowledge may be a legitimate concern*',[35] in and of itself, appointment as an arbitrator in these circumstances would not lead the fair-minded and informed observer to conclude that there was a real possibility of bias.[36] The importance of trust was emphasised in the sense that arbitrators should be trusted to approach the resolution of disputes with an appropriately open mind and to rely solely on the evidence put in front of them by the parties to the proceedings in question.[37]

The Court decided that '*objectively this is not affected by the fact that there is a common party*'[38] and stressed that '*something more*' of '*substance*' would be required for the threshold for bias to be met.[39] It was considered whether this requirement for '*something more*' existed in this case, and in this context, the Court analysed the degree of overlap between the references, which was found to be very limited.[40] The financial benefit received by M from his appointments was not considered relevant, given that it could not be determined at the outset which party would ultimately end up bearing the responsibility for the tribunal's costs.

The arbitrator did have a duty to disclose the subsequent overlapping references to the parties at the time that he was appointed in respect of those references, as the fair-minded and informed observer would conclude that there *might* be a possibility of bias and therefore disclosure was required.[41] It was recognised that Halliburton would then have been able to explore potential issues, express any concerns to the arbitrator and deal with any practical measures required to prevent problems arising as a result of the multiple references.[42]

The Court referred to the IBA Guidelines, noting that the Guidelines did not bind the Court but conceded that it was possible to say that the IBA Guidelines represented

31. *Ibid.*, 14-15.
32. *Ibid.*, 17.
33. *Ibid.*, 19.
34. *Ibid.*, 20.
35. *Ibid.*, 49.
36. *Ibid.*
37. *Ibid.*, 51 and 86.
38. *Ibid.*, 51.
39. *Ibid.*, 53.
40. *Ibid.*, 81.
41. *Ibid.*, 89.
42. *Ibid.*, 87.

general practice in international commercial arbitration.[43] The Court also said that in considering the question of whether circumstances should be disclosed, international practice was a relevant factor.[44] The circumstances of the case fell within the Orange List (specifically 3.1.5) of the IBA Guidelines.[45] Under the IBA Guidelines, these circumstances may, in the eyes of the parties, give rise to doubts about the arbitrator's independence or impartiality, and the arbitrator, therefore, has a duty to disclose in these circumstances.

Accordingly, as a matter of English law, disclosure was found to have been required at the time when the subsequent appointments were accepted, and that disclosure in these circumstances was recognised to be best practice in international arbitration. The Court also recognised that, at this early stage of the arbitration, the likely degree of overlap between the cases was unknown and that the previous disclosure of other appointments would lead to an expectation that subsequent appointments would also be disclosed.[46]

While the Court concluded that disclosure should have been made, however, this did not lead the Court to determine that the threshold for apparent bias had been met. The Court decided that non-disclosure does not necessarily constitute the '*something more*' required for finding apparent bias in the case of overlapping appointments.[47] The accidental nature of the failure to disclose was highlighted, along with the limited degree of overlap between the arbitrations, and the Court stated that 'the fair-minded and informed observer would not consider that mere oversight in such circumstances would give rise to justifiable doubts as to impartiality'.[48] The Court recognised that Halliburton had raised the issue of unconscious bias, but in this context, it referred to M's reputation as an eminent and highly experienced arbitrator. As the concerns had been raised before any substantive decision-making had proceeded in the arbitration between Halliburton and Chubb, the Court took the view that M would have guarded against any impact from the overlapping references.[49]

5. WHAT LIES BEYOND *HALLIBURTON*?

The *Halliburton* Court of Appeal judgment has been a highly controversial decision and has attracted widespread criticism from the international arbitration community. As a leading centre for international arbitration, London has long had a reputation as an arbitration-friendly jurisdiction, with supportive courts taking a non-interventionist approach. However, while the English courts have been reluctant to interfere with the arbitral process unnecessarily, the courts have nonetheless been unafraid to take

43. *Ibid.*, 68.
44. *Ibid.*, 89.
45. *Ibid.*, 88.
46. *Ibid.*, 90.
47. *Ibid.*, 96.
48. *Ibid.*
49. *Ibid.*, 100.

robust decisions in support of arbitration when required.[50] It is accordingly important for the international arbitration community to be able to have confidence that challenges to arbitrators in the English courts will be dealt with rigorously, consistently and in a way that is broadly aligned with international standards.

As a starting point, the *Halliburton* case has shown that there is currently a lack of clarity on how the test for apparent bias should be applied in an arbitration context. This may derive from the fact that many of the English cases on apparent bias came to court in a litigation context in relation to allegations of potential judicial conflicts of interest. The test for apparent bias is the same in both litigation and arbitration, and the *Halliburton* case did not address the important differences between arbitration and litigation, including the fact that arbitrators are often selected by the parties, there are more limited rights of appeal and that arbitration hearings occur in private. The *Halliburton* judgment did not consider whether knowledge about the conduct and ethical standards usually adopted in international arbitration should form part of the 'context' referred to in previous cases on apparent bias.

While it seems logical that in cases relating to international commercial arbitration, the objective informed observer should be considered to be reasonably knowledgeable about the generally accepted ethical standards in international arbitration, there is a distinct lack of guidance from the English courts on how the knowledge of the 'informed observer' should be delineated, or what the informed observer should be assumed to know. It has always been understood that the informed observer is not a lawyer but will know the facts that are relevant to the issue to be determined.[51] This individual is expected to know the way the legal profession works, employing a balanced approach and *'appreciates that context forms an important part of the material to be considered'*.[52] The Court of Appeal judgment in *Halliburton* did not address how much of this international arbitration context should be considered in order to apply the objective apparent bias test, and this is a weakness in the judgment.

There also continues to be controversy over exactly what circumstances would be sufficient to lead the fair-minded and informed observer to conclude that there is a real possibility that an arbitrator was biased. There was widespread concern in the arbitration community after the *Halliburton* Court of Appeal judgment that the correct approach had not been taken to the issues of undisclosed overlapping and multiple

50. For example, the English Courts have been willing to issue anti-suit injunctions in relation to litigation commenced in breach of an arbitration agreement. *See, e.g.*, Craig Tevendale et al., *High Court grants anti-suit injunction having found that the parties to an insurance policy had agreed to arbitration despite a Service of Suit clause* (2019) (https://hsfnotes.com/arbitration/2019/11/28/high-court-grants-anti-suit-injunction-having-found-that-the-parties-to-an-insurance-policy-had-agreed-to-arbitration-despite-a-service-of-suit-clause/). The Courts have also been willing to correct awards where an oversight with unintended consequences would otherwise lead to substantial injustice. *See* Craig Tevendale and R. Metsch, *English Commercial Court addresses the scope of a tribunal's power to correct arbitral awards under the LCIA Rules 1998* (2019) (https://hsfnotes.com/arbitration/2019/12/16/english-commercial-court-addresses-the-scope-of-a-tribunals-power-to-correct-arbitral-awards-under-the-lcia-rules-1998/).
51. *Cofely* (*see supra* n. 19), 72.
52. *Ibid.*

appointments that were raised in that case.[53] The Court of Appeal's permissive approach to repeat and overlapping appointments must be considered questionable. This is because an arbitrator's previous position in relation to certain issues in other cases is likely to be known by the repeat-appointing party but not to the other parties involved in the subsequent case, leading to an inequality of arms. In overlapping references, the common party may also gain a significant tactical advantage over other parties. The common party is able to test out arguments in another reference and will potentially know the arbitrator's position on certain issues in advance. The common party will also have access to evidence not known to the other party and have the ability to influence the arbitrator with communications or submissions, which the other party has not seen and will not even know to exist. The potential issues arising from appointment in multiple and related cases can be significant, and maintaining equality of arms is of supreme importance if international arbitration is to continue to be trusted by its users.

Moreover, the arbitrator concerned is unlikely to be able to ignore entirely the material learned from the other references, even when concerted efforts are made to do so. This can create an imbalance within the tribunal, with the arbitrator appointed on multiple references knowing more about the issues at stake than other members of the tribunal. Arbitrators themselves are aware of the risks of being unconsciously influenced by material, which should not properly form part of the evidence for their consideration, and this is why tribunals commonly appoint third party advisors to look at allegedly privileged material where there is a dispute as to whether or not it is appropriate for it to be seen by the tribunal. Clearly, there is general acknowledgement in the international arbitration community that material once seen is difficult to entirely ignore, however strenuous the efforts made to do so. Relying entirely on trust is unlikely to be realistic, given the potential for unconscious bias inherent in arbitrating overlapping references. The local reputation of the arbitrator in question, even when they are very eminent and experienced, should not affect the application of the test. In particular, there is no evidence that being a highly seasoned and widely trusted arbitrator will make it any easier for that arbitrator to prevent him or herself from being unconsciously affected by evidence seen and arguments raised in another connected case.[54]

There must also be a risk that 'frequent flyer' arbitrators will (even if unconsciously) be inclined to avoid alienating a source of potential future income. The Court of Appeal seemed to dismiss the relevance of the financial benefit received by an arbitrator, on the basis that appointment does not produce an immediate financial benefit and the question of who pays the arbitrators' fees is only decided by the tribunal at the end of the case.[55] However, there is some tension in this respect with earlier cases where the issue of financial benefit has been raised, regardless of the question of which

53. *See generally* Paul Stanley's case comment (*supra* n. 28), and Christopher Hancock QC, Daniel Bovensiepen, *Arbitral Appointments: broadening horizons or getting into deep water?* (2018) (https://twentyessex.com/wp-content/uploads/2019/06/Halliburton-v-Chubb-report.pdf) deta iling the concerns of the international arbitration community.
54. Paul Stanley (*see supra* n. 28), 10-11.
55. *Halliburton* (*see supra* n. 4), 82.

party ultimately pays the fees. In the *Cofely* case, for example, the Court held that the repeat appointments raised questions of significant financial dependence, which, cumulatively with other circumstances, would result in a fair-minded and informed observer concluding that there was a real possibility of bias.[56]

It is unclear from the *Halliburton* judgment why the non-disclosure itself did not amount to apparent bias and, while the judgment says '*something more*' would have been required, there is no guidance in the judgment on what factors would or would not satisfy the test.[57] This is unsatisfactory in circumstances where the acceptance of the overlapping appointments itself should surely have been a relevant factor. While the Court of Appeal judgment emphasised the accidental nature of the failure to disclose, this is also problematic, given that it will usually be extremely difficult for any party to prove a deliberate failure to disclose.[58] Giving weight to the accidental nature of the non-disclosure effectively makes it even more difficult to demonstrate apparent bias in cases where it is determined that there was a failure to disclosure.

The Court of Appeal's approach to the IBA Guidelines was also surprising. Despite recognising that the Guidelines set out expected practice in international arbitration, the Court effectively disregarded the failure to make the disclosure recommended by the Guidelines. This does not reflect the degree of use made of the IBA Guidelines by other courts, both within and outside England when deciding similar issues. For example, in *Sierra Fishing*, the English Court stated that assistance was gained from 'the [IBA Guidelines which]... provide illustrations of what the international arbitral community considers to be cases of conflict of interest and apparent bias'.[59] The Swiss Federal Supreme Court went further, commenting in a judgment that '[s]uch guidelines admittedly have no statutory value; yet they are a precious instrument ... .'[60]

It is true that the English courts have not limited their approach to match the IBA Guidelines, even in cases where the Guidelines have been cited. Indeed, the Courts will make a finding of apparent bias in situations that meet the English law test, regardless of whether the circumstances are listed in the IBA Guidelines. In *ASM*, for example, the Court looked at the IBA Guidelines in the context of a challenge to an award for serious irregularity under section 68 of the Act. The challenge related to the impartiality of the tribunal chair in respect of a key witness and was based on the fact that the chair had previously acted as counsel in a case where there was an allegation of inappropriate conduct by the same witness. While the Guidelines did not cover the situation, the Court pointed out that the Guidelines do not claim to be a comprehensive statement of all potential conflict situations. The Court quoted the statement from the Working Group that the Guidelines need to be 'applied with robust common sense and without pedantic and unduly formulaic interpretation' and stated that in any event, the lists had

56. *Cofely* (*see supra* n. 19), 103-116.
57. *Halliburton* (*see supra* n. 4), 76.
58. Paul Stanley (*see supra* n. 28), 16.
59. *Sierra Fishing Company and others v. Hasan Said Farran and others* [2015] EWHC 140 (Comm) [58].
60. Swiss Federal Supreme Court, 1st Civil Chamber, DFSC 4A 506/2007 of 20 March 2008. *See* ASA Bulletin 3, 588, 589 (2008).

'come close to the point in issue'. In that case, the court decided that there had been apparent bias on the part of the arbitrator.[61]

The English courts have also demonstrated a willingness to depart from the IBA's assessment in respect of the Non-Waivable Red List. In the *W Limited* case, an award was challenged because the arbitrator's firm regularly advised an affiliate company of one of the parties to the arbitration. This advice generated substantial income for the arbitrator's law firm. There was no suggestion either that the arbitrator personally had advised the affiliate or that the arbitrator had received any of the income concerned. At the time of the arbitrator's appointment, the company receiving the advice was not an affiliate, but a later acquisition meant this company came to be owned by the same parent company as one of the parties. The arbitrator had for some time been operating as a near full-time arbitrator, only using the law firm's administrative and secretarial services.[62] The Court reached the conclusion that the fair-minded observer would not conclude there was a real possibility of bias on the part of the arbitrator, and the award was upheld.

The Court in *W Limited* noted the importance of consulting the IBA Guidelines for assistance and commented that it was 'valuable and appropriate to examine them'.[63] However, there were perceived weaknesses in the Non-Waivable Red List, which included advice given by the arbitrator's firm (even if not given by the arbitrator him or herself) to any affiliate of a party, without any consideration of whether this could impact on impartiality and whether the arbitrator was aware of the connection. The Court concluded that the situation called for case-specific assessment and took the view that some of the circumstances listed in the Waivable Red List were potentially more serious (including where the arbitrator has advised a party in relation to the dispute or a close family member of the arbitrator has a significant financial interest in the outcome of the dispute). Despite the Court's criticisms, it was noted that the Guidelines 'make a distinguished contribution in the field of international arbitration [and their] objective, to assist in assessing impartiality and independence, is to be commended'.[64]

The decision in *W Limited* has attracted criticism for being out of step with international standards, including case law in France.[65] It is true that a recent and high profile case in the French *Cour de cassation* has set aside an award due to the fact that the arbitrator's firm was advising an affiliate of a party. However, the *W Limited* case arguably fell into different and more ambiguous territory, where the arbitrator's true connection with the law firm concerned was much more limited than in the French

61. *ASM Shipping Limited of India v. TTMI Limited of England* [2005] EWHC 2238 (Comm), 39.
62. *W Limited v. M SDN BHD* [2016] EWHC 422 (Comm) 10, 21.
63. *Ibid.*, 36.
64. *Ibid.*, 33.
65. *See, e.g.*, Dominic Corsini-Meek and Dhevine Chandrapala, *The IBA Guidelines on Conflicts of Interest: Evolution not revolution* (2016) (http://arbitrationblog.practicallaw.com/the-iba-guidelines-on-conflicts-of-interest-evolution-not-revolution/).

Cour de cassation case.[66] The IBA Guidelines themselves state that they are to be used with *'robust common sense'* and *'without unduly formalistic interpretation'*.[67]

While the English courts have not always followed the IBA Guidelines, in other cases, the Courts have clearly been influenced by the Guidelines. In *Sierra Fishing*, for example, the application to remove the arbitrator related to the legal and business connections between one of the parties and the arbitrator. The circumstances fell into one of the only four situations in the Non-Waivable Red List (at 1.4), as the arbitrator's law firm had acted for one of the parties in respect of matters from which the law firm received significant income.[68] The Court determined that the fair-minded observer would consider there was a real possibility that the arbitrator would be pre-disposed to decide in the connected party's favour.[69] A number of other factors engaged further provisions of the IBA Guidelines, and these were discussed, including a series of potential issues that fell under the Waivable Red List, along with an issue included in the Orange List.[70] The arbitrator's father was a member of the senior management at the bank chaired by one of the parties in the arbitration. The arbitrator had also drafted a relevant clause in an agreement that he would have been called upon to interpret as an arbitrator. It does not come as any surprise to see that the application for removal succeeded.[71]

In another recent case, *A and Others v. B and X*, the English Court dealt with both a challenge to an award and an application to remove a sole arbitrator in a situation that was alleged to be covered by the Waivable Red List (at 2.3.2). The arbitrator concerned had been instructed as counsel by a party's legal representatives in an unrelated case.[72] The Court took the view that the factual circumstances in paragraph 2.3.2 of the Waivable Red List did not apply, as paragraph 2.3.2 referred to the arbitrator representing 'the lawyer or law firm' themselves, not the arbitrator representing a client of the relevant law firm. The Court commented that, unlike the *ASM* case, the situation did not fall within either the spirit or letter of the Guidelines.[73] The IBA Guidelines were also followed in *Koshigi*, which commented that although 'this is in no sense binding on the court, it is a useful indication of what is accepted as international best practice'.[74] While there was a friendly relationship, this was 'a long way from the 'close personal friendship' referred to in the Orange List'. The relationship was very unlikely to have given rise to bias in the legal sense or to have required disclosure.

---

66. *See* Laurence Franc-Meneget and Peter Archer, *Cour de cassation upholds decision to set aside an award following an arbitrator's non-disclosure* (2019) (https://hsfnotes.com/arbitration/2019/12/17/cour-de-cassation-upholds-decision-to-set-aside-an-award-following-an-arbitrators-non-disclosure/). It is interesting to note that the French Courts did not refer to the IBA Guidelines at all in reaching their decision, as the situation was expressly covered in the relevant provision of the French procedural code.
67. IBA Guidelines (*see supra* n. 2), intro, 6.
68. *Sierra Fishing* (*see supra* n. 59), 7.
69. *Ibid.*, 59.
70. *Ibid.*
71. *Ibid.*, 81.
72. *A and Others v. B and X* [2011] EWHC 2345 (Comm) [8].
73. *Ibid.*, 74-75.
74. *Koshigi Ltd and another v. Donna Union Foundation and Another* [2019] EWHC 122 (Comm), 54.

These cases demonstrate that, even though the English courts have been at pains to uphold the primacy of the English law test, the IBA Guidelines have been extensively cited in cases on apparent bias and not simply confined to the question of whether disclosure of a particular issue should have been made. This position is in line with the approach in a number of other jurisdictions, including the United States, where courts have referred to the Guidelines on a number of occasions and have been prepared to give them weight, despite emphasising that the Guidelines are not binding. In *Applied Industrial Materials v. Sanayi*, for example, the US District Court for the Southern District of New York referred to the IBA Guidelines in deciding a case on arbitrator conflicts.[75] Although the Swiss Courts have recognised the relevance and importance of the IBA Guidelines, they have also sounded a warning note that it is important not to overestimate the significance of the Guidelines in reaching decisions. The Swiss Courts will always focus most of all on the particular facts of any case, along with the relevant Swiss case law, to reach decisions on conflicts.[76]

The extent to which the IBA Guidelines have been referenced in English cases on apparent bias demonstrates that the Guidelines have come to be seen as a guide to what is to be expected in international arbitration. The status of the Guidelines is also expressly recognised in the *Halliburton* judgment itself. However, the IBA Guidelines were only taken into account in considering the question of whether the disclosure should have been made and were not considered when determining the question of whether the overlapping appointments themselves amounted to apparent bias. The fact that overlapping appointments are addressed in the Orange List should have been accorded greater weight by the Court of Appeal as an indication that 'frequent flying' in these circumstances raises a justifiable concern.

It is important to note that the context of the *Halliburton* case is English-seated ad hoc arbitration. It has been suggested that concerns about the case may encourage parties who are currently using ad hoc arbitration to select institutional arbitration in future, where any challenge to an arbitrator will be considered in relation to the rules of the relevant institution. For example, in LCIA arbitration, the test for disclosure is set out in Article 5.4, which requires the arbitrator to disclose any circumstances which are likely to give rise in the mind of any party to any justifiable doubts as to his or her impartiality or independence and Article 5.5 makes this obligation a continuing one, lasting throughout the life of the arbitration. Selecting the more certain regime of institutional arbitration can accordingly avoid at least some of the uncertainty created by the *Halliburton* decision, even in relation to English-seated arbitration. A further advantage of institutional arbitration is that challenge applications are made to the relevant institution (at least in the first instance) so that decisions are taken by

75. *Applied Industrial Materials* (*see supra* n. 3), and Peter Halprin, Stephen Wah, *'Ethics in International Arbitration'* J. Disp. Resol. (2018) (https://scholarship.law.missouri.edu/jdr/vol2018/iss1/10/). *See also* the IBA Arbitration Guidelines and Rules Subcommittee, *Report on the reception of the IBA arbitration soft law products* (2016) (https://www.ibanet.org/Document/Default.aspx?DocumentUid=105D29A3-6261-4437-84E2-1C8637844BEB), 61.
76. There are a number of jurisdictions where it is rare for the IBA Guidelines to be referred to in the courts and, in their report of 2016, the IBA listed a number of jurisdictions where the Guidelines had never been referenced in the local courts. *See, e.g.*, IBA Soft Law Report (*see supra* n. 3), 60.

arbitration specialists with a good understanding of the ethical standards expected within the international arbitration community. Accordingly, there may be some degree of movement to institutional arbitration among users previously more inclined to use English-seated ad hoc arbitration clauses.[77]

6. CONCLUSION

Uncertainty has clouded the determination of apparent bias on the part of arbitrators in English-seated arbitration since 2017 when Halliburton first asked the English Court to remove the presiding arbitrator. However, although the litigation has been fairly protracted, the question at the heart of *Halliburton* is, in reality, a very simple one. It is abundantly clear that arbitrator 'frequent flying' carries risks and that accepting overlapping references of the kind that occurred in *Halliburton* without making a disclosure should be capable of meeting the test for apparent bias. In certain circumstances, the existence of multiple appointments (even when disclosed) should in and of itself be enough to meet the test. There should be no justification for non-disclosure of multiple appointments, and the fact of non-disclosure should be a key factor in applying the apparent bias test. The *Halliburton* case has been appealed to the Supreme Court, and it is expected that the judgment will provide welcome guidance on the threshold for apparent bias and how the fair-minded and informed observer test is to be applied in the future.

Addendum

The English Supreme Court has now handed down its decision in *Halliburton Company (Appellant) v. Chubb Bermuda Insurance Ltd* [2020] UKSC 48.

The Supreme Court was asked to decide two issues:

(1) Whether overlapping appointments could be accepted without this resulting in the appearance of bias on the part of the arbitrator?
(2) Could such appointments be accepted without giving disclosure?[78]

The Supreme Court had to decide whether there was an appearance of bias and confirmed that the test for this remains 'whether the fair-minded and informed observer, having considered the facts, would conclude that there was a real possibility that the tribunal was biased'.[79] The Supreme Court decided that when this test is applied to arbitrators, the unique features of arbitration must be taken into account,[80] including the private nature of arbitration,[81] the limited rights of appeal,[82] the

77. For commentary on these issues, *see* Paul Stanley (*see supra* n. 28), 9.
78. *Halliburton Company (Appellant) v. Chubb Bermuda Insurance Ltd (formerly known as Ace Bermuda Insurance Ltd) (First Respondent)* [2020] UKSC 48 [2].
79. *Ibid.* [52].
80. *Ibid.* [55].
81. *Ibid.* [56]-[57].
82. *Ibid.* [58].

appointment process[83] and the potential '*financial interest in obtaining further appointments as arbitrator*'.[84] The Supreme Court found that in English law, all arbitrators (whether party-appointed or not) are required to meet the same high standards of fairness and impartiality.[85]

The decision confirmed that arbitrators have a duty of disclosure under English law, which extends to facts and circumstances which would or might reasonably give rise to the appearance of bias.[86] The Supreme Court determined that acceptance of multiple overlapping appointments of the kind in question may need to be disclosed in accordance with usual practice in the relevant type of arbitration.[87] Failure to disclose such appointments may amount to apparent bias and will be one factor taken into account in deciding whether there was an appearance of bias.[88]

The Supreme Court decided that the arbitrator in question had been under a legal duty to disclose the multiple appointments.[89] This was because disclosure of this kind was expected in Bermuda Form arbitration and because the overlapping appointment 'might reasonably give rise to the real possibility of bias'.[90] However, having considered all the relevant factors, the Supreme Court found that there was no appearance of bias in this case, which was stated to be for five reasons:[91]

(1) At the relevant time, the law on arbitrator disclosure was unclear.[92]
(2) The time sequence of the three arbitrations in question may explain why the arbitrator 'saw the need to disclose reference 1 to Transocean but did not identify the need to tell Halliburton about reference 2'.[93]
(3) Both the later arbitrations were being decided by way of a preliminary issue, which meant there would be no overlap in evidence or submissions.[94] The arbitrator had offered to resign from the subsequent arbitrations if this did not prove to be the case.[95]
(4) The arbitrator had not received any secret financial benefit.[96]
(5) The arbitrator responded fairly, and there was nothing to suggest that he 'bore any animus towards Halliburton as a result'.[97]

As expected, the Supreme Court judgment has provided important guidance on this critical area of arbitration law, delivering a greater measure of certainty on how

83. *Ibid.* [59]-[60].
84. *Ibid.* [59].
85. *Ibid.* [62]-[63].
86. *Ibid.* [75]-[76] and [81].
87. *Ibid.* [133]-[136].
88. *Ibid.* [118].
89. *Ibid.* [137].
90. *Ibid.* [145].
91. *Ibid.* [149]-[150].
92. *Ibid.*
93. *Ibid.*
94. *Ibid.*
95. *Ibid.*
96. *Ibid.*
97. *Ibid.*

apparent bias will be assessed by the English courts in the arbitration-specific context. It is now clear that the distinctive qualities of the arbitration process must be taken into account in making a determination on apparent bias, which is a significant change.[98] In line with the submissions made by the LCIA and other interveners, the Supreme Court has confirmed the existence of a duty of arbitrator disclosure in English law, which is a welcome development. The Supreme Court noted that the 'existence of a legal duty promotes transparency in arbitration and is consistent with best practice as seen in the IBA Guidelines and in the requirements of institutional arbitrations such as those of ICC and LCIA'.[99] The judgment has also made it clear that there may be circumstances where arbitrator acceptance of multiple related appointments with one common party may in itself give rise to an appearance of bias. Importantly, the Supreme Court departed from the problematic requirement for there to be '*something more*', which was a much-criticised feature of the Court of Appeal case.[100]

98. In this regard, *see* my discussion on the Court of Appeal decision under '*What lies beyond Halliburton*' on the important differences between arbitration and litigation.
99. *Supra* n. 78, [80].
100. In this regard, *see* my comments in the conclusion on the status of overlapping references in regard to the test for apparent bias.

CHAPTER 11

The View from U.S. Courts on Conflicts of Interest

Laurence Shore & Federico Alberto Cabona

1. THE THRESHOLD FOR INDEPENDENCE AND IMPARTIALITY

Unlike many modern national arbitration acts, the U.S. Federal Arbitration Act ("FAA") deals exclusively with the issue of arbitrators' (lack of) impartiality and independence as a ground for the annulment of awards. Section 10(a)(2) FAA enables competent district courts to vacate an award "where there was evident partiality or corruption in the arbitrators."

There is no U.S. federal law defining independence or impartiality or requiring a statement of independence or impartiality by an arbitrator upon acceptance of an appointment. Moreover, there is no federal law entitling a party to challenge an arbitrator for perceived bias while the arbitration is ongoing. Domestic courts may not, as a general matter, interfere with the conduct of arbitral proceedings on alleged partiality grounds.[1] As a result, absent a statutory "interlocutory challenge" procedure,[2] case law has usually arisen from vacatur (or recognition) proceedings after a losing party's unsuccessful attempt to disqualify an arbitrator based on disclosed circumstances during the arbitration or the discovery of undisclosed information after the award has been rendered.

Thus, it must be appreciated that in international cases, where the FAA governs, disqualification of an arbitrator for failing to meet the standards of independence/impartiality means the setting aside of the award, not merely replacing the arbitrator. Coupled with the stringent textual language of "evident" partiality and

1. *Aviall, Inc. v. Ryder Sys.*, 110 F.3d 892 (2nd Cir. 1997).
2. Of course, this does not preclude a party from resorting to challenge procedures provided by the applicable arbitration rules.

the inconclusive guidance from the U.S. Supreme Court (*see* below), this has inevitably affected the requisite degree of bias for a motion alleging lack of independence or impartiality to be successful, and the general understanding of the threshold for independence and impartiality. In particular, this context has given leeway to Federal circuit courts to take different views on the threshold, with the Fifth, Seventh, and Tenth Circuits requiring proof of actual bias as the test for "evident partiality"—a remarkably high standard.

To date, the only Supreme Court case on the meaning of "evident partiality" is the 1968 *Commonwealth Coatings* judgment.[3] The Court vacated an award on the ground of evident partiality under FAA Section 10(a)(2) because the tribunal chair had failed to disclose that a party had been a regular customer of his engineering consulting business. It is disputed whether *Commonwealth Coatings* was a majority opinion (meaning that the reasoning and result were accepted) or a plurality opinion (meaning that there was no majority for the reasoning, just the result). Justice Black authored the opinion for the Court, Justice White authored a concurring opinion, and Justice Fortas delivered a dissent. As the Fourth Circuit subsequently commented, the only certain guidance that can be effectively derived from *Commonwealth Coatings* is that expressed by the parts where the Black and White opinions coincide.[4] Crucially, however, the two differ significantly on the threshold for evident partiality.

Justice Black stated that although arbitrators cannot be expected to sever all ties with the business world, a court should be "even more scrupulous to safeguard the impartiality of arbitrators than judges, since the former have completely free rein to decide the law as well as the facts and are not subject to appellate review."[5] Writing for the Court, he found that for an award not to survive an "evident partiality" challenge, arbitrators "not only must be unbiased but also must avoid even the appearance of bias."[6] Accordingly, arbitrators are expected to disclose any past and present dealings that "might create an impression of possible bias."[7]

On the other hand, Justice White reasoned that the effectiveness of arbitration rests, *inter alia*, on the fact that the adjudicators are "men of affairs, not apart from but of the marketplace."[8] As a consequence, arbitrators cannot be bound by the strict requirements of impartiality of judges. An arbitrator that has entertained a business relationship with a party should not be automatically disqualified if (a) both parties are aware of it or (b) the relationship is trivial.[9] Thus, an arbitrator may not be held to disclose "his complete and unexpurgated business biography," but only instances where he has a "substantial interest in a firm which has done more than trivial business" with a party. "Appearance of bias" therefore is not within the scope of the

3. *Commonwealth Coatings Corp. v. Continental Casualty Co. et al.*, 393 US 145 (1968) (Appendix I).
4. *ANR Coal Co., Inc. v. Cogentrix of N.C., Inc.*, 173 F.3d 493 (4th Cir. 1999).
5. *Commonwealth Coatings Corp. v. Continental Casualty Co. et al.*, 393 US 145, 148-149 (1968) (Appendix I).
6. *Id.*, 150.
7. *Id.*, 149.
8. *Id.*, 150.
9. *Id.*

arbitrator's disclosure obligation. White agreed with Black on the outcome in the particular case, but little else.

The Fortas dissent has received little attention from most scholarly commentators, but he took a middle ground between Black and White while disagreeing in the outcome. According to Fortas, it was not:

> either necessary, appropriate, or permissible to rule, as the Court does, that, regardless of the facts, innocent failure to volunteer information constitutes the "evident partiality" necessary under § 10(b) of the Arbitration Act to set aside an award. "Evident partiality" means what it says: conduct—or at least an attitude or disposition—by the arbitrator favoring one party rather than the other. This case demonstrates that to rule otherwise may be a palpable injustice, since all agree that the arbitrator was innocent of either "evident partiality" or anything approaching it.

Fortas comes close to a modern "justifiable doubts" standard.

The Supreme Court has yet to settle on the applicable standard. Consequently, as noted above, the circuits have taken different approaches. The Eighth[10] and Ninth[11] Circuits have effectively adopted the "appearance or impression of bias" approach advocated by Justice Black. This approach risks placing a disproportionate burden of disclosure upon arbitrators and relative ease of demonstrating "evident partiality" upon a party challenging for bias. This threshold is difficult to reconcile with the FAA text, which, by demanding *evident* partiality, points to a greater burden on the party that challenges for bias.

The Fifth,[12] Seventh,[13] Tenth,[14] Eleventh[15] and D.C.[16] Circuits have instead seemingly embraced Justice White's "actual bias" approach. The downside of this alternative is that it requires the petitioner to adduce clear evidence of an arbitrator's state of mind. Combined with the unavailability of interlocutory challenges, this makes a challenge for bias extremely difficult—an "insurmountable standard," according to the Second Circuit in *Morelite* (*see infra* n. 18).

10. *Montez v. Prudential Sec., Inc.*, 260 F.3d 980 (8th Cir. 2001); *Olson v. Merrill Lynch, Pierce, Fenner & Smith, Inc.*, 51 F.3d 157 (8th Cir. 1995).
11. *Monster Energy Company v. City Beverages, Llc*, 940 F.3d 1130 (9th Cir. 2019), cert. denied, No. 19-1333 (U.S. June 29, 2020) (Appendix V); *New Regency v. Nippon Herald Films*, 501 F.3d 1101 (9th Cir. 2007); *Schmitz v. Zilveti*, 20 F.3d 1043 (9th Cir. 1994).
12. *Positive Software Solutions Inc., v. New Century Mortgage Corporation*, 476 F.3d 278 (5th Cir. 2007) (Appendix II).
13. *Sphere Drake Insurance Limited v. All American Life Insurance Company*, Seventh Circuit, 307 F.3d 617 (7th Cir. 2002).
14. *Ormsbee Dev. Co. v. Grace*, 668 F.2d 1140 (10th Cir. 1982).
15. *Javier Aviles v. Charles Schwab & Co., Inc.*, 435 F. App'x 824 (11th Cir. 2011).
16. *Al-Harbi v. Citibank*, N.A., 85 F.3d 680 (D.C. Cir. 1996).

The First,[17] Second,[18] Third,[19] Fourth[20] and Sixth[21] Circuits have opted for an "objective, disinterested person" or "justifiable doubts" standard. This standard is also the one advocated by the 2019 American Law Institute's Restatement of the U.S. Law of International Commercial and Investor-State Arbitration ("Restatement"), an authoritative academic commentary on U.S. law. Section 4(18)(b) of the Restatement provides as follows:

> A showing of evident partiality requires proof that would cause an objective, disinterested observer who is fully informed of the relevant facts relating to the arbitrator's conduct or alleged conflicts of interest to have a serious doubt regarding the fundamental fairness of the arbitral proceedings.[22]

According to the Restatement approach, proof of actual partiality is not necessary, but a mere impression of bias is insufficient. What is demanded is that the fairness of the proceedings be put in "serious doubt." In addition, such doubt is to be weighed from the perspective of a fully informed but entirely disinterested reasonable person. This assessment is to be performed on a case-by-case basis, and as the Fourth Circuit and the Restatement point out, courts generally consider issues such as the extent or nature of the relationship or personal interest; its directness; the proximity in time with the arbitration; relevant industry practices; and the extent to which the arbitrator investigated potential conflicts.[23]

Although the question of how much partiality must be demonstrated has predominantly involved FAA Section 10(a)(2) petitions, the issue has recently arisen in another context, in an arbitration involving Mr. Shawn Carter, better known as Jay-Z. When a trademark infringement dispute was referred to New York-seated arbitration administered by the American Arbitration Association ("AAA"), Mr. Carter was presented with a list of 200 arbitrators from the AAA roster to choose from, only one of whom was an African-American. Mr. Carter argued that such an underrepresentation reflected racial bias and constituted, *inter alia*, a violation of the equal protection clause in the New York Constitution, thereby rendering the arbitration agreement void for violation of public policy. On these grounds, he obtained from the New York State Supreme Court a temporary stay of the arbitral proceedings, pending the presentation by the AAA of a more diverse list of neutrals. Although the case was later settled, it shows how impartiality concerns may affect arbitral proceedings even outside Section 10(a)(2).

---

17. *JCI Communications, Inc., D/B/A Netversant–New England, v. International Brotherhood of Electrical Workers*, Local 103, 324 F.3d 42 (1st Cir. 2003).
18. *Ometto v. Abengoa Bioeneregia Agricola Ltda.*, 549 Fed. Appx. 41 (2nd Cir. 2014) (Appendix IV); *Applied Industrial Materials Corp. v. Ovalar Makine Ticaret Ve Sanayi, A.S. and Ural Ataman*, 492 F.3d 132 (2nd Cir. 2007) (Appendix III); *Morelite Construction Corp v. New York City District Council Carpenters Benefit Funds*, 748 F.2d 79 (2nd Cir. 1984).
19. *Bapu Corp. v. Choice Hotels Int'l, Inc.*, 371 F. Appx. 306 (3rd Cir. 2012).
20. *ANR Coal Co., Inc. v. Cogentrix of N.C., Inc.*, 173 F.3d 493 (4th Cir. 1999).
21. *Uhl v. Komatsu Forklift Co.*, 512 F.3d 294 (6th Cir. 2007).
22. This rule appears to be modeled after the one formulated in the Second Circuit's 1984 *Morelite* decision, in which the evident partiality requirement is met "where a reasonable person would have to conclude that an arbitrator was partial to one party" (*see supra* n. 18).
23. *ANR Coal Co., Inc. v. Cogentrix of N.C., Inc.*, 173 F.3d 493 (4th Cir. 1999).

2. IS THERE A SPECIFIC THRESHOLD FOR DISCLOSURE?

The case law on the threshold(s) for disclosure is tied to the threshold for evident partiality. As discussed above, this is due to the statutory framework, in which the law concerns challenges of arbitrators in the context of awards that have already been rendered.

Although the FAA is silent on the issue of disclosure, both the Black and White opinions in *Commonwealth Coatings* are based on the assumption that arbitrators are held to disclose all circumstances that might be relevant to an annulment on partiality grounds. However, *what* these circumstances are depends on the impartiality (or evident partiality) threshold. According to Justice Black, the duty to disclose covers all past and present dealings that "might create an impression of possible bias." Not doing so creates a presumption against impartiality that could prove difficult to overcome. Thus, the thresholds for disclosure and vacatur for "evident partiality" tend to coincide, as nondisclosure of a known or willfully not investigated relationship indicates the appearance of partiality.[24]

Justice White, however, maintained that the disclosure obligation was limited to instances where the arbitrator has a "substantial interest in a firm which has done more than trivial business" with a party. Under this approach, the threshold for disclosure is higher, and nondisclosure will not necessarily be disqualifying (i.e., lead to vacatur).

As noted above, Justice Fortas held that the Black approach would lead to the annulment of all awards rendered in case of nondisclosure, regardless of whether the arbitrator was effectively trying to conceal information or innocently ignoring circumstances perceived as irrelevant.[25] Nondisclosure, therefore, becomes an element to assess whether a biased inclination exists, but it cannot alone constitute an *evident* lack of partiality.

The Circuit split on the meaning of "evident partiality" is paralleled by the standard for disclosure.[26] Thus, there is no "one-size-fits-all" disclosure rule in the U.S. Soft law instruments, discussed in the following Section, have also provided some guidance for the courts.

A brief comparison of the following precedents illustrates the wide rift between the Federal circuits' consideration of disclosure obligations.

In *Sphere Drake*,[27] the Seventh Circuit, which adheres to the actual bias approach, reviewed an award rendered by the tribunal majority. The majority included an arbitrator who had not disclosed the full extent of his past relationship with the

24. In *Positive Software Solutions*, the Fifth Circuit stated that "the 'mere appearance' standard would make it easier for a losing party to challenge an arbitration award for nondisclosure than for actual bias" (*see supra* n. 12).
25. In *Commonwealth Coatings*, the award was unanimous, and the petitioner had made no claim of actual bias on the part of the chair, which led Fortas to label the case "singularly inappropriate" to state the rule that the Court was aiming to state.
26. Victoria R. Orlowski, *FAA Section 10 Applications to Vacate an Award (Including "Manifest Disregard")*, in INTERNATIONAL ARBITRATION IN THE UNITED STATES, 517 (Kluwer Law International, L. Shore et al. eds., 2017).
27. *Sphere Drake Insurance Limited v. All American Life Insurance Company*, 307 F.3d 617 (7th Cir. 2002).

party that had appointed him—a 380-billable hour service as counsel given four years prior to a Bermuda subsidiary. The Court of Appeals reversed the District Court and confirmed the award. It held that disclosure is not "compulsory for its own sake," nor is it fatal in case the arbitrator meets the standard of impartiality that is requested of him/her, i.e., absence of evident partiality. This standard, the Court stated, is lower for arbitrators to meet than for judges, and lower still for party-appointed arbitrators in comparison with tribunal-presiding "neutrals."

On the opposite side of the spectrum, in *Monster Energy Company v. City Beverages*,[28] the Ninth Circuit found evident partiality of the sole arbitrator under FAA Section 10(a)(2), based on his nondisclosure of circumstances capable of generating a "reasonable impression of bias." The arbitrator had omitted to disclose his actual ownership interest in JAMS, the institution under which the arbitration was conducted. In the previous five years, JAMS had already administered ninety-seven arbitral proceedings involving one of the parties. Although holding such an interest was common to a third of JAMS arbitrators and, according to JAMS' testimony, had never resulted in dividends exceeding 0.1% of the institution's annual revenues, this was sufficient, according to the Ninth Circuit, to vacate the award.

The *AIMCOR* decision[29] offers an example of the middle-ground solution. The Second Circuit confirmed the District Court's vacatur on the ground that the arbitrator had failed to investigate and disclose the potential conflicts of interest between his company and one party's parent company. When the arbitrator became aware of the potential business ties between the two, he deliberately chose to be left uninformed of the details of the relationship and established an ethical wall—but he failed to inform the parties of the wall. The Court reasoned that "a reasonable person, looking at an arbitrator's decision not to investigate and his concomitant failure to inform the parties of the 'Chinese Wall' would conclude that evident partiality existed."[30] (There is little doubt that such behavior would *not* have constituted evident partiality under the actual bias approach.)

For an example of the application of the "reasonable person" standard leading to the opposite result, there is the *Abengoa* case.[31] Here, the Second Circuit found that the presiding arbitrator's failure to disclose, due to unawareness, a potential conflict was not sufficient to meet the "evident partiality" requirement. The arbitrator, a partner of Debevoise & Plimpton, had not disclosed that his Debevoise colleagues were providing legal advice to clients involved in several corporate transactions in which the Respondent was the counterparty. The Court reasoned that the arbitrator did not know of the conflict, but also that he "had no reason to believe that a nontrivial conflict might exist, and thus had no further duty to investigate."[32] Thus, to the extent there was administrative carelessness in conducting the conflict check, it did not amount to

28. *Monster Energy Company v. City Beverages, Llc*, 940 F.3d 1130 (9th Cir. 2019), cert. denied, No. 19-1333 (U.S. June 29, 2020) (Appendix V).
29. Applied Industrial Materials, 492 F.3d 132 (2nd Cir. 2007) (Appendix III).
30. *Id.*
31. *Ometto v. Abengoa Bioeneregia Agricola Ltda.*, 549 F. App'x. 41 (2nd Cir. 2014) (Appendix IV).
32. *Id.*, 42.

"willful blindness"[33] and, therefore, there was no basis for asserting that a reasonable person would have concluded that the chair was partial. Had the court decided to adopt the "impression of bias" approach, the same nondisclosure probably would have led to vacatur.

3. WHAT IS THE RELEVANCE OF THE IBA GUIDELINES ON CONFLICTS OF INTEREST IN INTERNATIONAL ARBITRATION ("IBA GUIDELINES") AND OTHER PRIVATE INSTRUMENTS?

Given the terseness of the FAA and the conflicting guidance of case law (e.g., the Second, Fifth, and Ninth Circuits' different approaches to "evident partiality"), soft law sources are often referred to by courts. Occasionally, those sources are made applicable by agreement of the parties. The IBA Guidelines are among them. Another influential instrument is the AAA/ABA Code of Ethics for Arbitrators in Commercial Disputes.

By way of example, in *New Regency Productions v. Nippon Herald Films*,[34] the Ninth Circuit made an express reference to the IBA Guidelines and, in particular, to General Standard 7(c)[35] when assessing the question of evident partiality of one of the arbitrators. In vacating the award, the Court held:

> [A]lthough these sources are not binding authority and do not have the force of law, when considered along with an attorney's traditional duty to avoid conflicts of interest, they reinforce our holding ... that "a reasonable impression of partiality can form when an actual conflict of interest exists and the lawyer has constructive knowledge of it". That the lawyer forgot to run a conflict check ... is not an excuse.[36]

Justice Hugo Black also referred to soft law in his famous *Commonwealth Coatings* opinion. He quoted the then applicable edition of the AAA Arbitration Rules (whereby an appointee must "disclose any circumstances likely to create a presumption of bias or which he believes might disqualify him as an impartial Arbitrator"), as well as the Canons of Judicial Ethics (whereby a judge should "avoid such action as may reasonably tend to awaken the suspicion that his social or business relations or friendships, constitute an element in influencing his judicial conduct") to support his conclusions.

However, codes of conduct remain nonbinding instruments, and their application by courts is unpredictable. The Fifth Circuit's reversal of itself regarding the standard for disclosure underscores the inconsistency. In its decision of January 11, 2006 in *Positive Software Solutions*,[37] the Fifth Circuit confirmed the District Court's vacatur decision on the ground of evident partiality of the sole arbitrator, holding that

33. *Id.*
34. *New Regency v. Nippon Herald Films*, 501 F.3d 1101 (9th Cir. 2007).
35. Pursuant to General Standard 7(c), "a party shall perform reasonable enquiries and provide any relevant information available to it."
36. *New Regency v. Nippon Herald Films*, 501 F.3d 1101, 1110 (9th Cir. 2007).
37. *Positive Software Solutions Inc., v. New Century Mortgage Corporation*, 436 F.3d 495 (5th Cir. 2006).

the nondisclosure of his prior relationship with the counsel in the case "created a reasonable impression of possible partiality."[38] This standard corresponded to Canon I of the AAA/ABA Code, which provides that evident partiality may be established in case of failure to disclose facts that might create a reasonable appearance of partiality.[39] However, by a decision of January 18, 2007, on rehearing *en banc*, the Fifth Circuit reversed itself and applied a strictly textual interpretation of FAA Section 10(a)(2).[40] The Court reasoned that "evident partiality" must be read as manifest, obvious and apparent bias and confirmed the award.[41]

The history of U.S. domestic arbitration includes a party's expectation that the arbitrator it appoints in a three-member tribunal would be its advocate, effectively endorsing/arguing its case against the opposing party's appointee, before the chair—the latter being characterized as the "neutral."[42] This expectation spilled over into international arbitrations seated in the U.S. However, by the early 1990s, that expectation had clearly changed, certainly in relation to international arbitration. The amendments implemented in the 1997 AAA International Arbitration Rules, 2003 AAA Commercial Arbitration Rules, and 2004 AAA/ABA Code of Ethics for Arbitrators in Commercial Disputes solidified the position that all tribunal members, not only the chair, must be impartial and independent. As such, they should all be subject to demanding disclosure requirements. Moreover, the overarching presumption in U.S. domestic arbitration similarly became that all arbitrators are neutrals (unless the parties expressly opt out of neutrality for party-appointed arbitrators).[43]

4. IS THERE A DUTY OF PARTIES TO INVESTIGATE?

U.S. courts have repeatedly held that the duty to investigate and disclose possible conflicts is a duty incumbent upon arbitrators *and* parties. Claims for vacatur of awards have been denied on the ground that the parties had a reasonable duty to investigate potential conflicts at an earlier stage and failed to do so.

In *Kiernan v. Piper Jaffray Cos.*,[44] the Fifth Circuit held that:

> While [the appellants] did not have full knowledge of all the relationships to which they now object, they did have concerns about [the arbitrator's] impartiality and yet chose to have her remain on the panel rather than spend time and money investigating further until losing the arbitration.[45]

38. *Id.*, 498.
39. *Id.*, 502.
40. *Positive Software Solutions Inc., v. New Century Mortgage Corporation*, 476 F.3d 278 (5th Cir. 2007).
41. *Id.*, 281.
42. *Sphere Drake Ins. Ltd v. All Am. Life Ins.*, 307 F.3d 617 (7th Cir. 2002), observing that "the main party-appointed arbitrators are supposed to be advocates."
43. Notably, Section R-18(b) of the 2013 AAA Commercial Arbitration Rules still allows parties to agree that arbitrators directly appointed by them "shall be non-neutral, in which case such arbitrators need not be impartial or independent and shall not be subject to disqualification for partiality or lack of independence."
44. *Kiernan v. Piper Jaffray Cos., Inc.*, 137 F.3d 588 (8th Cir. 1998).
45. *Id.*, 593.

The failure of the parties to investigate the arbitrator's potential conflict prevented them from later prevailing on a claim of "evident partiality," and the award was upheld.

The same reasoning was followed in *Dealer Computer Services, Inc. v. Michael Motor Company, Inc.*[46] The District Court had recognized that the losing party's failure to timely object to an arbitrator's appointment entails the waiver of the right to later challenge the arbitrator. Nonetheless, it had vacated the award on the ground that it would be "paradoxical" for a party to be deprived of its right to challenge the arbitrator because unaware of a conflict of interests that was the arbitrator's duty to disclose. On appeal, the Fifth Circuit reversed, holding that the arbitrator had disclosed sufficient elements to "put [the petitioner] on notice of a potential conflict."[47] Accordingly, it concluded that it was not the arbitrator that had not disclosed his conflict of interests, but rather the party that had not thoroughly fulfilled its duty to investigate the arbitrator's potential conflicts.

In *Lagstein*,[48] even the Ninth Circuit, generally a proponent of the "appearance of bias" doctrine, refused to annul an award rendered by an arbitrator who had not disclosed his and a fellow panel member's role in a past dispute, the details of which were publicly available. The court declined to "create a rule that encourages losing parties to challenge arbitration awards on the basis of pre-existing, publicly available background information on the arbitrators that has nothing to do with the parties to the arbitration."[49]

5. HOW SUCCESSFUL ARE CHALLENGES IN COURT AND ON WHAT GROUNDS?

According to a study published in 2005 that analyzed every decision reported in U.S. state and federal courts (either published or unpublished) between January 1, 2004 and October 31, 2004,[50] out of 182 challenges of awards, only 33 argued "evident partiality" (FAA Section 10(a)(2)). Of these 33 challenges, only 4 were successful—a 12.1% rate.[51] Evident partiality was the third most frequently used ground for challenge, behind manifest disregard of the law and misbehavior, but before refusal of evidence, fraud/corruption and refused postponement.

As discussed above, the chances of success of a challenge under Section 10(a)(2) are affected by the Circuit where it is brought, since the appellate courts have embraced different thresholds for unacceptable "bias." Indeed, the burden of proof carried by the petitioner may vary significantly from one Circuit to another.

46. *Dealer Computer Services, Inc. v. Michael Motor Company, Inc.*, No. 11-20053 (5th Cir. 2012).
47. *Id.*, 6.
48. *Lagstein, M.D. v. Certain Underwriters at Lloyd's, London*, 607 F.3d 634 (9th Cir. 2010).
49. *Id.*, 646.
50. Lawrence R. Mills et al., *Vacating Arbitration Awards: A Real-World View of the Case Law*, in Dispute Resolution Magazine, 23 (2015).
51. Baroness Gillian Sheppard, Jr, Stephen K. Huber, *AAA Yearbook on Arbitration and the Law—24th Edition*, 473-474, JurisNet LLC (2012).

APPENDIX I: *COMMONWEALTH COATINGS CORP. V. CONTINENTAL CASUALTY CO. ET AL.*: U.S. SUPREME COURT[52]

The U.S. Supreme Court, on November 18, 1968, vacated a final arbitration award between Commonwealth Coatings and Continental Casualty on the ground of evident partiality of the tribunal chair, pursuant to Section 10(a)(2) of the Federal Arbitration Act.

The original dispute arose out of an agreement between a subcontractor and prime contractor concerning a painting job. The subcontractor commenced arbitration. Each party nominated one arbitrator, and the co-arbitrators jointly nominated the chair. The latter, however, had a large engineering consulting business in Puerto Rico, and he had "repeated and significant"[53] business dealings with the prime contractor, involving fees of USD 12,000 within four or five years. Neither the arbitrator nor the prime contractor revealed this commercial relationship to the petitioner. Only after the tribunal issued the final award in favor of Continental Casualty did the petitioner become aware of the relationship.

Commonwealth applied to the U.S. District Court to set aside the award. The Court denied the petition. The petitioner then appealed, and the First Circuit affirmed. The Supreme Court granted certiorari.

Justice Black (there is controversy whether it is a majority or plurality opinion) reversed. Since neither the arbitrator nor the prime contractor had given "an intimation of the close financial relationship,"[54] this amounted to "a manifest violation of the strict morality and fairness Congress would have expected on the part of the arbitrator,"[55] The impartiality of arbitrators should be safeguarded even more than that of judges, since arbitrators have "completely free rein to decide the law as well as the facts and are not subject to appellate review."[56] Justice Black concluded that an arbitral tribunal must avoid any "appearance of bias."[57]

Justice White, though agreeing with Justice Black's result, stated that arbitrators cannot be held to the same impartiality standards as judges. This is because arbitrators are men of business affairs, often tied to specific markets, and the mere fact of having business relationship should not be sufficient to disqualify arbitrators. However, the parties should be informed when an arbitrator has a substantial interest in a firm that has done more than trivial business with a party; alternatively, the parties can remain unaware in case the relationship is trivial.

In dissent, Justice Fortas argued that the arbitrator's only fault was an "innocent failure to volunteer information."[58] Apart from this, the tribunal had acted fairly and impartially, and reached a proper determination of the facts before it. In his opinion, Justice Fortas denied that such failure to volunteer constitutes "evident partiality":

52. *Commonwealth Coatings Corp. v. Continental Casualty Co. et al.*, 393 US 145 (1968).
53. *Id.*, 146.
54. *Id.*, 148.
55. *Id.*
56. *Id.*, 149.
57. *Id.*, 150.
58. *Id.*, 152.

> I agree that failure of an arbitrator to volunteer information about business dealings with one party will, prima facie, support a claim of partiality or bias. But where there is no suggestion that the nondisclosure was calculated, and where the complaining party disclaims any imputation of partiality, bias, or misconduct, the presumption clearly is overcome.
>
> I do not believe that it is either necessary, appropriate, or permissible to rule, as the Court does, that, regardless of the facts, innocent failure to volunteer information constitutes the "evident partiality" necessary under § 10(b) of the Arbitration Act to set aside an award. "Evident partiality" means what it says: conduct—or at least an attitude or disposition—by the arbitrator favoring one party rather than the other. This case demonstrates that to rule otherwise may be a palpable injustice, since all agree that the arbitrator was innocent of either "evident partiality" or anything approaching it.

APPENDIX II: *POSITIVE SOFTWARE SOLUTIONS, INC. V. NEW CENTURY MORTGAGE CORPORATION*: U.S. COURT OF APPEALS FOR THE FIFTH CIRCUIT[59]

On January 11, 2006, the Fifth Circuit affirmed the holding of the District Court for the Northern District of Texas, which granted Positive Software's motion to vacate the award on the ground of evident partiality of the sole arbitrator, under Section 10(a)(2) of the FAA.

The original dispute arose out of a licensing agreement, in relation to which Positive Software claimed copyright infringement, theft of trade secrets and breach of contract.

The dispute was arbitrated under the AAA Rules. The sole arbitrator, Peter J. Shurn, III, found against Positive Software, concluding that New Century had neither infringed the copyright nor misappropriated trade secrets nor breached the contract.

Positive Software applied to the District Court to vacate the award on the ground that, after thorough investigation, it had discovered that the arbitrator and his former law firm had been involved in a professional relationship with Respondent's counsel.

The District Court vacated the award for evident partiality under Section 10(a)(2) of the FAA on the basis that Shurn had failed to disclose this relationship, which had created a reasonable impression of possible bias, and the failure to disclose had prevented parties from making an informed choice.

New Century appealed and lost; the Fifth Circuit affirmed the District Court. The Court reasoned that the evident partiality standard is met when there is a reasonable impression of partiality, which in turn is demonstrated by nondisclosure independently of whether actual bias is established.

The Court added that a complete disclosure of the arbitrator's past and present relationships is necessary to ensure that the parties can make an informed choice of the arbitrators, to safeguard the integrity of the arbitral process, and to minimize the courts' intervention on reviewing arbitrators' potential conflicts. This standard, the

59. *Positive Software Solutions Inc. v. New Century Mortgage Corporation*, 436 F.3d 495 (5th Cir. 2006).

Court said, comported with Canon II of the AAA's Code of Ethics. In the present circumstances, Shurn's failure to disclose a potential conflict of interest created an impression of possible partiality to a reasonable person, and prevented Positive Software from making an informed choice. Positive Software had not waived its right to object, since such waiver would have required that Positive Software had actual knowledge of the arbitrator's partiality.

BUT –

Positive Software Solutions, Inc., v. New Century Mortgage Corporation: U.S. Court of Appeals for the Fifth Circuit, rehearing en banc[60]

On January 18, 2007, the Fifth Circuit, on rehearing *en banc*, reversed its decision of January 11, 2006, on the ground that the evident partiality standard under Section 10(a)(2) of the FAA does *not* mandate vacatur of the award for the sole reason of nondisclosure of trivial past relationships.

The Court stated that "partiality" shall be interpreted as "bias" and "evident" a synonym of manifest, obvious and apparent; therefore, evident partiality shall mean more than a mere impression or appearance of bias. In cases of nondisclosure, the standard of evident partiality is met only when there is a concrete, and not speculative, impression of bias.

Vacatur of an award on the sole ground of nondisclosure of a past trivial relationship between the arbitrator and a party, or the arbitrator and a counsel, would not only jeopardize the finality of arbitration, but also subject arbitrators to higher ethical standards than federal judges.

APPENDIX III: *APPLIED INDUSTRIAL MATERIALS CORP. V. OVALAR MAKINE TICARET TE SANAYI, A.S. AND URAL ATAMAN*: U.S. COURT OF APPEALS FOR THE SECOND CIRCUIT[61]

The Second Circuit affirmed the decision of the Southern District, which had vacated the award in *AIMCOR v. Ovalar* on the ground of evident partiality under Section 10(a)(2) of the FAA.

The dispute arose out of a joint venture contract entered into in 1992, under which AIMCOR would purchase and deliver petroleum coke to Ovalar, which would then distribute it in Turkey. In 1997, as disputes relating to profit distribution escalated, the parties commenced arbitration.

On September 3, 2003, before the start of the proceedings, the arbitrators were informed that AIMCOR was being sold to Oxbox Industries. Each arbitrator ran a conflict check. Mr. Fabrikant, chair of the panel and president of a company called

60. *Id.*, 476.
61. *Applied Industrial Materials Corp. v. Ovalar Makine Ticaret Ve Sanayi, A.S. and Ural Ataman*, 492 F.3d 132 (2nd Cir. 2007).

Seacor Holdings, asserted that he had "no personal or business relationship with any of the parties to this proceeding, or their affiliates."[62]

On September 22, 2005, the Tribunal decided the liability claim in favor of AIMCOR. Two months later, during the bifurcated quantum phase, Ovalar requested Mr. Fabrikant to resign; it had emerged that SFC, a division of Seacor Holding, had been doing business with Oxbox since 2004.

Mr. Fabrikant revealed that, as soon as he had become aware that SFC was starting business with Oxbox, he had informed SFC's president that he wished to raise a "Chinese wall" and therefore to be kept outside of any business carried out by the two companies.

In February 2006, AIMCOR sought to confirm the award, while Ovalar sought to vacate it on the grounds that the "Chinese wall" raised by the arbitrator was insufficient to avoid a claim for evident partiality under Section 10(a)(2) of the Federal Arbitration Act.

The District Court found in favor of Ovalar on the grounds that (i) the arbitration agreement contained disclosure requirements; (ii) Mr. Fabrikant himself had initially excluded any conflict of interest; and (iii) he had only revealed the existence of the conflict at issue after being challenged. All these elements raised the parties' expectation that the arbitrator would inform them of any contractual relationship between SFC and Oxbox.

In particular, the Court found that, by raising the "Chinese wall" but by failing to tell the parties he had done so, the chairman had created an appearance of partiality sufficient to vacate the award.

The Court also referred to the American Arbitration Code of Ethics and the IBA Guidelines on Conflicts of Interest in International Arbitration, according to which "there must be continuous obligation on the part of the arbitrator to avoid partiality or the appearance of partiality."

AIMCOR appealed the District Court's decision.

The Second Circuit explored the scope of the arbitrator's duty to investigate and disclose potential unknown conflicts of interest. It held that if an arbitrator "has reason to believe that a nontrivial conflict of interest might exist, he must (1) investigate the conflict or (2) disclose his reasons for believing there might be a conflict and his intention not to investigate."[63] The Court did not intend to create a free-standing duty to investigate on arbitrators, but rather to establish a duty to choose between investigating or informing of the intention not to investigate, in case of potential conflicts. The Court then proceeded to apply to the circumstances of the case the "reasonable person" test developed in *Morelite*, i.e., "whether a reasonable person, looking at an arbitrator's decision not to investigate and his concomitant failure to inform the parties of the 'Chinese Wall,' would conclude that evident partiality existed."[64]

62. *Id.*, 135.
63. *Id.*, 138.
64. *Id.*

Under this objective test, the Second Circuit found "evident partiality" and affirmed the District Court's decision to vacate the award.

APPENDIX IV: *OMETTO ET AL. V. ABENGOA BIOENERGIA AGRICOLA LTDA. ET AL.*: U.S. COURT OF APPEALS FOR THE SECOND CIRCUIT[65]

On January 7, 2014, the Second Circuit issued a non-precedential summary order by which it affirmed the finding of the Southern District of New York denying Ometto's petition to vacate the award entered against it.

Ometto entered into a sugar cane purchase agreement with Abengoa. When a dispute arose on grounds of alleged errors and omissions in the auditing and negotiation process preceding the sale, the parties began two New York-seated ICC arbitration proceedings. Both ensuing awards were issued in favor of Abengoa.

Both arbitral proceedings were conducted before a three-member tribunal chaired by a partner of Debevoise & Plimpton. Since he had failed to disclose that some of his colleagues were providing legal advice to clients in several unrelated corporate transactions in which Abengoa was involved, Ometto sought to vacate the awards on the ground of the chair's evident partiality.

The District Court denied Ometto's petition. It did so reasoning that not only was the chairman unaware of the existence of the conflict at the time he issued the awards, but he also did not have any reason to believe that a possible conflict might exist and therefore he had no duty of further investigation. In other words, any administrative carelessness in which the chair and his law firm had carried out their duty of investigation did not amount to "willful blindness."

On appeal, the Second Circuit, applying a "reasonable person" test, confirmed the District Court's finding. It held that the arbitrator's failure to investigate could at best qualify as carelessness, without rising to the level of willful blindness. Accordingly, a reasonable person would not have concluded, in these circumstances, that the chairman was partial to one side.

Notably, the above ruling did not deter the Brazilian Superior Court of Justice from later rejecting Abengoa's petition to recognize the awards rendered in its favor.[66] An 8-to-1-majority of Brazil's highest court for non-constitutional matters ruled that an arbitrator's failure to disclose information capable of casting a reasonable doubt as to his impartiality amounts to a violation of Brazilian constitutional due process guarantees and, as such, of Brazil's public policy. This justified the re-examination of the awards, irrespective of the court of the seat's decision not to vacate them.

65. *Ometto v. Abengoa Bioeneregia Agricola Ltda.*, 549 Fed. Appx. 41 (2nd Cir. 2014).
66. STJ—SEC: 9412 EX 2013/0278872-5, April 19, 2017, CE—Corte Especial.

APPENDIX V: *MONSTER ENERGY COMPANY V. CITY BEVERAGES LLC (OPERATING AS OLYMPIC EAGLE DISTRIBUTING)*: U.S. COURT OF APPEALS FOR THE NINTH CIRCUIT[67]

By a majority decision dated October 22, 2019, the Ninth Circuit vacated a JAMS award issued by a sole arbitrator because of his failure to disclose the full extent of his involvement with JAMS.

The underlying controversy arose from Monster Energy Company's exercise of its contractual right to early termination of a long-term distribution agreement with Olympic. In response, Olympic invoked a statutory prohibition against termination of franchise agreements without good cause. The dispute was submitted to a JAMS-administered arbitration.

Before being appointed, the sole arbitrator, a member of the JAMS panel of "neutrals," disclosed a *general* economic interest in the success of the institution. He later issued an award in favor of Monster. It later emerged that he (as many other JAMS arbitrators) owned a shareholding interest in the arbitral institution and, therefore, was entitled to part of its profits. It also emerged that, as Monster's form contracts included JAMS arbitration clauses, the company had been involved in ninety-seven JAMS arbitrations in the previous five years. In light of this, Olympic petitioned the District Court to have the award vacated for the arbitrator's evident partiality towards a repeat-client of an institution he had failed to disclose his true interest in.

The District Court's decision to confirm the award was overruled on appeal by the Ninth Circuit. The majority opinion, authored by Justice Smith, found that, as a JAMS shareholder, the arbitrator entertained a nontrivial business relationship with Monster. In the eyes of the Court, this implied a personal expectation that far exceeded a general interest in JAMS's reputation and prosperity. The failure to disclose such information created a "reasonable impression of bias," which led to the vacatur of the award on evident partiality grounds.

In her dissenting opinion, Judge Friedland stressed that arbitrators, be they affiliated with institutions or not, all share an incentive to find in favor of repeat clients, irrespective of their direct participation in the institution's profit. Regrettable as this may be, she noted, such is the structure of the arbitration industry. Thus, parties accepting to waive their right to trial in favor of arbitration also accept such repeat players' competitive advantage and should not be allowed to challenge awards on this basis.

Following this ruling, JAMS announced that a revision of its disclosure process was in the making.

In June 2020, the Supreme Court denied Monster's petition to have the Ninth Circuit's decision reviewed.[68]

In December 2020, Olympic, now facing the prospect of commencing new arbitral proceedings against Monster, petitioned a federal District Court to compel

67. *Monster Energy Company v. City Beverages, Llc*, 940 F.3d 1130 (9th Cir. 2019).
68. *Monster Energy Company v. City Beverages, Llc*, 940 F.3d 1130 (9th Cir. 2019), cert. denied, No. 19-1333 (U.S. June 29, 2020).

arbitration before an arbitral institution other than JAMS, arguing that the latter's amicus briefs filed with the Ninth Circuit and Supreme Court, which were aligned with Monster's position, raised reasonable doubts as to its impartiality. The case is ongoing.

APPENDIX VI: *SHAWN C. CARTER, S. CARTER ENTERPRISES, MARCH MEDIA, LLC V. ICONIX BRAND GROUP, INC. AND ICON DE HOLDINGS, LLC*: NEW YORK STATE SUPREME COURT

Shawn Carter, also known as Jay-Z, sold his Rocawear clothing brand to Iconix as part of a USD 200 million deal. After selling the brand, he started producing baseball merchandise using the trademark of Roc Nation, a company that he had recently funded. Following this event, Iconix started an arbitration proceeding against Jay-Z for trademark infringement, breach of contract and unjust enrichment.

The dispute was to be settled under the auspices of the American Arbitration Association in New York.

On November 28, 2018, Jay-Z requested and obtained from the New York State Supreme Court a temporary stay of the arbitration,[69] pending his claim to declare the arbitration agreement void for violation of public policy. When choosing the arbitrators among a list of more than 200 neutrals on the AAA's National Roster, Jay-Z noted that only one was an African-American. The absence of African-American arbitrators, in Jay-Z's submission, constituted an infringement of the Equal Protection Clause of the New York State Constitution, of the New York State Human Rights Law, of the New York State Civil Rights Law, and of the New York City Human Rights Law, with these violations rendering the arbitration clause invalid.

The AAA then provided a new list containing a number of African-American arbitrators among which to choose. Jay-Z therefore agreed to proceed with the arbitration, and withdrew the petition to vacate the arbitration clause.

The parties eventually settled their dispute.

69. AAA Case No. 01-18-0003-6487.

PANEL 4 The Debate: Is There Enough Uniformity? Not Enough? More Than Enough?

CHAPTER 12

Transcript Panel 4 – The Debate: Is There Enough Uniformity? Not Enough? More than Enough?

Charles Kaplan, Nathalie Voser, Paula Hodges QC, Álvaro López de Argumedo Piñeiro & Alexander Fessas

1. INTRODUCTION

Charles Kaplan: Uniformisation is our topic. You have heard throughout the day that there are a number of significantly different answers to the various questions posed in relation to arbitrator disclosure, arbitrator conflicts, standards of disclosure, and standards of disqualification.

At this session, we are going to look together at what those differences are and how and whether we should be reducing them or just simply learning to live with them. The first part is about looking at these issues of differences and whether they are positive or harmful or need to be reduced in relation to national rules and State jurisprudence. That will be Nathalie Voser and Paula Hodges.

Then, we will move on to the non-State sources, guidelines, and their differences. In particular, we have been talking today about the IBA Guidelines, so here to talk to us about the relationship between guidelines and harder rules such as institutional rules we have Álvaro Lópcz de Argumedo Pineiro, who is the guidelines guy to go to at the IBA. Then the ICC's Alexander Fessas will present an institutional view.

On the first part: Nathalie, what are the main differences you have spotted in the national approach to the problems we are dealing with? Are they a good thing or a bad thing?

2. DIFFERENCES BETWEEN LEGAL SYSTEMS

Nathalie Voser: When it comes to disclosure and conflict of interest, I basically discerned two main differences and a third area that is less of a difference.

The two main differences are: *first*, how do courts deal with the facts of non-disclosures per se. *Second*, the difference in the standard applied. With regard to the latter, I think here there are three subtopics which are very important because they are particularly relevant for us: (i) How did courts assess the fact that the arbitrator concerned knew or did not know about circumstances about which the parties are concerned and which give rise to a potential setting aside? (ii) the issue of the affiliates within a group of companies; and (iii) the issue of the partners in law firms. The *third* area of difference is the investigation duty. Here, I will be extremely short because we see things coming together from what we heard.

Are these differences good or bad? To take this point ahead, I think they are really bad. I will give you very few reasons why and then I will pass on to Paula to see whether we can do something about it or not.

The first issue and difference in approach is, as mentioned, the question of how courts deal with the non-disclosure per se.

Summarising what we heard so far: in England, something more than the pure fact of non-disclosure is necessary for a successful challenge, but we do not know what. In the US, you have three different streams, black, white and grey. In New York, particularly, Judge Rakoff in the famous *Ometto* decision[1] assessed the issue of whether or not knowledge was relevant, and he basically said that the arbitrator did not really know what was going on (at least there was no evidence to prove he did know). This was an important factor not to accept the challenge of the arbitrator and not to set aside the award. In France, it is a bit of a strange situation. You have the principles which seem clear that there is a subjective approach, but if you look at the two most recent decisions which have been mentioned before – including the Audi decision involving a well-known German arbitrator[2] – the fact that there was a non-disclosure was probably the key factor in the decision for setting aside, in particular, because the non-disclosure happened, as we heard, after the constitution of the arbitral tribunal. Finally, in Switzerland, as we heard from Diana, it is established case law that the non-disclosure, as such, is not sufficient to constitute impartiality and a lack of independence, so we also need more. I think, in Switzerland, it is pretty clear what the 'more' is; it is actually the lack of independence and neutrality, so what is required are circumstances that show a lack of independence.

The IBA had addressed this issue. The IBA Guidelines on Conflict of Interest say that a later challenge based on the fact that an arbitrator did not disclose such facts or circumstances should not automatically result in a non-appointment, later disqualification or a successful challenge to any award. Here we have the answer. I think this

1. *Ometto v. Abengoa Bioeneregia Agricola Ltda.*, 549 Fed. Appx. 41 (2nd Cir. 2014) (above, Shore/Cabona, Chapter 11, Appendix IV).
2. *Volkswagen (Audi)*, Cour de cassation, Case No. 18-15.756 of 3 October 2019; *see* Gouiffès, Chapter 9 above.

should still be what courts should also apply, but, as I said before, they do not necessarily do so.

A brief comment with regard to what we heard earlier, from the point of view of legal logic if the criteria for disclosure and the criteria for the challenge were the same, as Alex explained, you would not have this issue because whenever you do not disclose something, it is automatically also a reason for a successful challenge. In other words, the problem we have with the non-disclosure is created by the different levels: one for disclosure and one for a successful challenge.

The underlying rationale to accept non-disclosure per se as a reason for challenge is that if you do not accept non-disclosure as a reason for the successful challenge, then there is no sanction to non-disclosure. That is the real issue, and that is why courts are inclined to accept the fact of non-disclosure as a general loss of confidence in this person, which amounts to a lack of necessary impartiality.

On the other hand, does this lack of not having any sanction really justify the outcome? I think we could see in the French case that I mentioned, the case involving Volkswagen/Audi and the German arbitrator, how questionable this is: There, we had three years of arbitration, 2013 to 2016. We had two years of proceedings before the Paris Court of Appeal. We had one and a half years before the Court of Cassation. In total, we had six and a half years of arbitration proceedings to come to the result that the case had to finally be set aside. We heard this morning from Jan-Michael Ahrens that this is what he called a 'disaster for a company'. I agree that such an outcome is a disaster. It is, in particular, a disaster because the parties who chose France as the seat could not expect an outcome like this one.

The second difference concerns the different standards as such from a substantive point of view. Earlier I posed the question – whether knowledge of the circumstances is relevant or not? Again, we see really different outcomes in the jurisdictions that were discussed. In the US *Ometto* case, Judge Rakoff said that lack of knowledge is an important factor of not assuming a conflict of interest. Similarly, the Swiss Supreme Court in the famous CMS decision[3] also gave quite a lot of weight to the subjective element of the lack of independence and said because the arbitrator did not know, i.e., was not aware of the circumstances, at least subjectively, he was still impartial and independent. Also, in the French case, it was undisputed that the arbitrator did not know about the circumstances. This was not considered by the court as an element in favour of not accepting this as a conflict, rather the pure objective elements that the law firm, within a certain period that the arbitration was going on, had been instructed by a subsidiary or an affiliate was sufficient to accept a conflict of interest. This shows that we have very different approaches to the question of whether or not the knowledge of the arbitrator is relevant.

Let us turn to the conflict standard regarding affiliates. Again, we can go back to some of the cases that we have heard. There is one more in Switzerland, which is a very important one, which is the so-called Nespresso decision.[4] It was not decided in the context of an arbitration, but the patent court in St Gallen referred to the case law and

3. DFSC 142 III 521 of 7 September 2016, *see* Akikol, Chapter 7 above.
4. DSC 139 III 433 dated 27 August 2013.

the literature in arbitration. This was about the well-known Nespresso capsules, and it involved a daughter company of the Migros Genossenschafts-Bund. One of the judges in St Gallen was also a partner of a law firm, and the law firm advised a sister company of one of the Migros daughter. The Supreme Court made a very careful analysis of whether this was sufficient or not, and in this case, it says, yes, it constitutes a conflict. Why? Because, in essence, the whole group, and in particular the mother company, was interested in the outcome because it concerned a very important patent right of the group.

By contrast, coming back to the French decision in the Audi case, there, we had a Middle Eastern company of the Volkswagen Group and the Austrian Porsche, a sister company. There is no discussion in the case of the Court of Appeal why the fact that the law firm, during a certain point of time, advised the Austrian sister should have any impact on the other party, which was a party to the arbitration. I think, from an objective standpoint, work for an affiliate of the law firm of the arbitrator needs to have a real impact on the parties in the arbitration in order to constitute a conflict.

Regarding the last sub-issue concerning different standards and members of the law firms, I want to start again with the Paris Court of Appeal example. The arbitrator was a partner of the law firm. It was not discussed whether or not another partner's activity had an impact on him. I want to contrast this with the famous CMS case in Switzerland where the Supreme Court said that because there was no income sharing between the arbitrator as a partner of CMS in Zurich and the German CMS, it was not a conflict. You can say CMS 'has the cake and eats it'. They are one brand, but in terms of conflict, appearing under one brand is not automatically considered a conflict. I think that exactly shows the point, the point being that it requires certain circumstances – other than just the fact that there is this connection of another law firm partner – that might influence the arbitrator to come to a decision rather than the other, which is not connected to the merits.

Let me skip the third issue mentioned at the outset, i.e., the duty to investigate. Here, besides the fact that when the duty ends, we have now more convergence.

By way of conclusion: as I already mentioned, from my point of view, a substantial difference in approaches by Courts is not good for arbitration. Arbitration is a global business and what parties do not like is unexpected outcomes. Where we stand today is that we have so many unexpected and unforeseeable outcomes when it comes to challenges of awards because of allegedly conflicted arbitrators not only in setting aside proceedings but also when it comes to the recognition of awards.

Yes, there is something that should be done.

Paula Hodges: You understood from Nathalie's presentation that she is very much in favour of uniformity. I do not think she has actually given us the solution for how you go about it, and that is actually a very difficult outcome to achieve. I am very much in favour of consistency when it comes to conflicts of interest and duties of disclosure. When you think the reason that parties turn to arbitration is that they want a neutral, fair hearing from arbitrators that they choose, and they have to have confidence in the system. They have to have faith that they are going to get a fair result.

I think it is incumbent on the arbitrators to realise that and to be very open and candid with the parties in order to wear that badge of impartiality that the English Court of Appeal referred to; but is it realistic to get all the various jurisdictions that are involved in arbitration – if you think, there are over 140, close to 150, parties to the New York Convention – to actually buy into a formal mandatory set of rules about this?

I absolutely think that the IBA Guidelines serve a very important purpose. Our courts in England and other courts refer to them, but it will be difficult to force courts to abide by them wholly. Some courts even apply criminal sanctions. For some time, the UAE included arbitrators in that criminal sanction if they did not act fairly.[5] If you want to unify all these things, I do not think it is possible. Also, I think you always have to look at the facts of the particular situation. I told you about the two cases earlier, which looked at paragraph 1.4 of the Guidelines,[6] non-waivable issues, where the courts reached very different conclusions based on the specific facts and how much the arbitrator was actually deriving benefit from the link between his law firm and the party.

There is another case in the UK called the ASM case, and this is a challenge to an award where the losing party had subsequently discovered that the arbitrator had been the counsel in a previous case where the losing party's principal witness had been involved as a witness again, and a very serious allegation of impropriety had been made against the witness.[7] The basis of the challenge was that the arbitrator knew about this, so would have had suspicions about the credibility of the principal witness, but failed to disclose this, and the English court set the award aside. It referred to the IBA Guidelines, but there was nothing that came close to this issue in the Guidelines. It said, 'In any event, we are not bound by that, and in this case, we are going to set aside.'

Charles Kaplan: Was it not the real reason, and it is a substantive reason, the court felt in that particular case that the arbitrator might have a pre-conditioned view of the witness and, therefore, the arbitrator was not impartial no matter what the guideline says?

Paula Hodges: We are now talking about unconscious basis. It is very difficult to legislate for that in advance. We can go to a certain degree, and that is why I think the Guidelines are an excellent starting point, but I think it is very difficult to cover every possible angle along the way.

Charles Kaplan: I would go further. I think that is conscious bias as opposed to unconscious. There is an obvious tension here about getting it absolutely right in terms of disclosing actual conflicts and potential conflicts because that is a way of consolidating confidence in the process and arguably a way of protecting the awards from being challenged. On the other hand, opening the door too wide is itself potentially a source of dispute and of new and more inventive ways of trying to challenge awards. Is there something to be said for jurisdictions, arguably like England, that say, 'No, we are not really interested in what the general standard may be and the fact that people

5. Article 257 of the UAE Penal Code, enacted in 2016, was amended as of 8 October 2018, removing arbitrators from its scope after broad outcry.
6. Hodges, Chapter 10 above.
7. *ASM Shipping Limited of India v. TTMI Limited of England* [2005] EWHC 2238 (Comm), 39; *see* Hodges, Chapter 10 above.

are being more and more demanding; we have more interest in the safety of awards and in looking at whether they deserve to survive in light of the specific facts in the specific case.' Is there not an argument for saying that national jurisdictions are a way of resisting the trend, the ratchet towards ever more bases to challenge and ever more bases to question the impartiality.

Nathalie Voser: At the end of the day, I would say for most of the jurisdictions, this is absolutely correct. If we look at the more robust line in the US, if we look at Switzerland and Germany, the one which falls outside of this line, yes, but I do not know what to do with France because that seems to go in a totally different direction with at least the latest two decisions.

Álvaro López de Argumedo Piñeiro: I think you have to find the right balance. The parties are entitled to know, but not everything, and you also have to protect the award. I do not think you can go either way. You have to be in the middle – where the issue is.

Alexander Fessas: Yes, of course, it should be State courts and not through the basis of legislation but through their case law. Is this not what we are seeing with Halliburton? You have a principle that might stand and hold well in the context of domestic arbitration, which we now risk seeing become an accepted part of arbitration law in the United Kingdom, and that is risky knowing that London is a hub for international disputes. I think the same thing happened in the context of the *Ometto* case.[8] Probably the Second Circuit decision in that case was correct, and if you look at the last chapter of that saga, which is the enforcement of the award in Brazil, the Brazilian courts have a fantastic track of showing deference to arbitral awards, yet this was one of three out of the seventy awards reviewed in the last five years where it was decided not to enforce the award. It does not necessarily mean that courts are doing the wrong thing just because they do not follow the same approach. I hate playing the devil's advocate for State courts, but that is true sometimes.

3. GUIDELINES AND INSTITUTIONAL RULES

Charles Kaplan: Let us move to the second part of our discussion, which is the role of non-State forces. On the one hand, you have the so-called soft law guidelines and the like, and on the other hand, you have institutional rules. Is uniformity to be found in guidelines? What happens when guidelines are in apparent contradiction to institutional rules? What about if you look at the IBA Guidelines that tell you what is disclosable and then fix it within a time frame? Famously arbitral appointments by the same party or the same counsel are fixed within a three-year time frame, whereas if you look at the notes to parties and arbitrators from the ICC providing guidelines on the same topic you find broad-ranging disclosure obligations without any limit in time whatsoever. Here is an apparent contradiction right there upfront and centre. How do we resolve it? Are we supposed to resolve it?

8. *Ometto v. Abengoa Bioeneregia Agricola Ltda.*, 549 F. App'x. 41 (2nd Cir. 2014), *see* Shore/Cabona, Chapter 11 above.

Álvaro López de Argumedo Piñeiro: I would first like to explain three main differences in the approach, the scope and lack of limitation in what is otherwise difficult to understand. The IBA Guidelines essentially follow an objective approach if there is any circumstance that may be disclosed in the eyes of any reasonable third party. Meanwhile, the ICC follows a subjective approach if that circumstance may be important or evident in the eyes of the parties and would give rise to reasonable doubts as to the arbitrator's impartiality or independence.

The scope is also different between the IBA Guidelines and the ICC note because under the ICC note, the broader the disclosure is, the better. You have to disclose and say everything that the arbitrator knows. The IBA Guidelines try to find the right balance between the right of the parties to know and the right of the parties to choose the arbitrators they prefer.

The implementation is very different as well. The IBA Guidelines follow a very detailed description of many scenarios with time limits, three years, which I think probably is too short, but in the ICC note, the range of circumstances is very broad, no time limit, so you have to disclose what happened fifteen years ago and also there is an obligation to make reasonable inquiries. Maybe the approach of the ICC is very demanding for arbitrators because the parties are entitled to know, but, as I said before, they are not entitled to learn about everything, only about significant or relevant matters. I also think that there should be a time limit. You cannot challenge your relationship back to fifteen or twenty years ago.

What I think is that the IBA Guidelines and the ICC rules are complementary. In fact, as Alexis Mourre has confirmed, the ICC note is very much based on and consistent with the IBA Guidelines. This is my impression, and I am sure that Alexis can add much more to this.

Alexander Fessas: I have a slightly different view. First of all, on the more positive side, I think there is an element of convergence that very often is forgotten and that there is a part in the IBA Guidelines that precedes the colour coding, i.e., the general principles. The principle on disclosure is General Standard 3. Please compare it with Article 11(2) of the ICC Arbitration Rules. They are both manifestations of the same subjectivised criterion with regard to disclosure – 'in the eyes of the parties'.

I do think that both the IBA Guidelines and many institutional rules actually have a very common denominator with regard to the disclosure standard. The lack of an express temporal restriction on disclosure under the ICC Arbitration Rules is not in and of itself a requirement to disclose everything back to time immemorial. A requirement whereby nearly everything needs to be disclosed is found in the AAA Commercial Arbitration Rules, Article 17, that state any person to be appointed as an arbitrator, as well as the parties and their representatives, shall disclose any circumstances likely to give rise to justifiable doubt, any bias, any financial or personal interest in the result of the arbitration or any past or present relationship with the parties or their representative, which is a blanket objective: throw everything that you know in a basket and send it to us and disclose it. I think that is a disclosure obligation that knows no temporal restriction.

The fact that, in addressing potential conflict in the context of repeat appointments, the IBA Guidelines introduce a temporal element is important, but again we need to approach it as guidance and not as a fixed rule. Should there be disclosure where you have four nominations by the same counsel in four years, for instance? Does the fact that the Orange List speaks of three years mean that disclosure is always unwarranted? Those are important issues. They are important to the parties, and probably that is why, in the context of the Orange List, what is there should be disclosed and probably would get you off the hook in case of an actual conflict but still necessary for the parties to know. I think there are many other examples of which we can speak.

Charles Kaplan: This approach is very broad. It does not distinguish between whether your partner in the Singapore office was involved with a party before your appointment or afterwards or whether it has anything to do with your case; it is blanket in that sense. You, as an arbitrator, have your first stab, and you take what you think is a reasonable approach under the ICC Rules, and then one of the parties says, 'No, I want you to go back ten years' or 'You did not tell us about this fact which happened not five years ago but twelve years ago which I think is significant. Why did you not tell us?' Then you are off onto a discussion which may very well end up with the ICC Secretariat playing it safe – we are talking about confirmation, not a challenge at the beginning – and saying, 'In the circumstances, perhaps we better not.' Here is my real gripe: is not the way the guidance is structured at the moment inviting litigious bad faith tacticians, lawyers to do their job in a way that is not necessarily conducive to reaching a fair result?

Nathalie Voser: I think it is worth looking back to the IBA Guidelines at that point in time. What Charles said was precisely the reason to have the IBA Guidelines. We wanted to set limits to what we call 'over-disclosure'. Why? Because we thought that this would impact a party's right to appoint his or her arbitrator. I think this right is undervalued. It was Gabrielle Kaufmann-Kohler and Arthur Marriott at the time who said that we have to say 'stop' to this tendency of over-disclosure, which was coming from the United States. We need a green list for facts that do not need to be disclosed.

I see the risk with the very broad ICC note that we are back to a no green-list scenario, to the disclosure of everything, and then, of course, you risk that your right to appoint your arbitrator is indeed not such a big right anymore because the attacks will come. Let me say something else regarding disclosure. You said that the disclosure, the subjective approach, is everywhere similar. I think there are two schools, and for me, it is the ICC and LCIA, which have this subjective party approach. The Swiss Rules, the Singapore Rules, the UNCITRAL Model Law and the UNCITRAL Arbitration Rules apply an objective approach. Even more importantly, I know of no state law that would apply a subjective approach to the disclosure, so the national laws seem to be much more contained in what needs to be disclosed than certain arbitral institutions.

Paula Hodges: To come back to the LCIA for a moment, yes, there is a duty to disclose issues that are likely – and we deliberately included 'likely' – to raise an issue in the eyes of the parties,[9] but that is not a completely subjective process. Yes, we take into account what the parties think, but it is still an objective assessment when it comes

9. *See* Article 5.4 LCIA Arbitration Rules.

down to upholding or rejecting a challenge. I would not want to think it has gone to a completely subjective viewpoint. It is taking into account the parties' views or what we think likely to be their views when you are making that objective assessment.

Alexander Fessas: It is indeed primarily the LCIA, the ICC and the IBA Guidelines. I do not know the history of General Standard 3, but I do believe there is something there that does in a way complement the way that the IBA Guidelines, later on, operate in.

In a way, it has to be subjectivised. It has to be the prospective arbitrator, or ultimately the decision maker in the case, positioning himself or herself in the context of the dimensions of the case and the parties. I have to say that I would share the concern if I had seen objections firmly adopting that broad-based blanket approach that sometimes we see in the context of US-style domestic arbitration proceedings, but that has not happened. Neither have we seen a rise of the objections or of the rate of successful objections against the confirmation of arbitrators.

I really believe this is something that works prospectively in fields where arbitration has not been used that often or where a certain level of homogeneity – and I am not speaking of uniformity but a certain homogeneity – within that jurisdiction has not yet been achieved. There are plenty of such jurisdictions around the world where arbitration is being used.

Charles Kaplan: You really think parties are not going to take advantage of that and ask for more? My worry is not so much blanket disclosure, it is maybe first disclosure, and then a party says, 'I found something else. Let us pull on the string. Let us pull a little more.' By the time we have finished, we have created a climate of suspicion around the prospective nominee such that it is probably better not to confirm them. That is the easiest solution. That is, to me, the way it is more likely to happen.

Álvaro López de Argumedo Piñeiro: My point is that the IBA Guidelines do not encourage the parties to submit more and more challenges or object confirmation. On the contrary, I think they provide certainty. You know which are the basic rules, the basic framework, on which you can challenge or object.

Nathalie Voser: I do not want people to believe that I am against the subjective approach. I am in favour of it because I think it is the first step to additional information to find out whether there is a conflict. With this regard, I came around with my view. In the drafting of the IBA Guidelines, we first went for an objective approach and then in discussions with the ICC, we were persuaded that the subjective approach, i.e., 'in the eyes of the parties', was preferable because it was a starting point of further inquiries and discussions.

Paula Hodges: I do worry, going along with Charles's suggestion, that the more disclosures that are out there, the more challenges there will be. Certainly wearing my LCIA hat, I have seen a number of arbitrators resign or withdraw because there has been an objection by one of the parties even before there is a formal application or formal challenge. It does worry me that the parties' right to choose an arbitrator is being eroded if we go too far down the disclosure route.

4. ISSUES RAISED FROM THE FLOOR

Charles Kaplan: Turning to the floor: is there anybody who like to put a question to our panel?

Giovanni Viglino: You talk about the relationship between soft law and institutional rules, but what about the relationship between national laws and institutional rules? One of the big problems in the Tecnimont saga is that the French judges did not care about the ICC rules on impartiality and independence, and this created huge problems. In my opinion, it is fundamental to achieve a sort of uniformity between institutional rules and national laws but is it possible? Is it desirable? What are your thoughts about that?

Alexander Fessas: It is telling that the last Court of Cassation decision and the last decision of the Court of Appeal of Paris actually speaks to that point by saying 'Parties, if you have elected to operate within an institutional setting, you are bound by it. Those are decisions that emanate from the institutions in the context or as a consequence of your agreement to abide by their rules, so you need to work with them and operate within the context that you agree to set up.' Therefore, if there is a process within which information has been made available to you, you need to make a timely challenge; this is the conclusion of Tecnimont. If you did not raise an issue in the context of the ICC process means that you have lost your chance. I think that is a very telling example of a move towards clarity and hopefully uniformity.

Eckart Brödermann: Assuming likelihood being the standard, and I am a fan of that, how do you determine the cultural danger that the word 'likelihood' will be understood differently depending on where you are in the world?

Paula Hodges: I think it is better to have it there as a benchmark rather than feel you have to disclose everything. Ultimately, the challenge will be decided upon whether or not there are justifiable doubts as to impartiality. In terms of disclosure, I think likelihood is a good thing.

Charles Kaplan: It means more than 50% probability, does it not?

Wolfgang Peter: I think a wide range of disclosure is good to create trust. I am really addressing that there is no time limit for the ICC Rules. I do not see any compelling reason why the ICC rules, in all their splendour, departed from the principles laid down in the universally accepted standard of the IBA Guidelines. Even though I know that the IBA Guidelines do not make the limitations absolute, there are exceptions, but what the ICC does, and I see it in practice, is opening the door to lawyers. We know how that works: you open the door 2 mm, and then the door is wide open. I spoke about the example of facts from seventeen years ago, and the ICC has the approach to say, 'Yes, we let the problem develop, but then we cure it. Do not worry.' That is what I said this morning: this is a problem that we see again and again in practice. It creates tensions and animosities. I do not see a compelling reason for the ICC to depart from a standard that has been widely accepted, is much more developed, has been around for much longer. I have seen months and months of exchanges between arbitrator, prospective arbitrator, the ICC Secretariat, the other counsel. Statistically, most formal challenges may be rejected, but that is not the issue.

Alexander Fessas: I do not think I am familiar with the example you are referring to, but obviously, if something needs to be addressed, it will be addressed. The standard has not changed, and it has been there since before the introduction of the IBA Guidelines. I think that the problem that has always existed is how far we go with regard to establishing or expanding a green list, which is a safe haven, or from the other side expanding or reducing the red list, which is the 'do not go to' zone. I think ultimately, what we are left with under either scenario is a field of disclosable material which, in principle, will not lead to situations of sanctionable conflict. I think we can, in broad terms, agree on that.

5. CLOSING REMARKS

Felix Dasser: With that, some closing remarks. Today's topic was: clear path or jungle. I dare say that today's search for a clear path met with maybe rather limited success, which, of course, raises the question: what is so bad about the jungle? Several among you might even have given money to some NGO to protect the jungle in the Amazon or in Africa or somewhere else, at least I do.

To be sympathetic to a legal jungle might strike you as odd or worse, but it reminds me of an anecdote when I taught a course at university many years ago. We discussed hypotheticals. After we had discussed all the pros and cons of a particular hypothetical, I saw everybody looking at me with the pen ready and said, 'What do you expect from me? I do not know the answer.' They looked at me, obviously thinking what an idiot I was, a professor who does not know the answer to a hypothetical. I told them, 'I am only a professor. How can I know what the Federal Supreme Court would decide in this case in maybe five years' time when the case had worked its way up to it. I am only a professor, I do not decide cases.' Then, of course, they looked at me even stranger, and I told them, 'You know what, if the law were as clear as you want to have it, the world would not need so many lawyers, and you would not find a job, so be happy about it.'

Maybe there is something similar here. There is a lot of grey area. We are not happy about the grey area, but it supports our livelihood. On that uplifting thought, I release you from this conference, and I thank everybody, all the panel members, moderators, all of you for coming here.

CHAPTER 13

Interaction Between the IBA Guidelines on Conflicts of Interest of Arbitrators and the ICC Arbitration Rules

Álvaro López de Argumedo Piñeiro

1. INTRODUCTION

The extraordinary development of international arbitration and its increased complexity have given rise to a significant proliferation of soft law in order to try to guide the conduct of those involved in arbitration proceedings: parties, counsels, arbitrators and institutions. This proliferation has been described by some authors as a 'pathology',[1] while others see it as a sign of the maturity of the arbitration community. Whatever the case, the coexistence of multiple soft law regulations does not necessarily imply an obstacle for the development of arbitration. The market (i.e., the arbitration practitioners) is de facto selecting the soft law rules it considers more convenient and, therefore, determining in practice which soft law rules prevail. Furthermore, the most successful soft law rules up to now do not present significant differences in their approach to the different fields they regulate.

Therefore, this proliferation of soft law should not be of concern to the arbitration community and should arguably be interpreted as proof of its continuous dynamism.

Out of the many soft law products in existence, only two have gained broad acceptance (and application) among arbitration circles. These soft law norms are the IBA Rules on the Taking of Evidence and the IBA Guidelines on Conflicts of Interest in International Arbitration (the '**IBA Guidelines**').[2]

1. Alexis Mourre, *Arbitral Institutions and Professional Organizations as Lawmakers*, in Evolution and Adaptation: The Future of International Arbitration, ICCA Congress Series No. 20, 87-88 (Kalicki and Raouf eds., Wolters Kluwer 2019).
2. *Ibid.* Mourre, *supra* n. 1, 96.

The extensive use of these rules is confirmed in the report on the reception of the IBA Arbitration soft law products prepared in 2016 by the IBA Arbitration Guidelines and Rules Subcommittee (the '**IBA Report**'):[3]

> The data collected shows that the Conflicts of Interest Guidelines have gained broad acceptance and were used often by the international arbitration community. Of the three IBA instruments surveyed, the Conflicts of Interest Guidelines were the most commonly referenced. By way of example, in the 3,201 arbitrations known to the respondents over the past five years in which issues of conflicts of interest arose (at the start of the arbitration), the Guidelines were referenced in 57 per cent of them.

This general acceptance has also been confirmed by the fact that those rules have been taken into account by many judicial courts across Europe and elsewhere when deciding matters covered under these soft law norms.[4]

In addition, there have been some efforts to convert guidelines such as the IBA Guidelines into 'hard' law. An example of this is Article 8.30[5] of the Canada-Europe Trade Agreement (CETA), which states:

> 1. The Members of the Tribunal shall be independent. They shall not be affiliated with any government. They shall not take instructions from any organisation, or government with regard to matters related to the dispute. They shall not participate in the consideration of any disputes that would create a direct or indirect conflict of interest. *They shall comply with the International Bar Association Guidelines on Conflicts of Interest in International Arbitration or any supplemental rules* adopted pursuant to Article 8.44.2. In addition, upon appointment, they shall refrain from acting as counsel or as partyappointed expert or witness in any pending or new investment dispute under this or any other international agreement.

This general acceptance obviously does not imply that these soft law rules are binding.[6] Only when the parties agree to be bound by a specific set of soft law rules will those rules be legally binding and therefore become 'hard' rules for the parties.

The purpose of this article is to explore the interaction between the IBA Guidelines and the ICC rules (including the ICC Note to Parties and Arbitral Tribunals on the Conduct of the Arbitration under the ICC Rules of Arbitration dated 1 January

3. *The IBA Arbitration Guidelines and Rules Subcommittee. Report on the reception of the IBA arbitration soft law products*, 31 (2016). *See also* the overview by Felix Dasser, *'Soft Law' in International Commercial Arbitration*, in Recueil des cours, Vol. 402 (2019), 503 et seqq. and 518 et seqq.
4. For example, *see* Swiss Federal Supreme Court DFSC 4A_506/2007 of 20 March 2008, the High Court of Justice of Madrid Judgment of 28 January 2015 (ECLI:ES:TSJM:2015:1286) and the Austrian Supreme Court Resolution of 19 April 2016, 18ONc3/15h (ECLI:AT:OGH0002:2016:018ONC00003.15H.0419.000).
5. Eric Picanyol, *Due Process and Soft Law in International Arbitration*, Spain Arbitration Review: Revista del Club Español del Arbitraje, 55, Issue 24 (2015).
6. Gabrielle Kaufmann-Kohler, *Soft Law in International Arbitration: Codification and Normativity*, Journal of International Dispute Settlement, Volume 1, Issue 2 (2010); *see also* Felix Dasser, *Soft Law in International Commercial Arbitration – A Critical Approach*, in Austrian Yearbook on International Arbitration, 112 (Klausegger, Klein et al. eds., 2019).

2019 – the '**ICC Note**') and verify whether both texts could be considered complementary in spite of the differences existing between them.

2. THE IBA GUIDELINES ON THE CONFLICT OF INTEREST OF ARBITRATORS AND THE ICC RULES: MAIN FEATURES AND DIFFERENCES

In order to be able to explain the interaction between the IBA Guidelines and the ICC rules (and, in particular, the ICC Note – jointly, the '**ICC Rules**'), it is important to first describe their main features (as regards their legal nature, legitimacy, goals and practical purposes) as well as their main differences.

2.1. Main Features

2.1.1. First: They Have a Different Legal Nature

The IBA Guidelines are soft law precisely because they are not compulsory and will only be binding if the parties so agree. In other words, the IBA Rules are soft law because they are norms 'that cannot be enforced through public force'.[7]

However, the ICC Rules cannot be characterized as soft law given that they are binding upon the parties as soon as they submit their conflicts to the ICC. As has been rightly suggested,[8] those instituted rules 'are deemed [to be] an offer to contract extended by the ICC, which the parties accept when they agree on ICC arbitration, not when they initiate arbitration proceedings'. As such, the ICC Rules should be considered as being contractually binding.[9]

2.1.2. Second: They Have a Different Source of Legitimacy

The legitimacy of the IBA Guidelines arises from the reputation of the IBA, its geographical diversity, the fact that it represents a large proportion of the arbitral community from both the common and the civil law systems, and the ensuing reality that the IBA Guidelines reflect a broad consensus with regard to the different solutions achieved under those two systems.[10] The legitimacy of the IBA Guidelines also comes from the openness and transparency of their drafting, which benefited from the participation of the main stakeholders of the arbitration community.[11]

7. *Ibid.* Kaufmann-Kohler, *supra* n. 6, 2.
8. *Ibid.* Kaufmann-Kohler, *supra* n. 6, 11.
9. *Ibid.* Dasser, *supra* n. 6, 112.
10. *Ibid.* Mourre, *supra* n. 1, 108.
11. At the very least, those instruments deemed to qualify as soft law must have: (1) institutional legitimacy, (2) be the result of a transparent procedure, and (3) receive wide acceptance by the arbitral community; *see ibid.* Dasser, *supra* n. 6, 116-118.

However, the legitimacy of the ICC Rules derives from the legal authority, tradition and prestige of the institution itself, and ultimately from the fact that once the parties submit to the ICC, these rules do have contractual force.[12]

Ultimately, the ICC Rules represent a pure implementation of the ICC's policies.[13]

2.1.3. *Third: They also Have Different Goals*

The purpose of the IBA Guidelines is 'to enhance confidence in the integrity of international arbitration, and to assist institutions and courts to make consistent, clear and coherent decisions about disqualification'.[14]

In essence, the aim of the IBA Guidelines is to promote and assist disclosure by arbitrators of certain types of information in order to enhance confidence in the integrity of international arbitration and to help institutions and courts to make consistent, clear and coherent decisions about disqualification and, as such, to reinforce overall trust in arbitration.

In contrast, the purpose of the ICC Rules is, in essence, to implement the ICC's policies, one of which is to protect the integrity of ICC arbitral awards (*inter alia*, to protect them from any ethical issue arising from any potential non-disclosure by arbitrators of relevant circumstances that could affect the validity of the award when being examined by a judicial court in a set-aside action).

2.1.4. *Fourth: Both Sets of Rules Have Different Practical Purposes*

The IBA Guidelines provide guidance to the arbitral community about what arbitrators should disclose and what the parties can request that arbitrators disclose. As the IBA Subcommittee reported:

> the Conflicts of Interest Guidelines have gained broad acceptance and were used often by the international arbitration community. Of the three IBA instruments surveyed, *the Conflicts of Interest Guidelines were the most commonly referenced.* By way of example, in the 3,201 arbitrations known to respondents over the past five years in which issues of conflicts of interest arose (at the start of the arbitration), *the Conflicts of Interest Guidelines were referenced in 57 per cent of them.*
>
> ...
>
> At the global scale, counsel made use of the Conflicts of Interest Guidelines when appointing arbitrators in 67 per cent of all reported cases. Arbitrators also appeared to make frequent use of the Conflicts of Interest Guidelines across all regions.
>
> The survey also confirms that the Conflicts of Interest Guidelines were often referenced by the relevant decision maker (arbitral institutions, tribunals, or courts) in reaching a pronouncement on the existence of a conflict of interest. At

12. *Ibid.* Dasser, *supra* n. 6, 112; *ibid.* Kaufmann-Kohler, *supra* n. 6, 11.
13. *Ibid.* Mourre, *supra* n. 1, 99-100.
14. Judith Gill, *The IBA Conflicts Guidelines – Who's using them and how?*, in Dispute Resolution International, 59 (2007).

a global level, the Conflicts of Interest Guidelines were referenced in 67 per cent of decisions resolving issues of conflicts of interest. Perhaps more importantly, in 69 per cent of the decisions that referenced the Conflicts of Interest Guidelines in solving a conflicts of interest issue, the decision maker chose to follow the guidelines.[15]

The Federal Swiss Court has stressed the fact that the IBA Guidelines are a working tool to determine when arbitrators are conflicted:

> These guidelines have certainly not force of law … . They nonetheless constitute a valuable working tool ['instrument de travail'], susceptible at contributing to harmonization and unification of standards that are applicable in the area of international arbitration for the regulation of conflicts of interest, which tool [sic] will not fail to exert an influence on the practice of arbitration institutions and courts … .[16]

However, the ICC Rules are hard law per se, and their purpose is to organize and administer basic aspects of the arbitral proceedings submitted to the ICC.

2.2. What Are the Main Differences Between The IBA Guidelines and the ICC Rules with Respect to the Duty of Disclosure by Arbitrators?

We examine below the main differences that can be found between the IBA Guidelines and the ICC Rules with respect to disclosure in order to subsequently analyse how they may be considered complementary in spite of those differences.

2.2.1. Scope

2.2.1.1. IBA Guidelines

In order to determine the scope of disclosure, the IBA Guidelines seek a balance between:[17]

(1) the parties' right to be informed of circumstances that could call into question the impartiality or independence of the arbitrator; and
(2) the right of the parties to choose the arbitrators they prefer.

The IBA Guidelines were the product of a working group of nineteen experts in international arbitration from fourteen countries, and they attempt to strike the delicate balance between the two circumstances mentioned above. In order to achieve that balance, the circumstances which in principle cannot lead to disqualification should not be disclosed, as they lack any relevance for determining the impartiality and

15. *Ibid.* IBA, *supra* n. 3, 31.
16. Federal Court decision 4A_506/2007 of 20 March 2008, cons. 3.3.2.2; *ibid.* Dasser, *supra* n. 6, 125; Dasser, *supra* n. 3, 523 et seqq.
17. *Ibid.* Gill, *supra* n. 14, 59.

independence of the arbitrators. Furthermore, if arbitrators were encouraged to inform the parties of circumstances that could in no way affect their independence or impartiality, this could cause an increase in unfounded challenges, which would be detrimental to arbitration as an institution.

2.2.1.2. ICC Rules

The standard for disclosure under the ICC Rules is far more extensive: it may be summarized in the following terms: 'the broader, the better'. Paragraphs 20 and 21 of the ICC Note are very clear in this respect:

> 'The parties have a legitimate interest in being *fully informed* of all facts and circumstances that may be relevant in their views.' (paragraph 20).
>
> 'Any doubt must be resolved in favour of disclosure.' (paragraph 21).

This approach is inspired by the previously mentioned aim of protecting the integrity of the award and the trust in arbitration overall.

2.2.2. Practical Implementation

The IBA Guidelines go very much into specifics and provide detailed descriptions of situations and circumstances that should (or should not) be disclosed. This is so because they are not intended to be interpreted by a single institution; on the contrary, the idea is that they should be applicable to all kinds of arbitration proceedings, regardless of which institution is in charge of their administration.

As a consequence, the IBA Guidelines try to address as many scenarios as possible (in a list that is intended to be comprehensive though not exhaustive) and provide general principles and explanations about the different situations they address.

All those scenarios are classified following a traffic light system:

- ***Red***: for circumstances that do not allow the appointment of the arbitrator (except for those which can be waived by the parties by means of express consent). These scenarios are numbered 1.X for the non-waivable red list and 2.X for the waivable red list.
- ***Orange***: for situations in which there are justifiable doubts as to whether the arbitrator can act as an impartial and independent arbitrator in the eyes of the parties. As a consequence, the arbitrator has an obligation to disclose those relevant circumstances. These scenarios are numbered 3.X.
- ***Green***: for those situations where no appearance and no actual conflict of interest exist, and there is, therefore, no obligation to disclose. These scenarios are numbered 4.X.

In contrast, and as described in section 2.1.2 above, the ICC Note describes the situations and circumstances that should be disclosed by an arbitrator in a broader manner, thus intensifying the arbitrator's duty of disclosure.

2.2.3. *Time Limit for Circumstances Subject to Disclosure*

Another important difference between the IBA Guidelines and the ICC Rules is that the latter do not impose a time limit for the circumstances that should be disclosed. In other words, arbitrators are encouraged to disclose any circumstance that, in the eyes of the parties, could give rise to doubts as regards their independence or impartiality, regardless of the time that circumstance dates from. Further, under the ICC Note, an arbitrator or prospective arbitrator must 'make reasonable enquiries in his or her records, those of his or her law firm and, as the case may be, in other readily available materials'.[18] Arbitrators are therefore encouraged to be comprehensive in their disclosures and to actively ascertain the existence of circumstances subject to disclosure.

However, the IBA Guidelines establish a clear time limit (generally, occurrence or existence within the three years prior to appointment as an arbitrator) for a circumstance to be subject to disclosure. This obviously imposes a more limited duty of disclosure.

It is important to note that the obligation to disclose does not end upon appointment as an arbitrator under the ICC Rules or the IBA Guidelines. In both cases, the obligation is an ongoing one, and it covers new circumstances that could affect their independence or impartiality as well as previously existing circumstances not disclosed for any reason.

3. INTERACTION BETWEEN THE IBA GUIDELINES AND THE ICC RULES

The two sets of provisions are arguably complementary. The ICC Rules set a general rule for arbitrators in favour of a broad standard of disclosure with some specific circumstances that should be considered by arbitrators. Meanwhile, the IBA Guidelines go into more detail and cover different and diverse scenarios, giving the arbitrators and the parties a particular checklist to guide them as to disclosure.[19] These sets of rules, therefore, do not have an opposing relationship.

In fact, as Alexis Mourre has pointed out, 'the ICC Rules are largely inspired by, and consistent with, the IBA Guidelines',[20] although they depart from them in certain instances.

Moreover, the IBA Arbitration Guidelines and Rules Subcommittee mentioned in its 2016 report that:

18. ICC Note to Parties and Arbitral Tribunals on the Conduct of the Arbitration under the ICC Rules of Arbitration (2019), para. 29.
19. Nathalie Voser and Angelina M. Petti, *The Revised IBA Guidelines on Conflicts of Interest in International Arbitration*, 33 ASA Bulletin, 14 (2015).
20. Mourre, *supra* n. 1, 99.

(1) the IBA Guidelines are commonly invoked by the parties in ICC arbitration proceedings to challenge an arbitrator, as well as by arbitrators to explain their non-disclosures;[21] and
(2) the ICC takes the IBA Guidelines into account when deciding whether to confirm an arbitrator or uphold a challenge, although it is obviously not bound by the IBA Guidelines and is entirely free to come to its own decisions.[22]

Tables 13.1-13.9 provide an overview of the current correspondence (imperfect, but existing nonetheless) and interaction between the disclosure criteria established in the ICC Note and the relevant sections of the IBA Guidelines.

Table 13.1 On the Arbitrator or His or Her Law Firm Advising One of the Parties

ICC Note[a]	*IBA Guidelines*
The arbitrator or prospective arbitrator or his or her law firm represents or advises, or has represented or advised, one of the parties or one of its affiliates.	**1.4** The arbitrator or his or her firm regularly advises the party, or an affiliate of the party, and the arbitrator or his or her firm derives significant financial income therefrom. **2.3.1** The arbitrator currently represents or advises one of the parties, or an affiliate of one of the parties. **2.3.7** The arbitrator regularly advises one of the parties, or an affiliate of one of the parties, but neither the arbitrator nor his or her firm derives a significant financial income therefrom.

a ICC, *supra* n. 18, para. 23, first bullet point.

Under the IBA Guidelines, representation of a party or an affiliate by the arbitrator or the arbitrator's firm implies that the arbitrator cannot accept the appointment or can only accept it with the express consent of the parties (non-waivable red list or waivable red list). But, according to the ICC Note, this circumstance must be disclosed and will in all likelihood lead to the arbitrator not being confirmed.

In fact, as confirmed by Andrea Carlevaris and Rocío Digón:[23]

> The ICC has accepted such challenges when (i) the former counsel of a party joined the arbitrator's law firm; (ii) the arbitrator's new law firm is representing the non-challenging party in two ongoing litigations; or (iii) counsel to a party has nominated the arbitrator five times in twelve years.

21. IBA, *supra* n. 3, 41.
22. IBA, *supra* n. 3, 41.
23. Andrea Carlevaris and Rocío Digón, *Arbitrator Challenges under the ICC Rules and Practice*', ICC Dispute Resolution Bulletin, Issue 1, 33-34 (2016).

Table 13.2 On the Arbitrator or His or Her Law Firm Acting Against One of the Parties

ICC Note[a]	*IBA Guidelines*
The arbitrator or prospective arbitrator or his or her law firm acts or has acted against one of the parties or one of its affiliates.	**3.1.4** The arbitrator's law firm has, within the past three years, acted for or against one of the parties, or an affiliate of one of the parties, in an unrelated matter without the involvement of the arbitrator. **3.4.1** The arbitrator's law firm is currently acting adversely to one of the parties, or an affiliate of one of the parties.

a ICC, *supra* n. 18, para. 23, second bullet point.

Here, circumstances that must be disclosed according to the ICC Note fall under the orange list of the IBA Guidelines. As such, they must be disclosed. However, if they affect the arbitrator's firm rather than the actual arbitrator, the latter is not prevented from accepting the appointment as long as the parties do not object. Despite this theoretical possibility, in practice, it remains improbable that the ICC would confirm an arbitrator whose law firm is acting or has recently acted against one of the parties or its affiliates unless both parties accept it.

Table 13.3 On the Business, Commercial, Financial or Personal Relationship Between the Arbitrator or His or Her Law Firm and the Parties

ICC Note[a]	*IBA Guidelines*[b]
The arbitrator or prospective arbitrator or his or her law firm has a business relationship with one of the parties or one of its affiliates, or a personal interest of any nature in the outcome of the dispute.	**1.1** The arbitrator is a legal representative or employee of an entity that is a party in the arbitration. **1.3** The arbitrator has a significant, financial or personal interest in one of the parties, or the outcome of the case. **2.2.1** The arbitrator holds shares either directly or indirectly, in one of the parties, or an affiliate of one of the parties, this party or an affiliate being privately held. **2.2.2** A close family member of the arbitrator has a significant financial interest in the outcome of the dispute. **2.2.3** The arbitrator, or a close family member of the arbitrator, has a close relationship with a non-party who may be liable to recourse on the part of the unsuccessful party in the dispute.

ICC Note[a]	*IBA Guidelines*[b]
	2.3.6 The arbitrator's law firm currently has a significant commercial relationship with one of the parties, or an affiliate of one of the parties. **2.3.8** The arbitrator has a close family relationship with one of the parties, or with a manager, director or member of the supervisory board, or any person having a controlling influence in one of the parties, or an affiliate of one of the parties, or with a counsel representing a party. **2.3.9** A close family member of the arbitrator has a significant financial or personal interest in one of the parties, or an affiliate of one of the parties. **3.4.2** The arbitrator has been associated with a party, or an affiliate of one of the parties, in a professional capacity, such as a former employee or partner. **3.4.3** A close personal friendship exists between an arbitrator and a manager or director or a member of the supervisory board of a party; an entity that has direct economic interest in the award to be rendered in the arbitration; or any person having a controlling influence, such as a controlling shareholder interest, on one of the parties or an affiliate of one of the parties or a witness or expert. **3.5.1** The arbitrator holds shares, either directly or indirectly, that by reason of number or denomination constitute a material holding in one of the parties, or an affiliate of one of the parties, this party or affiliate being publicly listed. **3.5.4** The arbitrator is a manager, director or member of the supervisory board, or has a controlling influence on an affiliate of one of the parties, where the affiliate is not directly involved in the matters in dispute in the arbitration.

a ICC, *supra* n. 18, para. 23, third bullet point.
b For the meaning of the numbering, *see* section 2.2.2.

The short statement included in the ICC Note covers a wide range of circumstances expressly listed in the IBA Guidelines, which are specifically categorised within the red or the orange list. Most are classified as waivable subjects or as merely subject to disclosure. Arbitrators whose circumstances fall within red-list categories under the IBA Guidelines will not normally be appointed in ICC proceedings. With respect to the orange-list categories, ICC decisions will be taken on more of a case-by-case basis.

Table 13.4 On Professional Relationships Between the Arbitrator or His or Her Law Firm and One of the Parties

ICC Note[a]	*IBA Guidelines*
The arbitrator or prospective arbitrator or his or her law firm acts or has acted on behalf of one of the parties or one of its affiliates as director, board member, officer, or otherwise.	**1.2** The arbitrator is a manager, director or member of the supervisory board, or has a controlling influence on one of the parties or an entity that has a direct economic interest in the award to be rendered in the arbitration. **2.3.4** The arbitrator is a manager, director or member of the supervisory board, or has a controlling influence in an affiliate of one of the parties, if the affiliate is directly involved in the matters in dispute in the arbitration.

a ICC, *supra* n. 18, para. 29, fourth bullet point.

The ICC criterion is fully aligned with the IBA Guidelines, and therefore, an arbitrator in any of these situations would not be appointed by the ICC unless that appointment was accepted by both parties (again, however, the ICC would take such a decision on a case-by-case basis).

Table 13.5 On the Relationship Between the Arbitrator or His or Her Law Firm and the Dispute Itself

ICC Note[a]	*IBA Guidelines*
The arbitrator or prospective arbitrator or his or her law firm is or has been involved in the dispute, or has expressed a view on the dispute in a manner that might affect his or her impartiality.	**2.1.1** The arbitrator has given legal advice, or provided an expert opinion, on the dispute to a party or an affiliate of one of the parties. **2.1.2** The arbitrator had a prior involvement in the dispute. **2.3.5** The arbitrator's law firm had a previous but terminated involvement in the case without the arbitrator being involved himself or herself. **3.5.2** The arbitrator has publicly advocated a position on the case whether in a published paper, or speech, or otherwise.

a ICC, *supra* n. 18, para. 29, fifth bullet point.

If an arbitrator has previously been involved in the case, he or she will be unable to accept an appointment unless both parties consent or make no objection. Under those circumstances, it would also be unlikely that the ICC confirms an appointment.

Table 13.6 On the Relationship Between Arbitrators and Counsel

ICC Note[a]	*IBA Guidelines*
The arbitrator or prospective arbitrator has a professional or close personal relationship with counsel to one of the parties or the counsel's law firm.	**2.3.2** The arbitrator currently represents or advises the lawyer or law firm acting as counsel for one of the parties. **2.3.3** The arbitrator is a lawyer in the same law firm as the counsel to one of the parties. **3.3.1** The arbitrator and another arbitrator are lawyers in the same law firm. **3.3.2** The arbitrator and another arbitrator, or the counsel for one of the parties, are members of the same barristers' chambers. **3.3.3** The arbitrator was, within the past three years, a partner of, or otherwise affiliated with, another arbitrator or any of the counsel in the arbitration. **3.3.5** A close family member of the arbitrator is a partner or employee of the law firm representing one of the parties, but is not assisting with the dispute. **3.3.6** A close personal friendship exists between an arbitrator and a counsel of a party.

a ICC, *supra* n. 18, para. 29, sixth bullet point.

Again, the generic requirement for disclosure provided by the ICC Note is developed into different specific scenarios in the IBA Guidelines, all of which are included either in the waivable red list or in the orange list. It is once more doubtful that the ICC would confirm the arbitrator under these circumstances, although – once again – this will be decided on a case-by-case basis.

Table 13.7 On Multiple Appointments of the Arbitrator by One of the Parties

ICC Note[a]	*IBA Guidelines*
The arbitrator or prospective arbitrator acts or has acted as arbitrator in a case involving one of the parties or one of its affiliates.	**3.1.3** The arbitrator has within the past three years been appointed as arbitrator on two or more occasions by one of the parties, or an affiliate of one of the parties.

a ICC, *supra* n. 18, para. 29, seventh bullet point.

Again, there is close alignment between the circumstances established for disclosure in each case, the main point of difference being the time limit established under the IBA Guidelines. An example of the ICC's less time-constrained approach is provided by Carlevaris and Digón,[24] who confirm that the ICC has accepted a challenge to an arbitrator appointment where the counsel to a party had nominated the arbitrator five times in the previous twelve years.

Table 13.8 On the Relationship Between the Arbitrator and Related Arbitration Proceedings

ICC Note[a]	*IBA Guidelines*
The arbitrator or prospective arbitrator acts or has acted as arbitrator in a related case.	**3.1.5** The arbitrator currently serves, or has served within the past three years, as arbitrator in another arbitration on a related issue involving one of the parties, or an affiliate of one of the parties.

a ICC, *supra* n. 18, para. 29, eighth bullet point.

The above circumstances are subject to a very similar approach under the IBA Guidelines and the ICC Note. Both sets of provisions consider the proximity between the arbitrator and the specific case as a circumstance that should be disclosed and could eventually lead to the non-confirmation of the arbitrator.

Table 13.9 On Multiple Appointments of the Arbitrator by the Same Counsel

ICC Note[a]	*IBA Guidelines*
The arbitrator or prospective arbitrator has in the past been appointed as arbitrator by one of the parties or one of its affiliates, or by counsel to one of the parties or the counsel's law firm.	**3.3.8** The arbitrator has, within the past three years, been appointed on more than three occasions by the same counsel, or the same law firm.

a ICC, *supra* n. 18, para. 29, ninth bullet point.

In this case, the time limit is joined by the number of appointments as points of difference between the two provisions. In any event, both provisions treat the fact that arbitrators have been appointed in the past by the same counsel as a significant circumstance and, therefore, one subject to disclosure.

In conclusion, substantially all of the circumstances that an arbitrator must take into account when deciding what to disclose in ICC arbitration proceedings are already

24. *Ibid.* Carlevaris and Digón, *supra* n. 23, 33-34.

reflected in the IBA Guidelines. The provisions do not match perfectly. Nonetheless, the IBA Guidelines can be interpreted as a more detailed description and specification of the circumstances established in the ICC Note. The texts have a complementary relationship and jointly offer a helpful guide not only for arbitrators and the ICC but also for parties. It is true that the three-year time limit generally provided for in the IBA Guidelines is not reflected in the ICC Note. Nevertheless, practice will probably help to find the right balance between these two different approaches to the same reality.

4. CONCLUSION

There has been a great proliferation of soft law in recent years in order to govern certain aspects of international arbitration (particularly the taking of evidence and conflicts of interest). Rather than causing concern, this proliferation should be seen as proof of the dynamism of the arbitral community.

The IBA Guidelines are one of the most successful and widely applied sets of soft law rules. They are a helpful tool for arbitrators and institutions, as well as for the parties and even judicial courts when considering the difficult issues involving conflicts of interest. Despite the fact that the ICC Note and the IBA Guidelines present some different approaches in certain aspects (e.g., the time limit applicable to the circumstances that should be disclosed), they can work in a highly complementary manner: the ICC Note establishes the general framework for the circumstances that should be disclosed by arbitrators and the IBA Guidelines outline the particular scenarios that develop this general framework and that arbitrators should carefully consider.

APPENDIX

Selected Rules and Regulations on Conflicts of Interest

1. LEGISLATION

1.1 International Treaties

1.1.1 United Nations Convention on the Recognition and Enforcement of Foreign Arbitral Awards (New York, 10 June 1958) (New York Convention, NYC)

Article V

1. Recognition and enforcement of the award may be refused, at the request of the party against whom it is invoked, only if that party furnishes to the competent authority where the recognition and enforcement is sought, proof that:

   [...]

   (b) The party against whom the award is invoked was not given proper notice of the appointment of the arbitrator or of the arbitration proceedings or was otherwise unable to present his case; or

   [...]

   (d) The composition of the arbitral authority or the arbitral procedure was not in accordance with the agreement of the parties, or, failing such agreement, was not in accordance with the law of the country where the arbitration took place; or

   [...]

2. Recognition and enforcement of an arbitral award may also be refused if the competent authority in the country where recognition and enforcement is sought finds that:

   [...]

(b) The recognition or enforcement of the award would be contrary to the public policy of that country.

1.1.2 UNCITRAL Model Law on International Commercial Arbitration (1985/2006)

Article 12 Grounds for challenge

1. When a person is approached in connection with his possible appointment as an arbitrator, he shall disclose any circumstances likely to give rise to justifiable doubts as to his impartiality or independence. An arbitrator, from the time of his appointment and throughout the arbitral proceedings, shall without delay disclose any such circumstances to the parties unless they have already been informed of them by him.
2. An arbitrator may be challenged only if circumstances exist that give rise to justifiable doubts as to his impartiality or independence, or if he does not possess qualifications agreed to by the parties. A party may challenge an arbitrator appointed by him, or in whose appointment he has participated, only for reasons of which he becomes aware after the appointment has been made.

1.1.3 Investment Treaties

(a) Convention on the Settlement of Investment Disputes Between States and Nationals of Other States (ICSID Convention)

Article 14

(1) Persons designated to serve on the Panels shall be persons of high moral character and recognized competence in the fields of law, commerce, industry or finance, who may be relied upon to exercise independent judgment. Competence in the field of law shall be of particular importance in the case of persons on the Panel of Arbitrators.

Article 57

A party may propose to a Commission or Tribunal the disqualification of any of its members on account of any fact indicating a manifest lack of the qualities required by paragraph (1) of Article 14. A party to arbitration proceedings may, in addition, propose the disqualification of an arbitrator on the ground that he was ineligible for appointment to the Tribunal under Section 2 of Chapter IV.

(b) *Comprehensive Economic and Trade Agreement between the EU and Canada (CETA) of October 30, 2016*

Article 8.30(1)

The Members of the Tribunal shall be independent. They shall not be affiliated with any government. They shall not take instructions from any organisation, or government with regard to matters related to the dispute. They shall not participate in the consideration of any disputes that would create a direct or indirect conflict of interest. They shall comply with the International Bar Association Guidelines on Conflicts of Interest in International Arbitration or any supplemental rules adopted pursuant to Article 8.44.2. In addition, upon appointment, they shall refrain from acting as counsel or as party-appointed expert or witness in any pending or new investment dispute under this or any other international agreement.[1]

(c) *Agreement between the United States of America, the United Mexican States, and Canada (USMCA) of November 30, 2018*

Article 14.D.6

5. Arbitrators appointed to a tribunal for claims submitted under Article 14.D.3.1 shall: (a) comply with the International Bar Association Guidelines on Conflicts of Interest in International Arbitration, including guidelines regarding direct or indirect conflicts of interest, or any supplemental guidelines or rules adopted by the Annex Parties; [...].

(d) *Comprehensive and Progressive Agreement for Trans-Pacific Partnership of March 8, 2018, Chapter 9 Section B Code of Conduct for Investor-State Dispute Settlement*

Article 3

(e) An arbitrator shall comply with internationally recognised standards or guidelines regarding direct or indirect conflicts of interest, such as the International Bar Association Guidelines on Conflicts of Interest in International Arbitration.

1.2 China (People's Republic of)

1.2.1 Arbitration Law 1994

Article 34

An arbitrator shall withdrawn and the parties concerned have the right to request withdrawal, in one of the following circumstances:

1. This provision is subject to subsequent replacement or supplementation by a code of conduct, see Article 8.44(2) and the Code of Conduct in Annex 29-B.

1. The arbitrator is a party involved in the case or a blood relation or relative of the parties concerned or their attorneys.
2. The arbitrator has vital personal interests in the case.
3. The arbitrator has other relations with the parties or their attorneys involved in the case that might effect the fair ruling of the case.
4. The arbitrator meets the parties concerned or their attorneys in private or has accepted gifts or attended banquets hosted by the parties concerned or their attorneys.

Article 35

In requesting for withdrawal, the parties concerned shall state reasons before the first hearing of the tribunal. If the reasons are known only after the first hearing, they may be stated before the end of the last hearing.

Article 36

The withdrawal of an arbitrator shall be decided upon by the chairman of the arbitration commission. Whereas the chairman of the arbitration commission serves as an arbitrator, the withdrawal shall be decided upon collectively by the arbitration commission.

1.3 England

1.3.1 Arbitration Act 1996

Section 24 – Power of court to remove arbitrator

(1) A party to arbitral proceedings may (upon notice to the other parties, to the arbitrator concerned and to any other arbitrator) apply to the court to remove an arbitrator on any of the following grounds—
  (a) that circumstances exist that give rise to justifiable doubts as to his impartiality;
  (b) that he does not possess the qualifications required by the arbitration agreement;
  (c) that he is physically or mentally incapable of conducting the proceedings or there are justifiable doubts as to his capacity to do so;
  (d) that he has refused or failed—
    (i) properly to conduct the proceedings, or
    (ii) to use all reasonable despatch in conducting the proceedings or making an award,
    and that substantial injustice has been or will be caused to the applicant.

(2) If there is an arbitral or other institution or person vested by the parties with power to remove an arbitrator, the court shall not exercise its power of

removal unless satisfied that the applicant has first exhausted any available recourse to that institution or person.

(3) The arbitral tribunal may continue the arbitral proceedings and make an award while an application to the court under this section is pending.

(4) Where the court removes an arbitrator, it may make such order as it thinks fit with respect to his entitlement (if any) to fees or expenses, or the repayment of any fees or expenses already paid.

(5) The arbitrator concerned is entitled to appear and be heard by the court before it makes any order under this section.

(6) The leave of the court is required for any appeal from a decision of the court under this section.

Section 33 – General duty of the tribunal

(1) The tribunal shall–

(a) act fairly and impartially as between the parties, giving each party a reasonable opportunity of putting his case and dealing with that of his opponent, and

(b) adopt procedures suitable to the circumstances of the particular case, avoiding unnecessary delay or expense, so as to provide a fair means for the resolution of the matters falling to be determined.

(2) The tribunal shall comply with that general duty in conducting the arbitral proceedings, in its decisions on matters of procedure and evidence and in the exercise of all other powers conferred on it.

Section 68 – Challenging the award: serious irregularity

(1) A party to arbitral proceedings may (upon notice to the other parties and to the tribunal) apply to the court challenging an award in the proceedings on the ground of serious irregularity affecting the tribunal, the proceedings or the award.

A party may lose the right to object (see section 73) and the right to apply is subject to the restrictions in section 70(2) and (3).

(2) Serious irregularity means an irregularity of one or more of the following kinds which the court considers has caused or will cause substantial injustice to the applicant–

(a) failure by the tribunal to comply with section 33 (general duty of tribunal);

[...]

1.4 France

1.4.1 Code of Civil Procedure – Book IV – Arbitration (2011)

Title I Domestic Arbitration

Article 1456

The constitution of an arbitral tribunal shall be complete upon the arbitrators' acceptance of their mandate. As of that date, the tribunal is seized of the dispute.

Before accepting a mandate, an arbitrator shall disclose any circumstance that may affect his or her independence or impartiality. He or she also shall disclose promptly any such circumstance that may arise after accepting the mandate.

If the parties cannot agree on the removal of an arbitrator, the issue shall be resolved by the person responsible for administering the arbitration or, where there is no such person, by the judge acting in support of the arbitration to whom application must be made within one month following the disclosure or the discovery of the fact at issue.

Title II International Arbitration

Article 1506

Unless the parties have agreed otherwise, and subject to the provisions of the present Title, the following Articles shall apply to international arbitration:

[...]
(2) 1452 through 1458 and 1460 regarding the constitution of the arbitral tribunal and the procedure governing application to the judge acting in support of the arbitration;
[...]

Article 1520

An award may only be set aside where:

(1) the arbitral tribunal wrongly upheld or declined jurisdiction; or
(2) the arbitral tribunal was not properly constituted; or
(3) the arbitral tribunal ruled without complying with the mandate conferred upon it; or
(4) due process was violated; or
(5) recognition or enforcement of the award is contrary to international public policy.

1.4.2 Code de l'organisation judiciaire (as of 2018)

Article L111-6

Subject to provisions specific to certain jurisdictions, an application may be made for the disqualification of a judge:

1° If he or his spouse has a personal interest in the challenge;
2° If he or his spouse is a creditor, debtor, presumptive heir or donee of one of the parties;
3° If he or his spouse is a relative or ally of one of the parties or of his spouse up to the fourth degree inclusively;
4° If there has been or is being a procedure between him or his spouse and one of the parties or his spouse;
5° If he has previously heard the case as a judge or arbitrator or if he has advised one of the parties;
6° If the judge or his spouse is in charge of administering the property of one of the parties;
7° If there is a relationship of subordination between the judge or his spouse and one of the parties or his spouse;
8° If there is a known friendship or enmity between the judge and one of the parties;
9° If there is a conflict of interest, within the meaning of article 7-1 of Ordinance No. 58-1270 of 22 December 1958 on the Basic Law on the Status of the Judiciary.

Magistrates of the Public Prosecutor's Office, joined party, may be challenged in the same cases.

1.5 Sweden

1.5.1 Arbitration Act (2019)[2]

Section 8

An arbitrator shall be impartial and independent.

If a party so requests, an arbitrator shall be released from appointment if there exists any circumstance that may diminish confidence in the arbitrator's impartiality or independence. Such a circumstance shall always be deemed to exist:

1. if the arbitrator or a person closely associated with the arbitrator is a party, or otherwise may expect noteworthy benefit or detriment as a result of the outcome of the dispute;

2. Translation from: https://sccinstitute.com/media/408924/the-swedish-arbitration-act_1march2019_eng.pdf.

2. if the arbitrator or a person closely associated with the arbitrator is the director of a company or any other association which is a party, or otherwise represents a party or any other person who may expect noteworthy benefit or detriment as a result of the outcome of the dispute;
3. if the arbitrator, in the capacity of expert or otherwise, has taken a position in the dispute, or has assisted a party in the preparation or conduct of its case in the dispute; or
4. if the arbitrator has received or demanded compensation in violation of Section 39, second paragraph.

Section 9

A person who is asked to accept an appointment as arbitrator shall immediately disclose all circumstances which, pursuant to Sections 7 or 8, might be considered to prevent the person from serving as arbitrator. An arbitrator shall inform the parties and the other arbitrators of such circumstances as soon as all arbitrators have been appointed and thereafter in the course of the arbitral proceedings as soon as the arbitrator has learned of any new circumstance.

Section 10

A challenge of an arbitrator on account of a circumstance set forth in Section 8 shall be presented within fifteen days from the date on which the party became aware both of the appointment of the arbitrator and of the existence of the circumstance. The challenge shall be adjudicated by the arbitrators, unless the parties have decided that it shall be determined by another party.

If the challenge is successful, the decision shall not be subject to appeal.

A party who is dissatisfied with a decision denying a challenge or dismissing a challenge as untimely may file an application with the District Court that the arbitrator be released from appointment. The application must be submitted within thirty days from the date on which the party was notified of the decision. The arbitrators may continue the arbitral proceedings pending the determination of the District Court.

Section 11

The parties may agree that a challenge as referred to in Section 10, first paragraph, shall be conclusively determined by an arbitration institution.

1.6 Switzerland

1.6.1 Federal Private International Law Act (PILA, 1987)[3]

Article 179 – IV. Arbitrators 1. Appointment and replacement

[...]

6 A person who has been approached to serve as arbitrator must promptly disclose any circumstances that may give rise to justifiable doubts as to his or her independence or impartiality. This obligation shall persist for the duration of the proceedings.

Article 180 – 2. Challenge a. Grounds

1 An arbitrator may be challenged:
  a) if that arbitrator does not meet the qualifications agreed upon by the parties;
  b) if a ground for challenge exists under the arbitration rules agreed upon by the parties;
  c) if circumstances exist that give rise to justifiable doubts as to that arbitrator's independence or impartiality.

2 A party may challenge an arbitrator whom it has appointed or in whose appointment it has participated only for reasons of which, despite having exercised due diligence, it became aware of only after the appointment.

Article 180a – b. Procedure

1 Unless the parties have agreed otherwise and if the arbitral proceedings are not yet concluded, the request for challenge shall be addressed, with reasons and in writing, to the challenged arbitrator and notified to the other arbitrators within 30 days of the requesting party becoming aware, or exercising due diligence ought to have become aware, of the ground for challenge.

2 The requesting party may, within 30 days of the submission of the request for challenge, challenge the arbitrator before the state court. The decision of the state court is final.

3 Unless the parties have agreed otherwise, during the challenge procedure the arbitral tribunal may proceed with the arbitration and render an award, with the participation of the challenged arbitrator.

3. Including 2020 revisions. Unofficial translation by the Swiss Arbitration Association (https://www.swissarbitration.org/swiss-arbitration/swiss-arbitration-laws).

1.7 United States of America

1.7.1 Federal Arbitration Act (9 U.S. Code Title 9)

9 U.S. Code §10. Same[4]; vacation; grounds; rehearing

(a) In any of the following cases the United States court in and for the district wherein the award was made may make an order vacating the award upon the application of any party to the arbitration—

[...]

(2) where there was evident partiality or corruption in the arbitrators, or either of them;

[...]

1.7.2 Restatement of the Law, The U.S. Law of International Commercial and Investor-State Arbitration (Approved Final Draft 2019[5])

Section 4(18)(b)

A showing of evident partiality requires proof that would cause an objective, disinterested observer who is fully informed of the relevant facts relating to the arbitrator's conduct or alleged conflicts of interest to have a serious doubt regarding the fundamental fairness of the arbitral proceedings.

2. ARBITRATION RULES

2.1 UNCITRAL Arbitration Rules (1976/2010/2013)

Article 12

1. Any arbitrator may be challenged if circumstances exist that give rise to justifiable doubts as to the arbitrator's impartiality or independence.
2. A party may challenge the arbitrator appointed by it only for reasons of which it becomes aware after the appointment has been made.
3. In the event that an arbitrator fails to act or in the event of the de jure or de facto impossibility of his or her performing his or her functions, the procedure in respect of the challenge of an arbitrator as provided in article 13 shall apply.

4. Referring to §9 "Award of arbitrators; confirmation; jurisdiction; procedure".
5. Subject to final editing.

Article 13

1. A party that intends to challenge an arbitrator shall send notice of its challenge within 15 days after it has been notified of the appointment of the challenged arbitrator, or within 15 days after the circumstances mentioned in articles 11 and 12 became known to that party.
2. The notice of challenge shall be communicated to all other parties, to the arbitrator who is challenged and to the other arbitrators. The notice of challenge shall state the reasons for the challenge.
3. When an arbitrator has been challenged by a party, all parties may agree to the challenge. The arbitrator may also, after the challenge, withdraw from his or her office. In neither case does this imply acceptance of the validity of the grounds for the challenge.
4. If, within 15 days from the date of the notice of challenge, all parties do not agree to the challenge or the challenged arbitrator does not withdraw, the party making the challenge may elect to pursue it. In that case, within 30 days from the date of the notice of challenge, it shall seek a decision on the challenge by the appointing authority.

2.2 China International Economic and Trade Arbitration Commission (CIETAC)

2.2.1 CIETAC Arbitration Rules (2015)

Article 24 Duties of Arbitrator

An arbitrator shall not represent either party, and shall be and remain independent of the parties and treat them equally.

Article 31 Disclosure

1. An arbitrator nominated by the parties or appointed by the Chairman of CIETAC shall sign a Declaration and disclose any facts or circumstances likely to give rise to justifiable doubts as to his/her impartiality or independence.
2. If circumstances that need to be disclosed arise during the arbitral proceedings, the arbitrator shall promptly disclose such circumstances in writing.
3. The Declaration and/or the disclosure of the arbitrator shall be submitted to the Arbitration Court to be forwarded to the parties.

Article 32 Challenge to Arbitrator

1. Upon receipt of the Declaration and/or the written disclosure of an arbitrator, a party wishing to challenge the arbitrator on the grounds of the disclosed facts or circumstances shall forward the challenge in writing within ten (10) days from the date of such receipt. If a party fails to file a challenge within the above

time period, it may not subsequently challenge the arbitrator on the basis of the matters disclosed by the arbitrator.

2. A party having justifiable doubts as to the impartiality or independence of an arbitrator may challenge that arbitrator in writing and shall state the facts and reasons on which the challenge is based with supporting evidence.
3. A party may challenge an arbitrator in writing within fifteen (15) days from the date it receives the Notice of Formation of the Arbitral Tribunal. Where a party becomes aware of a reason for a challenge after such receipt, the party may challenge the arbitrator in writing within fifteen (15) days after such reason has become known to it, but no later than the conclusion of the last oral hearing.
4. The challenge by one party shall be promptly communicated to the other party, the arbitrator being challenged and the other members of the arbitral tribunal.
5. Where an arbitrator is challenged by one party and the other party agrees to the challenge, or the arbitrator being challenged voluntarily withdraws from his/her office, such arbitrator shall no longer be a member of the arbitral tribunal. However, in neither case shall it be implied that the reasons for the challenge are sustained.
6. In circumstances other than those specified in the preceding Paragraph 5, the Chairman of CIETAC shall make a final decision on the challenge with or without stating the reasons.
7. An arbitrator who has been challenged shall continue to serve on the arbitral tribunal until a final decision on the challenge has been made by the Chairman of CIETAC.

2.3 Deutsches Institut für Schiedsgerichtsbarkeit (DIS)

2.3.1 DIS Arbitration Rules (2018)

Article 9 Impartiality and Independence of the Arbitrators, Duties of Disclosure

9.1 Every arbitrator shall be impartial and independent of the parties throughout the entire arbitration and shall have all of the qualifications, if any, that have been agreed upon by the parties.

9.2 Subject to Article 9.1, the parties may nominate any person of their choice to act as an arbitrator. The DIS may propose names of potential arbitrators to any party upon such party's request.

9.3 Every prospective arbitrator shall declare in writing whether they accept to act as arbitrator.

9.4 In case of acceptance, the prospective arbitrators shall sign a declaration in which they shall state that they are impartial and independent of the parties, that they have all of the qualifications, if any, that have been agreed upon by the parties, and that they will be available throughout the arbitration. In addition, each prospective arbitrator shall disclose any facts or circumstances that could cause a reasonable person in the position of a party to have doubts as to the arbitrator's impartiality and independence.

9.5 The DIS shall send each prospective arbitrator's declaration and any disclosures pursuant to Articles 9.3 and 9.4 to the parties and shall set a time limit for the parties to provide any comments regarding the appointment of the prospective arbitrator.

9.6 Every arbitrator shall have a continuing obligation throughout the entire arbitration to promptly disclose in writing to the parties, the other arbitrators and the DIS any facts or circumstances in the sense of Article 9.4.

[...]

Article 15 Challenge of an Arbitrator

15.1 Any party who seeks to challenge an arbitrator, on the grounds that the arbitrator has failed to comply with one or more of the requirements of Article 9.1, shall file a request for challenge ("Challenge") pursuant to Article 15.2.

15.2 The Challenge shall describe the facts and circumstances on which it is based and shall specify when the party filing the Challenge first obtained knowledge of the same. The Challenge shall be filed with the DIS no later than 14 days after the party filing the Challenge first obtained knowledge of the facts and circumstances on which it is based.

15.3 The DIS shall transmit the Challenge to the challenged arbitrator, the other arbitrators and the other party, and shall set a time limit for comments. The DIS shall send any comments that it receives to the parties and to each arbitrator.

15.4 The Arbitration Council shall decide upon the Challenge.

15.5 The arbitral tribunal may proceed with the arbitration, unless and until the Challenge is accepted.

2.4 Hong Kong International Arbitration Centre

2.4.1 HKIAC Administred Arbitration Rules (2018)

Article 11 – Qualifications and Challenge of the Arbitral Tribunal

11.1 An arbitral tribunal confirmed under these Rules shall be and remain at all times impartial and independent of the parties.

[...]

11.4 Before confirmation or appointment, a prospective arbitrator shall (a) sign a statement confirming his or her availability to decide the dispute and his or her impartiality and independence; and (b) disclose any circumstances likely to give rise to justifiable doubts as to his or her impartiality or independence. An arbitrator, once confirmed or appointed and throughout the arbitration, shall disclose without delay any such circumstances to the parties unless they have already been informed by him or her of these circumstances.

11.5 No party or its representatives shall have any ex parte communication relating to the arbitration with any arbitrator, or with any candidate to be designated as arbitrator by a party, except to advise the candidate of the general nature of the dispute, to discuss the candidate's qualifications, availability, impartiality or independence, or to discuss the suitability of candidates for the designation of a third arbitrator where the parties or party-designated arbitrators are to designate that arbitrator. No party or its representatives shall have any ex parte communication relating to the arbitration with any candidate for the presiding arbitrator.

11.6 Any arbitrator may be challenged if circumstances exist that give rise to justifiable doubts as to the arbitrator's impartiality or independence, or if the arbitrator does not possess qualifications agreed by the parties, or if the arbitrator becomes de jure or de facto unable to perform his or her functions or for other reasons fails to act without undue delay. A party may challenge the arbitrator designated by it or in whose appointment it has participated only for reasons of which it becomes aware after the designation has been made.

11.7 A party that intends to challenge an arbitrator shall send notice of its challenge within 15 days after the confirmation or appointment of that arbitrator has been communicated to the challenging party or within 15 days after that party became aware of the circumstances mentioned in Article 11.6.

11.8 The notice of challenge shall be communicated to HKIAC, all other parties, the challenged arbitrator and any other members of the arbitral tribunal. The notice of challenge shall state the reasons for the challenge.

11.9 Unless the arbitrator being challenged resigns or the non-challenging party agrees to the challenge within 15 days from receiving the notice of challenge, HKIAC shall decide on the challenge. Pending the determination of the challenge, the arbitral tribunal (including the challenged arbitrator) may continue the arbitration.

11.10 If an arbitrator resigns or a party agrees to a challenge under Article 11.9, no acceptance of the validity of any ground referred to in Article 11.6 shall be implied.

2.4.2 Practice Notes on Challenges to Arbitrators (2019)

See https://www.hkiac.org/sites/default/files/ck_filebrowser/PDF/arbitration/20190311_Practice_Note_on_Challenges_of_Arbitrators.pdf[6]

2.5 International Center for Dispute Resolution (ICDR)

2.5.1 International Dispute Resolution Procedures (2021)

Article 14: Impartiality and Independence of Arbitrator

1. Arbitrators acting under these Rules shall be impartial and independent and shall act in accordance with these Rules, the terms of the Notice of Appointment provided by the Administrator, and with *The Code of Ethics for Arbitrators in Commercial Disputes*.
2. Upon accepting appointment, an arbitrator shall sign the Notice of Appointment provided by the Administrator affirming that the arbitrator is available to serve and is independent and impartial. The arbitrator shall disclose any circumstances that may give rise to justifiable doubts as to the arbitrator's impartiality or independence and any other relevant facts the arbitrator wishes to bring to the attention of the parties.
3. If, at any stage during the arbitration, circumstances arise that may give rise to such doubts, an arbitrator or party shall promptly disclose such information to all parties and to the Administrator. Upon receipt of such information from an arbitrator or a party, the Administrator shall communicate it to all parties and to the tribunal.
4. Disclosure by an arbitrator or party does not necessarily indicate belief by the arbitrator or party that the disclosed information gives rise to justifiable doubts as to the arbitrator's impartiality or independence.
5. Failure of a party to disclose any circumstances that may give rise to justifiable doubts as to an arbitrator's impartiality or independence within a reasonable period after the party becomes aware of such information constitutes a waiver of the right to challenge an arbitrator based on those circumstances.
6. No party or anyone acting on its behalf shall have any ex parte communication relating to the case with any arbitrator, or with any candidate for party-appointed arbitrator, except to advise the candidate of the general nature of the controversy and of the anticipated proceedings and to discuss the candidate's qualifications, availability, or impartiality and independence in relation to the parties, or to discuss the suitability of candidates for selection as a presiding arbitrator where the parties or party-appointed arbitrators are to participate in that selection. No party or anyone acting on its behalf shall have any ex parte communication relating to the case with any candidate for presiding arbitrator.

6. Last visited 23 May 2021.

7. On the application of a party, or on its own initiative after consulting the parties, the tribunal may require the parties to disclose:
   a. Whether any non-party (such as a third-party funder or an insurer) has undertaken to pay or to contribute to the cost of a party's participation in the arbitration, and if so, to identify the person or entity concerned and to describe the nature of the undertaking.
   b. Whether any non-party (such as a funder, insurer, parent company, or ultimate beneficial owner) has an economic interest in the outcome of the arbitration, and if so, to identify the person or entity concerned and to describe the nature of the interest.

Article 15: Challenge of an Arbitrator

1. A party may challenge an arbitrator whenever circumstances exist that give rise to justifiable doubts as to the arbitrator's impartiality or independence, or for failing to perform the arbitrator's duties. Unless a shorter time period is otherwise agreed by the parties, specified by law, or determined by the Administrator, a party shall send a written notice of the challenge to the Administrator within 15 days after being notified of the appointment of the arbitrator or within 15 days after the circumstances giving rise to the challenge become known to that party. The challenge shall state in writing the reasons for the challenge. The party shall not send this notice to any member of the arbitral tribunal.
2. Upon receipt of such a challenge, the Administrator shall notify the other party of the challenge and give such party an opportunity to respond. The Administrator shall not send the notice of challenge to any member of the tribunal but shall notify the tribunal that a challenge has been received, without identifying the party challenging. When an arbitrator has been challenged by a party, the other party may agree to the acceptance of the challenge and, if there is agreement, the arbitrator shall be removed. The Administrator may advise the challenged arbitrator of the challenge and request information from the challenged arbitrator relating to the challenge. The challenged arbitrator, after consultation with the Administrator, also may withdraw in the absence of such agreement. In neither case does withdrawal imply acceptance of the validity of the grounds for the challenge.
3. If the other party does not agree to the challenge or the challenged arbitrator does not withdraw, the Administrator shall make the decision on the challenge.
4. The Administrator, on its own initiative, may remove an arbitrator for failing to perform or if the arbitrator becomes incapable of performing the duties of an arbitrator.

2.5.2 *The Code of Ethics for Arbitrators in Commercial Disputes (American Arbitration Association 2004)*

See https://adr.org/sites/default/files/document_repository/Commercial_Code_of_Ethics_for_Arbitrators_2010_10_14.pdf[7]

2.6 International Chamber of Commerce (ICC)

2.6.1 *ICC Arbitration Rules (2021)*

Article 11: General Provisions

1) Every arbitrator must be and remain impartial and independent of the parties involved in the arbitration.
2) Before appointment or confirmation, a prospective arbitrator shall sign a statement of acceptance, availability, impartiality and independence. The prospective arbitrator shall disclose in writing to the Secretariat any facts or circumstances which might be of such a nature as to call into question the arbitrator's independence in the eyes of the parties, as well as any circumstances that could give rise to reasonable doubts as to the arbitrator's impartiality. The Secretariat shall provide such information to the parties in writing and fix a time limit for any comments from them.
3) An arbitrator shall immediately disclose in writing to the Secretariat and to the parties any facts or circumstances of a similar nature to those referred to in Article 11(2) concerning the arbitrator's impartiality or independence which may arise during the arbitration.
4) The decisions of the Court as to the appointment, confirmation, challenge or replacement of an arbitrator shall be final.
5) By accepting to serve, arbitrators undertake to carry out their responsibilities in accordance with the Rules.
6) Insofar as the parties have not provided otherwise, the arbitral tribunal shall be constituted in accordance with the provisions of Articles 12 and 13.
7) In order to assist prospective arbitrators and arbitrators in complying with their duties under Articles 11(2) and 11(3), each party must promptly inform the Secretariat, the arbitral tribunal and the other parties, of the existence and identity of any non-party which has entered into an arrangement for the funding of claims or defences and under which it has an economic interest in the outcome of the arbitration.

7. Last visited 23 May 2021.

Article 14: Challenge of Arbitrators

1) A challenge of an arbitrator, whether for an alleged lack of impartiality or independence, or otherwise, shall be made by the submission to the Secretariat of a written statement specifying the facts and circumstances on which the challenge is based.
2) For a challenge to be admissible, it must be submitted by a party either within 30 days from receipt by that party of the notification of the appointment or confirmation of the arbitrator, or within 30 days from the date when the party making the challenge was informed of the facts and circumstances on which the challenge is based if such date is subsequent to the receipt of such notification.
3) The Court shall decide on the admissibility and, at the same time, if necessary, on the merits of a challenge after the Secretariat has afforded an opportunity for the arbitrator concerned, the other party or parties and any other members of the arbitral tribunal to comment in writing within a suitable period of time. Such comments shall be communicated to the parties and to the arbitrators.

2.6.2 Note to Parties and Arbitral Tribunals on the Conduct of the Arbitration under the ICC Rules of Arbitration (2021)

III - Arbitral Tribunal

A - Statement of Acceptance, Availability, Impartiality and Independence

22. All arbitrators, including emergency arbitrators, have the duty to act at all times in an impartial and independent manner (Articles 11 and 22(4)).
23. The Court requires all prospective arbitrators to complete and sign a Statement of Acceptance, Availability, Impartiality and Independence ("Statement") (Article 11(2)).
24. The parties have a legitimate interest in being fully informed of all facts or circumstances that may be relevant in their view to be satisfied that an arbitrator or prospective arbitrator is and remains independent and impartial or, if the parties so wish, to explore the matter further and/or take the initiatives contemplated by the Rules.
25. An arbitrator or prospective arbitrator must disclose in his or her Statement, at the time of his or her appointment and as the arbitration is ongoing, any circumstance that might be of such a nature as to call into question his or her independence in the eyes of any of the parties or give rise to reasonable doubts as to his or her impartiality. Any doubt must be resolved in favour of disclosure.
26. A disclosure does not imply the existence of a conflict. On the contrary, arbitrators who make disclosures consider themselves to be impartial and independent, notwithstanding the disclosed facts, or else they would decline to serve. In the event of an objection or a challenge, it is for the Court to assess

whether the matter disclosed is an impediment to service as arbitrator. Although failure to disclose is not in itself a ground for disqualification, it will however be considered by the Court in assessing whether an objection to confirmation or a challenge is well founded.

27. Each arbitrator or prospective arbitrator must assess what circumstances, if any, are such as to call into question his or her independence in the eyes of the parties or give rise to reasonable doubts as to his or her impartiality. In making such assessment, an arbitrator or prospective arbitrator should consider all potentially relevant circumstances, including but not limited to the following:
    - The arbitrator or prospective arbitrator or his or her law firm represents or advises, or has represented or advised, one of the parties or one of its affiliates.
    - The arbitrator or prospective arbitrator or his or her law firm acts or has acted against one of the parties or one of its affiliates.
    - The arbitrator or prospective arbitrator or his or her law firm has a business relationship with one of the parties or one of its affiliates, or a personal interest of any nature in the outcome of the dispute.
    - The arbitrator or prospective arbitrator or his or her law firm acts or has acted on behalf of one of the parties or one of its affiliates as director, board member, officer, or otherwise.
    - The arbitrator or prospective arbitrator or his or her law firm is or has been involved in the dispute, or has expressed a view on the dispute in a manner that might affect his or her impartiality.
    - The arbitrator or prospective arbitrator has a professional or close personal relationship with counsel to one of the parties or the counsel's law firm.
    - The arbitrator or prospective arbitrator acts or has acted as arbitrator in a case involving one of the parties or one of its affiliates.
    - The arbitrator or prospective arbitrator acts or has acted as arbitrator in a related case.
    - The arbitrator or prospective arbitrator has in the past been appointed as arbitrator by one of the parties or one of its affiliates, or by counsel to one of the parties or the counsel's law firm.

    In assessing whether a disclosure should be made, an arbitrator or prospective arbitrator should consider relationships with non-parties having an interest in the outcome of the arbitration, such as third-party funders as well as relationships with other members of the arbitral tribunal, as well as experts or witnesses in the case.

28. To assist prospective arbitrators, the Secretariat endeavours to identify, at the outset of the case, entities and individuals in the arbitration that may be relevant for purposes of disclosures. Such an indication does not release an arbitrator or prospective arbitrator from his or her duty to disclose with respect to other relevant entities and individuals he or she may be aware of.

In case of doubt with respect to such an indication made by the Secretariat, an arbitrator or prospective arbitrator is encouraged to consult the Secretariat.

29. The duty to disclose is of an ongoing nature and it therefore applies throughout the duration of the arbitration.
30. Although an advance declaration or waiver in relation to possible conflicts of interest arising from facts and circumstances that may arise in the future may or may not in certain circumstances be taken into account by the Court, such advance declaration or waiver does not discharge an arbitrator from his or her ongoing duty to disclose.
31. When completing his or her Statement and identifying whether he or she should make a disclosure, both at the outset of the arbitration and subsequently, an arbitrator or prospective arbitrator should make reasonable enquiries in his or her records, those of his or her law firm and, as the case may be, in other readily available materials.
32. For the scope of disclosures, an arbitrator is considered to bear the identity of his or her law firm, and a legal entity will include its affiliates. In addressing possible objections to confirmation or challenges, the Court will consider the activities of the arbitrator's law firm and the relationship of the law firm with the arbitrator in each individual case. In each case, arbitrators should consider disclosing relationships with another arbitrator or counsel who is a member of the same barristers' chambers. Arbitrators should also consider relationships between arbitrators, as well as relationships with any entity having a direct economic interest in the dispute or an obligation to indemnify a party for the award.
33. Arbitrators have a duty to devote to the arbitration the time necessary to conduct the proceedings as diligently, efficiently and expeditiously as possible. Accordingly, prospective arbitrators must indicate in the Statement the number of arbitrations in which they are currently acting, specifying whether they are acting as president, sole arbitrator, co-arbitrator or counsel to a party, as well as any other commitments and their availability over the next 24 months.
34. If one or more parties object to the confirmation of a prospective arbitrator, or in case of a challenge, the Secretariat will invite the other party or parties and the arbitrator or prospective arbitrator to comment.
35. Arbitrators are encouraged to ensure that they have appropriate insurance to cover their liability. In assessing whether they should seek insurance, arbitrators may want to consider the circumstances of the case, including the amount in dispute, the currencies used, the parties' nationality and location, the place of arbitration and the location of hearings.
36. By signing the Statement, prospective arbitrators acknowledge that their name and contact details, as well as their curriculum vitae, may be communicated to the members of the Court, the Secretariat at its various offices, and to ICC National Committees and Groups to perform the functions assigned to them under the Rules. By signing the Statement, prospective arbitrators also acknowledge that their names and related information, as well as their

award(s), procedural order(s) and dissenting or concurring opinion(s) may be published pursuant to sections IV(B) and (C), to (a) further the legitimate interests of the parties, arbitrators and the public in accessing transparent information about ICC arbitration; (b) assist them in their decision making and in pursuing their legitimate interests; (c) safeguard the parties' fundamental procedural rights through arbitration and (d) ensure the rendering of high quality awards. The prospective arbitrator may object to the publication if his/her interests and fundamental rights override such legitimate interests.

2.7 Japan Commercial Arbitration Association (JCAA)

2.7.1 JCAA Commercial Arbitration Rules (2019)

Article 24 Impartiality and Independence of Arbitrators

1 A person who is not impartial and independent shall decline to accept an appointment as an arbitrator. An arbitrator shall be, and remain at all times, impartial and independent during the arbitral proceedings.

2 When a person is approached in connection with his or her possible appointment as an arbitrator, he or she shall conduct a reasonable investigation into any circumstances which may, in the eyes of the Parties, give rise to justifiable doubts as to his or her impartiality or independence. If he or she finds such circumstances, he or she shall decline to accept the appointment or disclose in writing such circumstances to enable the approaching person to decide whether or not to withdraw its request for appointment.

3 When a person is appointed as an arbitrator, he or she shall promptly submit in writing to the Parties and the JCAA his or her undertaking to disclose any circumstances which may give rise to justifiable doubts as to his or her impartiality or independence, or to declare that there are no such circumstances (the "**Declaration of Impartiality and Independence**").

4 During the course of the arbitral proceedings, an arbitrator shall have an ongoing duty to make reasonable investigation into any circumstances which may, in the eyes of the Parties, give rise to justifiable doubts as to the arbitrator's impartiality or independence. If the arbitrator finds such circumstances, the arbitrator shall promptly disclose to the Parties and the JCAA in writing such circumstances, unless the arbitrator has already disclosed such circumstances. An advance declaration in relation to such circumstances that may possibly arise in the future does not discharge the arbitrator's ongoing duty of disclosure.

Article 34 Challenge to Arbitrators

1 A Party may challenge an arbitrator if circumstances give rise to justifiable doubts as to the arbitrator's impartiality or independence.
2 A Party may challenge an arbitrator it has appointed, or whose appointment the Party has participated in by way of recommendation or any similar acts, only for reasons which the Party becomes aware of after the appointment has been made.
3 A Party that intends to challenge an arbitrator shall submit in writing to the JCAA a request for challenge (the "**Request for Challenge**") within two weeks from the date of its receipt of the notice by the JCAA confirming the appointment of the arbitrator (the Notice of Appointment of the arbitrator, if the arbitrator is appointed by the JCAA) or the date when it became aware of any circumstance under Article 34.1, whichever comes later.
4 On receipt of the Request for Challenge, the JCAA shall promptly notify the other Party and the challenged arbitrator, supplying them with a copy thereof.
5 The JCAA shall make a decision on the challenge without giving reasons, after giving the other Party and the challenged arbitrator an opportunity to comment.

2.8 Korean Commercial Arbitration Board

2.8.1 KCAB Arbitration Rules (2016)

Article 10. General Provisions

1. Arbitrators under the Rules shall be, and remain at all times, impartial and independent.
2. An arbitrator who accepts an appointment or nomination shall sign and submit a Statement of Acceptance and a Statement of Impartiality and Independence in the form provided by the Secretariat. An arbitrator shall disclose to the Secretariat any circumstances likely to give rise to justifiable doubts as to the arbitrator's impartiality or independence, and if at any stage during the arbitration, new circumstances arise that may give rise to such doubts as to the arbitrator's impartiality or independence, the arbitrator shall immediately disclose such circumstances in writing to the parties and to the Secretariat.
3. The Secretariat shall provide to the parties the Statement of Acceptance and the Statement of Impartiality and Independence immediately upon receipt.
4. The decisions of the Secretariat on any matter related to the appointment, replacement or removal of arbitrators shall be final and not subject to appeal.

Article 14. Challenge of Arbitrators

1. A party may challenge an arbitrator if circumstances give rise to justifiable doubts as to the arbitrator's impartiality or independence. A party that nominates an arbitrator may challenge such arbitrator only for reasons of which the party becomes aware after the nomination.
2. A challenge of an arbitrator for lack of impartiality or independence, or for other reasons, shall be made by submitting a written statement to the Secretariat specifying the facts and circumstances on which the challenge is based. Such statement shall be copied to the Arbitral Tribunal and to each other party.
3. A challenge shall be considered valid only if it is made within 15 days from either of the following:
   a) the date of receipt of the confirmation if the parties nominated the arbitrator, or the date of receipt of the appointment if the Secretariat appointed the arbitrator; or
   b) the date on which the party making the challenge becomes aware of the facts and circumstances giving rise to such challenge.
4. The challenged arbitrator, the other party or parties, and any other member of the Arbitral Tribunal may submit written comments on the challenge to the Secretariat within 15 days of their receipt of the challenge. Such comments shall be copied to the Arbitral Tribunal and each other party.
5. When an arbitrator has been challenged by one party, the arbitrator shall withdraw if all of the parties so agree. The challenged arbitrator may also withdraw voluntarily. In neither case does withdrawal imply acceptance of the validity of the grounds for the challenge. If all of the parties do not agree to the challenge, and the challenged arbitrator does not withdraw voluntarily, the Secretariat shall decide upon the challenge.

2.9 London Court of International Arbitration

2.9.1 LCIA Arbitration Rules (2020)

Article 5 Formation of the Arbitral Tribunal

[...]

5.3 All arbitrators shall be and remain at all times impartial and independent of the parties; and none shall act in the arbitration as advocate for or authorised representative of any party. No arbitrator shall give advice to any party on the parties' dispute or the conduct or outcome of the arbitration.

5.4 Before appointment by the LCIA Court, each arbitrator candidate shall furnish to the Registrar (upon the latter's request) a brief written summary of his or her qualifications and professional positions (past and present); the candidate shall also agree in writing fee rates conforming to the Schedule of Costs; the candidate shall sign a written declaration stating: (i) whether there are any circumstances currently known to the candidate which are likely to give rise in the mind of any party to any justifiable doubts as to his or her impartiality or independence and, if so, specifying in full such circumstances in the declaration; and (ii) whether the candidate is ready, willing and able to devote sufficient time, diligence and industry to ensure the expeditious and efficient conduct of the arbitration. The candidate shall promptly furnish such agreement and declaration to the Registrar.

5.5 Each arbitrator shall assume a continuing duty, until the arbitration is finally concluded, forthwith to disclose in writing any circumstances becoming known to that arbitrator after the date of his or her written declaration (under Article 5.4) which are likely to give rise in the mind of any party to any justifiable doubts as to his or her impartiality or independence, to be delivered to the LCIA Court, any other members of the Arbitral Tribunal and all parties in the arbitration.

[...]

Article 10 Revocation and Challenges

10.1 The LCIA Court may revoke any arbitrator's appointment upon its own initiative, at the written request of all other members of the Arbitral Tribunal or upon a written challenge by any party if: (i) that arbitrator gives written notice to the LCIA Court of his or her intent to resign as arbitrator, to be copied to all parties and all other members of the Arbitral Tribunal (if any); (ii) that arbitrator falls seriously ill, refuses or becomes unable or unfit to act; or (iii) circumstances exist that give rise to justifiable doubts as to that arbitrator's impartiality or independence.

10.2 The LCIA Court may determine that an arbitrator is unfit to act under Article 10.1 if that arbitrator: (i) acts in deliberate violation of the Arbitration Agreement; (ii) does not act fairly or impartially as between the parties; or (iii) does not conduct or participate in the arbitration with reasonable efficiency, diligence and industry.

10.3 A party challenging an arbitrator under Article 10.1 shall, within 14 days of the formation of the Arbitral Tribunal or (if later) within 14 days of becoming aware of any grounds described in Article 10.1 or 10.2, deliver a written statement of the reasons for its challenge to the LCIA Court, the Arbitral Tribunal and all other parties. A party may challenge an arbitrator whom it has nominated, or in whose appointment it has participated, only for reasons of which it becomes aware after the appointment has been made by the LCIA Court.

10.4 If all other parties agree in writing to the challenge within 14 days of receipt of the written statement, the LCIA Court shall revoke that arbitrator's appointment (without reasons).

10.5 Unless the parties so agree or the challenged arbitrator resigns in writing within 14 days of receipt of the written statement, the LCIA Court shall decide the challenge. The LCIA Court may conduct the challenge proceedings in any manner it considers to be appropriate in the circumstances but shall in any event provide the other parties and the challenged arbitrator a reasonable opportunity to comment on the challenging party's written statement. The LCIA Court may require at any time further information and materials from the challenging party, the challenged arbitrator, other parties, any authorised representative of a party, other members of the Arbitral Tribunal and the tribunal secretary (if any).

10.6 The LCIA Court's decision shall be made in writing, with reasons; and a copy shall be transmitted by the Registrar to the parties, the challenged arbitrator and other members of the Arbitral Tribunal (if any). If the challenge is upheld, the LCIA Court shall revoke that arbitrator's appointment. A challenged arbitrator who resigns in writing prior to the LCIA Court's decision shall not be considered as having admitted any part of the written statement.

10.7 The LCIA Court shall determine the amount of fees and expenses (if any) to be paid for the former arbitrator's services, as it may consider appropriate in the circumstances. The LCIA Court may also determine whether, in what amount and to whom any party should pay all or any part of the costs of the challenge; and the LCIA Court may also refer all or any part of such costs to the later decision of the Arbitral Tribunal and/or the LCIA Court under Article 28.

2.9.2 LCIA Notes for Arbitrators[8]

2. INDEPENDENCE AND IMPARTIALITY

6. Parties to arbitrations are entitled to expect of the process a just, well-reasoned and enforceable award. To that end, they are entitled to expect arbitrators: to disclose possible conflicts of interest at the outset; to avoid putting themselves in a position where conflicts will arise during the course of the proceedings; to conduct the arbitration fairly, in a timely manner and with careful regard to due process; to maintain the confidentiality of the arbitration; and to reach their decision in an impartial manner.
7. Under Article 5.4 of the LCIA Rules, all arbitrators are, before appointment, required to sign a declaration that there are no circumstances known to them likely to give rise to any justifiable doubts as to their impartiality or independence.
8. In completing their statements of independence, arbitrators should take into account, amongst other things, the existence and nature of any past or present relationships, direct or indirect, with any of the parties or their counsel. Any

8. Note by the LCIA: "These guidance notes reference the LCIA Rules (2014). In line with the LCIA Rules (2020) updated guidance notes and other related resources will be available from the LCIA website in due course."

doubt as to whether a relationship should be disclosed must be resolved in favour of disclosure.

9. There is a continuing obligation on all arbitrators immediately to disclose any further circumstance of which they become aware at any time during the course of the arbitration, which might give rise to conflicts.

2.10 Shanghai International Arbitration Center (SHIAC)

2.10.1 SHIAC Arbitration Rules (2015)

Article 19 Duties of Arbitrator(s)

An arbitrator shall not represent either party, and shall remain independent of the parties and treat them equally.

Article 25 Disclosure

1. The arbitrator(s) shall sign a Declaration and disclose to SHIAC in writing any facts or circumstances which may give a rise to justifiable doubts as to his/her impartiality or independence.
2. If circumstances that need to be disclosed arise during the arbitration proceedings, the relevant arbitrator shall promptly disclose such circumstances in writing to SHIAC.
3. The arbitrator shall submit the Declaration and/or the disclosure to the Secretariat. The Secretariat shall forward the arbitrator's submissions to the parties.

Article 26 Challenge to Arbitrator(s)

1. Upon receipt of the Declaration and/or written disclosure of an arbitrator communicated by the Secretariat, a party who intends to challenge the arbitrator on the grounds of the facts or circumstances disclosed by the arbitrator shall forward the challenge in writing to SHIAC within ten (10) days upon the date of such receipt. If a party fails to raise a challenge within the aforesaid time limit, it shall not challenge an arbitrator later on the basis of facts disclosed by the arbitrator.
2. A party who has justifiable doubts as to the impartiality or independence of arbitrator(s) may make a request in writing to SHIAC for that arbitrator's withdrawal. In the request, the facts and reasons on which the request is based shall be stated with supporting evidence. The aforesaid challenge of arbitrator shall be made in writing within fifteen (15) days upon the date of receipt of the Notice of the Constitution of the Tribunal. Where a party becomes aware of the facts and reasons for a challenge after that time, the party may challenge the arbitrator in writing within fifteen (15) days after such facts and reasons

become known to the party, but no later than the conclusion of the last hearing.

3. The Secretariat shall communicate the challenge promptly to the other party, the arbitrator being challenged and the other members of the tribunal, who subsequently may all provide their comments on such challenge.
4. Where an arbitrator is challenged by one party and the other party agrees to the challenge, or the arbitrator being challenged withdraws from his/her office, such arbitrator shall no longer act as an arbitrator. Neither circumstance shall imply that the challenge made by the party is sustainable.
5. In circumstances other than those specified in Article 26.4, the Chairman of SHIAC shall render a decision on the challenge with or without stating the reasons thereof.
6. An arbitrator who has been challenged shall continue to perform his/her functions as arbitrator until a decision on the challenge has been made by the Chairman of SHIAC.

2.11 Singapore International Arbitration Center (SIAC)

2.11.1 SIAC Rules (2016)

Rule 13: Qualifications of Arbitrators

13.1 Any arbitrator appointed in an arbitration under these Rules, whether or not nominated by the parties, shall be and remain at all times independent and impartial.

[...]

13.4 A nominated arbitrator shall disclose to the parties and to the Registrar any circumstances that may give rise to justifiable doubts as to his impartiality or independence as soon as reasonably practicable and in any event before his appointment.

13.5 An arbitrator shall immediately disclose to the parties, to the other arbitrators and to the Registrar any circumstances that may give rise to justifiable doubts as to his impartiality or independence that may be discovered or arise during the arbitration.

13.6 No party or person acting on behalf of a party shall have any ex parte communication relating to the case with any arbitrator or with any candidate for appointment as party-nominated arbitrator, except to advise the candidate of the general nature of the controversy and of the anticipated proceedings; to discuss the candidate's qualifications, availability or independence in relation to the parties; or to discuss the suitability of candidates for selection as the presiding arbitrator where the parties or party-nominated arbitrators are to participate in that selection. No party or person acting on behalf of a party shall have any ex parte communication relating to the case with any candidate for presiding arbitrator.

Rule 14: Challenge of Arbitrators

14.1 Any arbitrator may be challenged if circumstances exist that give rise to justifiable doubts as to the arbitrator's impartiality or independence or if the arbitrator does not possess any requisite qualification on which the parties have agreed.

14.2 A party may challenge the arbitrator nominated by it only for reasons of which it becomes aware after the appointment has been made.

2.11.2 Code of Ethics for an Arbitrator

2. Disclosure

2.1 A prospective arbitrator shall disclose all facts or circumstances that may give rise to justifiable doubts as to his impartiality or independence, such duty to continue throughout the arbitral proceedings with regard to new facts and circumstances.

2.2 A prospective arbitrator shall disclose to the Registrar and any party who approaches him for a possible appointment:

(a) any past or present close personal relationship or business relationship, whether direct or indirect, with any party to the dispute, or any representative of a party, or any person known to be a potentially important witness in the arbitration;

(b) the extent of any prior knowledge he may have of the dispute.

3. Bias

3.1 The criteria for assessing questions relating to bias are impartiality and independence. Partiality arises when an arbitrator favours one of the parties or where he is prejudiced in relation to the subject matter of the dispute. Dependence arises from relationships between an arbitrator and one of the parties, or with someone closely connected with one of the parties.

3.2 Any close personal relationship or current direct or indirect business relationship between an arbitrator and a party, or any representative of a party, or with a person who is known to be a potentially important witness, will normally give rise to justifiable doubts as to a prospective arbitrator's impartiality or independence. Past business relationships will only give rise to justifiable doubts if they are of such magnitude or nature as to be likely to affect a prospective arbitrator's judgment. He should decline to accept an appointment in such circumstances unless the parties agree in writing that he may proceed

2.12 Stockholm Chamber of Commerce (SCC)

2.12.1 Arbitration Rules of the Arbitration Institute of the Stockholm Chamber of Commerce (2017)

Article 18 Impartiality, independence and availability

(1) Every arbitrator must be impartial and independent.
(2) Before being appointed, a prospective arbitrator shall disclose any circumstances that may give rise to justifiable doubts as to the prospective arbitrator's impartiality or independence.
(3) Once appointed, an arbitrator shall submit to the Secretariat a signed statement of acceptance, availability, impartiality and independence, disclosing any circumstances that may give rise to justifiable doubts as to the arbitrator's impartiality or independence. The Secretariat shall send a copy of the statement of acceptance, availability, impartiality and independence to the parties and the other arbitrators.
(4) An arbitrator shall immediately inform the parties and the other arbitrators in writing if any circumstances that may give rise to justifiable doubts as to the arbitrator's impartiality or independence arise during the course of the arbitration.

Article 19 Challenge to arbitrators

(1) A party may challenge any arbitrator if circumstances exist that give rise to justifiable doubts as to the arbitrator's impartiality or independence or if the arbitrator does not possess the qualifications agreed by the parties.
(2) A party may challenge an arbitrator it has appointed, or in whose appointment it has participated, only for reasons it becomes aware of after the appointment was made.
(3) A party wishing to challenge an arbitrator shall submit a written statement to the Secretariat stating the reasons for the challenge, within 15 days from the date the circumstances giving rise to the challenge became known to the party. Failure to challenge an arbitrator within the stipulated time constitutes a waiver of the party's right to make the challenge.
(4) The Secretariat shall notify the parties and the arbitrators of the challenge and give them an opportunity to submit comments.
(5) If the other party agrees to the challenge, the arbitrator shall resign. In all other cases, the Board shall take the final decision on the challenge.

2.13 Swiss Arbitration Centre (the Centre)[9]

2.13.1 Swiss Rules of International Arbitration (Swiss Rules) (2012)

INDEPENDENCE AND CHALLENGE OF ARBITRATORS

Article 9

1. All arbitrators conducting an arbitration under these Rules shall be and remain at all times impartial and independent of the parties.
2. Prospective arbitrators shall disclose to those who approach them in connection with a possible appointment any circumstances likely to give rise to justifiable doubts as to their impartiality or independence. An arbitrator, once designated or appointed, shall disclose such circumstances to the parties, unless they have already been so informed.

Article 10

1. Any arbitrator may be challenged if circumstances exist that give rise to justifiable doubts as to the arbitrator's impartiality or independence.
2. A party may challenge the arbitrator appointed by it only for reasons of which it becomes aware after the appointment has been made.

Article 11

1. A party intending to challenge an arbitrator shall send a notice of challenge to the Secretariat within 15 days after the circumstances giving rise to the challenge became known to that party.
2. If, within 15 days from the date of the notice of challenge, all of the parties do not agree to the challenge, or the challenged arbitrator does not withdraw, the Court shall decide on the challenge.
3. The decision of the Court is final and the Court has no obligation to give reasons.

2.13.2 Swiss Rules of International Arbitration (Swiss Rules) (2021)

INDEPENDENCE, IMPARTIALITY AND DISCLOSURES OF ARBITRATORS

9. As of 1 June 2021, the Swiss Chambers' Arbitration Institution (SCAI) was converted into the Swiss Arbitration Centre Ltd under the leadership of ASA. The Swiss Rules were revised by the same time. See https://swissarbitration.org.

Article 12

1. Any arbitrator conducting an arbitration under these Rules shall be and shall remain impartial and independent throughout the proceedings.
2. Before appointment or confirmation, prospective arbitrators shall disclose to the Secretariat any circumstances likely to give rise to justifiable doubts as to their impartiality or independence. The Secretariat shall provide such information to the parties and set a time limit within which they may comment.
3. After appointment or confirmation, each arbitrator shall have the duty to promptly disclose to the Secretariat and to the parties any such circumstances arising in the course of the proceedings.
   CHALLENGE OF AN ARBITRATOR

Article 13

1. Any arbitrator may be challenged if circumstances exist that give rise to justifiable doubts as to the arbitrator's impartiality or independence.
2. A party intending to challenge an arbitrator shall send a notice of challenge to the Secretariat with a copy to the other parties and the arbitral tribunal within 15 days after the circumstances giving rise to the challenge became known to that party.
3. If, within 15 days from the date of the notice of challenge, the parties do not agree to the challenge, or the challenged arbitrator does not withdraw, the Court shall decide on the challenge.

2.14 Vienna International Arbitral Center (VIAC)

2.14.1 Vienna Rules (2018)

Article 16 – General Provisions

[...]

(2) The arbitrators shall perform their mandate independently of the parties, and impartially and, to the best of their knowledge and ability, and they shall not be bound by any instruction. They have the duty to keep confidential all information acquired in the course of their duties.

(3) If a person intends to accept an appointment as an arbitrator, he shall sign and submit a declaration to the Secretary General before his appointment confirming his (i) impartiality and independence; (ii) availability; (iii) qualification; (iv) acceptance of office; and (v) submission to the Vienna Rules.

(4) An arbitrator shall disclose in writing all circumstances that could give rise to doubts as to his impartiality, independence or availability or that conflict with

the agreement of the parties. The duty to immediately disclose such circumstances continues to apply throughout the arbitration.
[...]

Article 20 Challenge of Arbitrators

(1) After his appointment, an arbitrator may be challenged only if circumstances exist that give rise to justifiable doubts as to his impartiality or independence, or if he does not fulfil the qualifications agreed by the parties. A party may challenge the arbitrator whom it nominated, or in whose nomination it has participated, only for reasons of which the party became aware after the nomination or its participation in the nomination.
(2) A party's challenge of an appointed arbitrator shall be submitted to the Secretariat within 15 days from the date the party making the challenge became aware of the grounds for the challenge. The challenge shall specify the grounds for the challenge and include corroborating materials to substantiate the challenge.
(3) If the challenged arbitrator does not resign, the Board shall rule on the challenge. Before the Board makes a decision, the Secretary General shall request comments from the challenged arbitrator and the other party/parties. The Board may also request comments from other persons. All comments shall be communicated to the parties and the arbitrators.
(4) The arbitral tribunal, including the challenged arbitrator, may continue the arbitration while the challenge is pending. The arbitral tribunal may not issue an award until after the Board has ruled on the challenge.

3. VARIOUS REGULATIONS AND GUIDELINES

3.1 International Bar Association (IBA)

3.1.1 Guidelines on Conflicts of Interest in International Arbitration (2014)

(1) General Principle

Every arbitrator shall be impartial and independent of the parties at the time of accepting an appointment to serve and shall remain so until the final award has been rendered or the proceedings have otherwise finally terminated.

(2) Conflicts of Interest

(a) An arbitrator shall decline to accept an appointment or, if the arbitration has already been commenced, refuse to continue to act as an arbitrator, if he or she has any doubt as to his or her ability to be impartial or independent.

(b) The same principle applies if facts or circumstances exist, or have arisen since the appointment, which, from the point of view of a reasonable third person having knowledge of the relevant facts and circumstances, would give rise to justifiable doubts as to the arbitrator's impartiality or independence, unless the parties have accepted the arbitrator in accordance with the requirements set out in General Standard 4.

(c) Doubts are justifiable if a reasonable third person, having knowledge of the relevant facts and circumstances, would reach the conclusion that there is a likelihood that the arbitrator may be influenced by factors other than the merits of the case as presented by the parties in reaching his or her decision.

(d) Justifiable doubts necessarily exist as to the arbitrator's impartiality or independence in any of the situations described in the Non-Waivable Red List.

(3) Disclosure by the Arbitrator

(a) If facts or circumstances exist that may, in the eyes of the parties, give rise to doubts as to the arbitrator's impartiality or independence, the arbitrator shall disclose such facts or circumstances to the parties, the arbitration institution or other appointing authority (if any, and if so required by the applicable institutional rules) and the co-arbitrators, if any, prior to accepting his or her appointment 7 or, if thereafter, as soon as he or she learns of them.

(b) An advance declaration or waiver in relation to possible conflicts of interest arising from facts and circumstances that may arise in the future does not discharge the arbitrator's ongoing duty of disclosure under General Standard 3(a).

(c) It follows from General Standards 1 and 2(a) that an arbitrator who has made a disclosure considers himself or herself to be impartial and independent of the parties, despite the disclosed facts, and, therefore, capable of performing his or her duties as arbitrator. Otherwise, he or she would have declined the nomination or appointment at the outset, or resigned.

(d) Any doubt as to whether an arbitrator should disclose certain facts or circumstances should be resolved in favour of disclosure.

(e) When considering whether facts or circumstances exist that should be disclosed, the arbitrator shall not take into account whether the arbitration is at the beginning or at a later stage.

(4) Waiver by the Parties

[...]

(5) Scope

(a) These Guidelines apply equally to tribunal chairs, sole arbitrators and co-arbitrators, howsoever appointed.

(b) Arbitral or administrative secretaries and assistants, to an individual arbitrator or the Arbitral Tribunal, are bound by the same duty of independence and impartiality as arbitrators, and it is the responsibility of the Arbitral Tribunal to ensure that such duty is respected at all stages of the arbitration.

(6) Relationships

(a) The arbitrator is in principle considered to bear the identity of his or her law firm, but when considering the relevance of facts or circumstances to determine whether a potential conflict of interest exists, or whether disclosure should be made, the activities of an arbitrator's law firm, if any, and the relationship of the arbitrator with the law firm, should be considered in each individual case. The fact that the activities of the arbitrator's firm involve one of the parties shall not necessarily constitute a source of such conflict, or a reason for disclosure. Similarly, if one of the parties is a member of a group with which the arbitrator's firm has a relationship, such fact should be considered in each individual case, but shall not necessarily constitute by itself a source of a conflict of interest, or a reason for disclosure.

(b) If one of the parties is a legal entity, any legal or physical person having a controlling influence on the legal entity, or a direct economic interest in, or a duty to indemnify a party for, the award to be rendered in the arbitration, may be considered to bear the identity of such party.

(7) Duty of the Parties and the Arbitrator

[...]

(d) An arbitrator is under a duty to make reasonable enquiries to identify any conflict of interest, as well as any facts or circumstances that may reasonably give rise to doubts as to his or her impartiality or independence. Failure to disclose a conflict is not excused by lack of knowledge, if the arbitrator does not perform such reasonable enquiries.

Part II: Practical Application of the General Standards

[...]

3.2 Chartered Institute of Arbitrators (CIArb)

3.2.1 CIArb Code of Professional and Ethical Conduct (2009)

Rule 3 Conflicts of Interest

Both before and throughout the dispute resolution process, a member shall disclose all interests, relationships and matters likely to affect the member's independence or impartiality or which might reasonably be perceived as likely to do so.

Where a member is or becomes aware that he or she is incapable of maintaining the required degree of independence or impartiality, the member shall promptly take such steps as may be required in the circumstances, which may include resignation or withdrawal from the process.

3.3 Draft Code of Conduct for Adjudicators in Investor-State Dispute Settlement, Version Two (ICSID/UNCITRAL, 2021)

Article 3 Independence and Impartiality

1. Adjudicators shall be independent and impartial, and shall take reasonable steps to avoid bias, conflict of interest, impropriety, or apprehension of bias;
2. In particular, Adjudicators shall not:
   (a) be influenced by self-interest, fear of criticism, outside pressure, political considerations, or public clamor;
   (b) be influenced by loyalty to a Treaty Party to the applicable treaty, or by loyalty to a disputing party, a non-disputing party, or a non-disputing Treaty Party in the proceeding;
   (c) take instruction from any organization, government or individual regarding the matters addressed in the IID;
   (d) allow any past or existing financial, business, professional or personal relationship to influence their conduct or judgement;
   (e) use their position to advance any personal or private interest; or
   (f) assume an obligation or accept a benefit during the proceeding that could interfere with the performance of their duties.

Article 10 Disclosure Obligations

1. Adjudicators shall disclose any interest, relationship or matter that may, in the eyes of the parties, give rise to doubts as to their independence or impartiality, or demonstrate bias, conflict of interest, impropriety or an appearance of bias. To this end, they shall make reasonable efforts to become aware of such interest, relationship, or matter.
2. Adjudicators shall make disclosures in accordance with paragraph (1) and shall include the following information:

(a) Any financial, business, professional, or personal relationship within [the past five years] with:
   (i) the parties, and any subsidiary, affiliate or parent entity identified by the parties;
   (ii) the parties' legal representatives, including all appointments as Arbitrator, [Judge], counsel, or expert witness made by the parties' legal representative in any IID [and non-IID] proceedings;
   (iii) the other Arbitrators, Judges or expert witnesses in the proceeding; and
   (iv) any third-party funder with a financial interest in the outcome of the proceeding and identified by a party;

(b) Any financial or personal interest in:
   (i) the proceeding or its outcome; and
   (ii) any administrative, domestic court or other international proceeding involving substantially the same factual background and involving at least one of the same parties or their subsidiary, affiliate, or parent entity as are involved in the IID proceeding; and

(c) All IID [and non IID] proceedings in which the Adjudicator has been involved in the past [5/10] years or is currently involved in as counsel, expert witness, or Adjudicator.

3. Adjudicators shall make any disclosures in the form of Annex 1 prior to or upon accepting appointment, and shall provide it to the parties, the other Adjudicators in the proceeding, the administering institution and any other person prescribed by the applicable rules or treaty.
4. Adjudicators shall have a continuing duty to make further disclosures based on newly discovered information as soon as they become aware of such information.
5. Adjudicators should err in favor of disclosure if they have any doubt as to whether a disclosure should be made. The fact of disclosure by an Adjudicator does not establish a breach of this Code.

ASA SPECIAL SERIES[*]

1. *Le nouveau droit suisse de l'arbitrage international*, 1989.
2. *The New Swiss Law on International Arbitration*, 1990.
3. Michael E. Schneider (ed.), *Verträge und Schiedsverfahren im europäischen Umbruch*, 1990.
4. *Dispute Resolution on International Markets*, 1993.
5. *Investing in Eastern-European Countries – And Arbitration*, 1993.
6. Marc Blessing (ed.), *Objective Arbitrability – Antitrust Disputes – Intellectual Property Disputes*, 1994.
7. *Profiles of ASA Members (1994)*, 1994.
8. Marc Blessing (ed.), *The Arbitration Agreement: Its Multifold Critical Aspects*, 1994.
9. Marc Blessing (ed.), *The New York Convention of 1958*, 1996.
10. *Profiles of ASA Members (1998)*, 1998.
11. *Arbitration of Sports-Related Disputes*, 1998.
12. Pierre Karrer (ed.), *International Arbitration Do's and Don'ts*, Second Edition, 1998.
13. Pierre Karrer (ed.), *The Claims Resolution Process on Dormant Accounts in Switzerland*, 2000.
14. *Profiles of ASA Members (2000)*, 2000.
15. Pierre Karrer (ed.), *Arbitral Tribunals or State Courts: Who Must Defer to Whom?*, 2001.
16. Pierre Karrer (ed.), *Glossary of Arbitration and ADR Terms and Abbreviations*, First Edition, 2001.
17. Pierre Karrer (ed.), *International Arbitration Do's and Don'ts*, Third Edition, 2001.
18. Pierre Karrer (ed.), *Conflicts of Interest in International Commercial Arbitration*, 2001.
19. *Profiles of ASA Members (2002)*, 2002.
20. Gabrielle Kaufmann-Kohler & Viviane Frossard (eds), *Arbitration in Banking and Financial Matters*, 2003.
21. Pierre Karrer (ed.), *International Arbitration Do's and Don'ts*, Forth Edition, 2004.
22. Gabrielle Kaufmann-Kohler & Blaise Stucki (eds), *The Swiss Rules of International Arbitration*, 2004.
23. *Profiles of ASA Members (2005)*, 2005.
24. Gabrielle Kaufmann-Kohler & Alexandra Johnson (eds), *Arbitration of Merger and Acquisition Disputes*, 2005.
25. Pierre Karrer (ed.), *International Arbitration Do's and Don'ts*, Fifth Edition, 2005.
26. Markus Wirth (ed.), Best Practices in International Arbitration, 2006.

---

* Volumes 47 and onward are published by Wolters Kluwer.

27. Pierre Karrer (ed.), Glossary of Arbitration and ADR Terms and Abbreviations, Second Edition, 2006.
28. Pierre Karrer (ed.), Glossary of Arbitration and ADR Terms and Abbreviations, Third Edition, 2008.
29. Markus Wirth (ed.), *The Resolution of the Dispute, from the Hearing to the Award*, 2007.
30. Michael E. Schneider & Joachim Knoll (eds), *Performance as a Remedy: Non-Monetary Relief in International Arbitration*, 2011.
31. Pierre Karrer (ed.), *International Arbitration Do's and Don'ts*, Sixth Edition, 2009.
32. Pierre Karrer (ed.), *Glossary of Arbitration and ADR Terms and Abbreviations*, Fourth Edition, 2009.
33. *Profiles of ASA Members (2009)*, 2009.
34. Anne K. Hoffmann (ed.), *Protection of Foreign Investments through Modern Treaty Arbitration: Diversity and Harmonisation*, 2010.
35. Markus Wirth, Christina Rouvinez & Joachim Knoll (eds), *Search for "Truth" in Arbitration: Is Finding the Truth What Dispute Resolution Is About?*, 2011.
36. Elliott Geisinger & Guillaume Tattevin (eds), *Advocacy in International Commercial Arbitration*, 2013.
37. Daniele Favalli (ed.), *Sense and Non-sense of Guidelines, Rules and Other Para-regulatory Texts in International Arbitration*, 2015.
38. Pierre Tercier (ed.), *Post Award Issues*, 2012.
39. **Not published**.
40. Philipp Habegger, Daniel Hochstrasser, Gabrielle Nater-Bass & Urs Weber-Stecher (eds), Arbitral Institutions under Scrutiny, 2013.
41. Elliott Geisinger & Elena Trabaldo de Mestral (eds), *Sports Arbitration: A Coach for Other Players*, 2014.
42. Bernhard Berger & Michael E. Schneider (eds), *Inside the Black Box: How Arbitral Tribunals Operate and Reach Their Decisions*, 2013.
43. Elliott Geisinger (ed.), *Confidential and Restricted Access Information in International Arbitration*, 2016.
44. Nathalie Voser (ed.), *10 Years of Swiss Rules of International Arbitration*, 2014.
45. Domitille Baizeau & Frank Spoorenberg (eds), *Arbitrators' Initiative: When, Why and How Should It Be Used?*, 2016.
46. Sebastien Besson & Harold Frey (eds), *Expert Evidence: Conflicting Assumptions and How to Handle Them in Arbitration*, 2020.
47. Andrea Meier & Christian Oetiker (eds), *Arbitration and Corruption*, 2021.
48. Felix Dasser (ed.), *Clear Path or Jungle in Commercial Arbitrators' Conflict of Interest?*, 2021.